Glimpses of Mennonite History and Doctrine

This book is dedicated
to my parents
AARON MARTIN WENGER
MARTHA A. ROCK WENGER
Best of all my teachers
in the doctrines of the church

Glimpses of Mennonite History and Doctrine

By

JOHN CHRISTIAN WENGER

Professor of Theology and Philosophy
Goshen College Biblical Seminary

WIPF & STOCK · Eugene, Oregon

Wipf and Stock Publishers
199 W 8th Ave, Suite 3
Eugene, OR 97401

Glimpses of Mennonite History
By Wenger, John C.

ISBN 13: 978-1-57910-465-8
ISBN 10: 1-57910-465-7
Publication date 10/3/2000
Previously published by Herald Press, 1949

Preface to the First Edition

In this little volume, I have tried to tell the story of the rise of the Mennonite Church in Switzerland and Holland and of its subsequent history in the various countries in which Mennonites have lived. In writing of the Mennonites in America I have given chief attention to the main body of the denomination, known officially as the "Mennonite Church." The literature at the end of each chapter directs the student to the more important articles, particularly those to which the average Mennonite youth has access, on the subjects covered by the chapter. At the end of the book will be found a fairly exhaustive bibliography of the publications, chiefly monographs, which deal with the history of the Mennonites and which appeared for the most part since the year 1880.

It is a pleasure to acknowledge my indebtedness to the editors of the *Mennonitisches Lexikon,* Christian Hege and Christian Neff, for the constant help received from their indispensable encyclopedia. The literature cited at the close of each chapter indicates how largely I have also drawn upon almost every number of *The Mennonite Quarterly Review* for reliable data and sound historical interpretation. Two of my teachers deserve especial mention. It was during my undergraduate study at Goshen College that Dean Harold S. Bender kindled in me a warm love for Mennonite history, and he has been my counselor and friend ever since. While a graduate student in the theological faculty of the University of Zurich, Switzerland, I received much help and inspiration in Professor Fritz Blanke's seminar, "The Anabaptists of the Sixteenth Century." John Horsch, the well-known Mennonite historian, of Scottdale, Pennsylvania, and Dean H. S. Bender of Goshen College, have given liberally of their time to read thoroughly the manuscript of this book, and each has offered valuable suggestions for improvement.

May this book find a wide reading by the youth of the Mennonite Church to the end that they may be inspired to a higher level of Christian living by the story here told. The volume is intended for use in Mennonite Schools, including Winter Bible Schools. The more advanced classes can well be given reading assignments in the literature listed throughout the book.

Goshen College
Goshen, Indiana
April, 1940

John Christian Wenger

THE LORD OUR GOD BE WITH US

As He was with our fathers;
Let Him not leave us
Nor forsake us:
That He may incline our hearts
Unto Him
To walk in all His ways
And to keep His commandments
And His statutes
And His judgments
Which He commanded our fathers.

Preface to the Second Edition

The printing of a second edition of this book has afforded me the welcome opportunity of re-writing it completely. In addition to the acknowledgements made in the preface to the first edition special mention should be made of my indebtedness to C. Henry Smith of Bluffton College. I have used his writings considerably in the preparation of this revised edition.

There are numerous points where the decisions made will undoubtedly please some readers and displease others. This concerns not only the selection and organization of the material, but such minor items as the spelling of proper names. I have generally Anglicized names, particularly first names. The reader will kindly bear with me in all mistakes in judgment.

In this revision I have made no attempt to treat the vicissitudes of the European Mennonites during the second world war. It is impossible at this point to get all the facts, much less to achieve any historical perspective.

My wife, Ruth Detweiler Wenger, prepared the indexes for this second edition.

I hope that in its enlarged form this book may better serve as an introduction to the field of Mennonite history for the general reader and as a useful compendium of denominational history for Mennonites.

Goshen, Indiana
April, 1946

J. C. Wenger

O Christe hilf du deinem Volk
Welch's dir in aller Treu nachfolgt,
Daß es durch deinen bittern Tod
Erlöset werd aus aller Not.

Lob sei dir Gott in deinem Thron,
Darzu auch deinem lieben Sohn:
Auch dem Heiligen Geist zugleich,
Der zieh noch viel zu seinem Reich.

Michael Sattler,† 1527

Contents

Illustrations

CHAPTER I

The Decline of New Testament Christianity

A practical question for us to consider is, Why did there need to be a Mennonite Church? Why did the Mennonite founding fathers not remain in the Roman Catholic Church? And why were they not satisfied with the other Protestant churches of continental Europe—the Lutheran and the Reformed? In this chapter an attempt will be made to answer briefly the first of these questions: Why did the founders of the Mennonite Church withdraw from the Roman Catholic Church?

At the outset, it should be clearly understood that there is an organizational continuity from the New Testament Church of the apostles to the Catholic Church of today. The complex ritual and elaborate organization of the Catholic Church are the result of a long development from the simplicity of the apostolic church, as it is portrayed in the Acts of the Apostles and in the New Testament epistles. Furthermore, the sixteenth-century reformers and present-day Protestants share alike the conviction that Catholics have lost the purity of faith and life which obtained in the church of the first century. Protestants in general believe that Roman Catholics do not teach soundly Biblical doctrines; that they have added more and more tradition to the original truth of the gospel until the message of God's Word is seriously obscured and defeated. This can be seen most clearly by a study of the changes which the centuries have brought to the church.

From the founding of the church at Pentecost, A.D. 30, until the death of the apostle John, a little before A.D. 100, the outstanding thing about the Christian Church was its rapid growth. This is clearly reflected in the Acts of the Apostles. It has been pointed out that the history of the first-century church can be divided into three periods. For the first fifteen years, the church was largely Jewish, with its spiritual center at Jerusalem, where Peter and John served as the leaders. At the time of the choosing of Matthias, the disciples numbered one hundred and twenty (Acts 1:15). On the day of Pentecost, accessions numbered approximately three thousand (Acts 2:41). At the imprisonment of Peter and John a little later, the believers totaled about five thousand (Acts 4:4). And shortly thereafter, the account states that "multitudes" were added to the church (Acts 5:14). By the time of Paul's arrest in Jerusalem, the Jewish believers were, it would seem, numbered by the tens of thousands (Acts 21:20).

From about A. D. 41 to 65 the active center of the church was Antioch in Syria. It was from this city that Paul set out on all three of his missionary expeditions (Acts 13:1-3; 15:35, 36; 18:22, 23), expeditions which resulted in the establishment of a remarkable chain of Christian congregations in the cities where Paul evangelized: Antioch, Iconium, Lystra, Derbe, Philippi, Thessalonica, Corinth, Ephesus. Gentile missions have the apostle Paul as their pioneer founder.

From about A.D. 65 to 95, the leading center of influence in the church was undoubtedly Ephesus in Asia Minor. Here the apostle John labored on after his fellow apostles were martyred. Christianity, it should be noted, was moving northward and westward around the eastern end of the Mediterranean Sea. Paul himself went as far as Rome (Acts 28:16), if not to Spain (Romans 15:28). By 180 A.D. Christianity had surrounded the Mediterranean Sea, being especially strong in the cities. At the Council of Arles, in 314 A.D., bishops from England were present. The Roman world was being rapidly won for Christ.

Along with the rapid numerical growth of Christianity, however, came also a sad spiritual decline. The gospel soon lost its glorious purity. The simple evangel of free forgiveness through faith in a crucified and risen Saviour was early contaminated by human admixtures of various kinds. The matchless grace of God, in which the apostles had gloried, was soon obscured by the church's prescribing stages to penance and by teaching the merit of good deeds. By 200 A.D., asceticism was highly regarded; greater merit with God could be achieved, the Christians then thought, by denying themselves of the pleasures of a normal life in society. In the third century, a man named Anthony took up his abode in the desert. There he lived, separated physically from the temptations of society, but doing nothing to minister to the needs of men. Yet his life as a hermit excited the admiration of many Christians of that time. They thought his asceticism was surely a meritorious way of life.

In the early centuries of the Christian era, the adoration of saints and images had also begun. In the post-Nicene period (after 325) people prayed to Peter, Thomas, James, and other deceased saints, hoping to receive help from them. Making the sign of the cross over one's bosom was thought to provide great spiritual protection. The worship of the virgin Mary was practiced devoutly; she was thought to be an effective intercessor with her Son, Jesus. Angels also came to be worshiped, especially Michael. The church also made use of relics—such things as bones of deceased saints, various objects from the life of holy martyrs, and especially items purported to have come from the life of Christ. Pieces of wood from the cross were scattered all over Europe. It was finally believed that the cross had the unusual power of being able to multiply itself.

During the early centuries of the church, the ecclesiastical organization became quite elaborate. There were deacons, archdeacons, subdeacons, acolytes, bishops, archbishops, patriarchs. Ultimately the bishop of Rome won out in his contention that he was over and above all other ecclesiastical officers. The church then had a human head, the pope, the spiritual "father" of the faithful, who was regarded as the vicar or deputy of Christ on earth. By 600 A.D. the pope's power was great. By 1200 A.D. it was enormous. Down through the so-called "Dark Ages," the pope was not only the supreme head of the church; he was also a temporal ruler with a throne, a crown, and an army, vying with earthly kings for political power. All this secularization was a far cry from the New Testament office of elder or bishop. But there were other deviations which Catholicism made from Biblical truth. Let us examine some of these deviations.

The New Testament teaches clearly that all Christian believers, or "saints," are priests in the sense that they have direct access to God (I Peter 2:9). No earthly priesthood, such as Catholics thought essential, is acceptable to God. Christ is the eternal "high priest" for all true believers (Heb. 3:1; 4:14; 5:5; 5:10; 6:20). No mere human being, on earth or in heaven, can intercede for other human beings before God; there is but one Mediator, the Man Christ Jesus (I Tim. 2:5). Hence the worship of saints and the adoration of images are sinful idolatry, an insult to Christ, in the judgment of Protestants. Further, it is not Scriptural to require lay Christians to confess sins to ordained "priests."

The New Testament also prescribes various practices, such as baptism (Matt. 28:19, 20), and the Lord's Supper (I Cor. 11:23-26), not that any supernatural power automatically accompanies the water to wash away sin, or that the elements of the Supper are in themselves efficacious to confer grace to the soul. Baptism does not cleanse from sin (I Peter 3:21); only the blood of Christ can take away sin (I John 1:7). The Lord's Supper is kept "in remembrance of" Jesus (I Cor. 11:24, 25); the bread and the "fruit of the vine" are memorial symbols only, not direct and automatic means of grace, as Catholics teach.

The New Testament also teaches that salvation is "by grace . . . through faith . . . not of works" (Eph. 2:8). No human accomplishments achieve any merit whatsoever with God, as the epistles to the Romans and to the Galatians clearly teach and emphasize. Yet Catholics believe that Christ and various outstanding saints had actually achieved more merit than they themselves needed. They therefore believe that prayer to such saints in heaven may result in the transfer of their surplus credits to the account of the supplicant. Indeed the church can sell, for money, "indulgences"; that is, the amount of suffering in "purgatory" can be diminished by the purchase of an indulgence from the church. Catholics believe that the atonement of Jesus covered only the guilt of sin, not the necessity of temporal suffering for one's sins. If one dies before suffering sufficiently, either directly or by making equivalent sacrifices, the balance of the debt, Catholics believe, must be paid in purgatory. The church can prevent the faithful from going to hell, and it can lighten or remit the suffering in purgatory by drawing upon the surplus credits stored in the "treasury of merit." Therefore the church is, for Catholics, in a very real sense, the institution of salvation, not merely the fellowship of saved believers.

Why then did the sixteenth-century founders of the Mennonite Church withdraw from the Roman Catholic Church? The answer is that they were determined by God's grace to get back to the Bible, back to the faith of the apostles of Christ, back to the faith of the church of the New Testament. A brief summary will perhaps help to clarify the issues:

1. The Bible teaches that salvation is by the grace of God, conditioned on faith alone, not determined by affiliation with any human organization. Grace is granted to each man by virtue of his faith in Christ, not by his mere partaking of "sacraments."

2. Every Christian is a priest in the same sense. Some Christians are ordained to preach the Word and to assume the oversight of the congregations of the brotherhood, but no Christian stands over his brethren as a dispenser of God's grace or as a "priest" with God.

3. Justification is by faith alone. There are no deeds which bring merit in God's sight. The whole conception of merit, surplus merit, and indulgences is unbiblical.

4. The essential character of the Christian life is holy obedience to Christ and His Word, not ceremonialism, church fasts, pilgrimages, adoration of relics, making the sign of the cross, using the rosary, and the like.

5. The church is the fellowship of the saints, the brotherhood of those who have been redeemed by Christ from a life of sin. It is not a great hierarchical organization linked up with earthly governments and participating in state affairs.

6. God, and God alone, is to be worshiped through Christ Jesus, the Mediator. Neither Mary, wife of Joseph, nor the apostles, nor martyrs, nor angels shall be prayed to, nor shall images be given veneration.

7. Baptism is an external rite, symbolizing the washing away of the convert's sins. It is not a supernatural instrument of grace to regenerate infants. Infant baptism is unscriptural, as is also the idea of baptismal regeneration.

8. The bread of the Lord's Supper is a symbol of Christ's death for the redemption of sinners. It is a memorial only; it is not changed into Christ's body, nor is it to be worshiped.

9. Jesus told His disciples when He took the communion cup, "Drink ye all of it" (Matt. 26:27), but for several centuries prior to the Protestant reformation the Catholic Church had given communion in "one kind," withholding the cup from the laity. This is still Catholic practice.

10. The New Testament condemns the prohibiting of marriage (I Tim. 4:3), but Roman Catholic priests are forbidden to enter the married state, a practice which has often led to unhappy consequences.

11. The Bible knows of only two destinies in the life after death, heaven and hell. But Catholics teach the existence of purgatory, as well as a limbo or two.

12. The New Testament clearly teaches that the Christian shall love all men, whether evil or good, and that his every action must be directed to the salvation of men, not to their destruction. Personal suffering is to be preferred to retaliation. Mennonites, like the Christians of the first two centuries, therefore refuse all military service, as well as the magistracy, while Catholics have long employed both.

13. The final authority in faith and life is the Word of Christ as it is found in the New Testament. But Catholics elevate the church and tradition as equal to, in effect actually above, the Scriptures.

A long list of reformers tried to lead the Catholic Church away from many of its unscriptural views and practices, but at the Council of Trent (1545 1563) the Catholics reaffirmed their "authoritative" traditions. By that time, however, the "Protestants" had left the fold of Rome. In the eleventh century, the Greek Orthodox schism had broken the unity of the Catholic Church. In the sixteenth century, the several Protestant denominations, Anabaptist, Lutheran, Reformed, and Anglican, broke permanently the unity of the church. But in the process, the Gospel of Christ was rediscovered. The matchless grace of God was once more clearly seen. Justification by faith again became the ground of assurance for thousands of Christians. The faith of the apostles was the joy of many hearts. Yet the Anabaptists were not satisfied with the Lutheran and Reformed churches; their conscience compelled them to set up their own church organization. The reason for this will be discussed in the next chapter.

READINGS

Bender, H. S.: *Mennonite Origins in Europe,* M.C.C., Akron, Pennsylvania, 1942, 3-7.

Fisher, G. P.: *History of the Christian Church,* Charles Scribner's Sons, New York, 1916, 17-286.

Horsch, John: *Mennonites in Europe,* Mennonite Publishing House, Scottdale, Pennsylvania, 1942, 1-3.

McGlothlin, W. J.: *The Course of Christian History,* The Macmillan Company, New York, 1918, 8-107.

Newman, A. H.: *A History of Anti-Pedobaptism from the Rise of Pedobaptism to A.D. 1609,* American Baptist Publication Society, Philadelphia, 1897, 1-14.

Nichols, R. H.: *The Growth of the Christian Church,* The Westminster Press, Philadelphia, 1939, Volume I, 17-156; Volume II, 1-20.

Qualben, Lars P.: *A History of the Christian Church,* Thomas Nelson and Sons, New York, 1933, 24-184.

Reproduced from "Die Taufgesinnten-Gemeinden," Karlsruhe, 1931

Christian Neff, 1863-1946; German Mennonite Bishop and Historian

The University of Basle Overlooking the Rhine
Conrad Grebel studied in this building, 1514-15

Ulrich Zwingli's Church in Zurich
The Great Minster

Chur, the Grisons; the Home of George Blaurock

CHAPTER II

The Reformation and the Founding of Swiss Anabaptism

1. The Founder of Swiss Anabaptism

The serious study of Mennonite history has been undertaken only in comparatively recent years. Mennonites themselves have generally been more concerned with practical Christian living than with writing histories about themselves. Much of the writing of Mennonite history has actually been done by writers who knew little about the life and faith of Mennonites. When Mennonites finally did begin to write about the history of their church they tended to follow in the trails which poorly informed guides had blazed. Before taking up the story of the Reformation and the rise of the Mennonite Church it will be necessary to inspect some of the false theories of its origin.

(1) *False Theories of Anabaptism*

Some of the older historians imagined a connection between the radical Zwickau prophets of Saxony, Germany, led by Nicholas Storch in the early 1520's, and the Swiss Anabaptists. But for this supposed connection there is no evidence. Indeed, Storch, who died in 1525, seems never to have practiced believers' baptism.

Another ill-founded notion, which goes back ultimately to Heinrich Bullinger, 1504-78, Zwingli's successor in Zurich, is that the radical Thomas Münzer of Saxony, another Zwickau "prophet," had established contact with the Swiss Brethren. It is true that Conrad Grebel wrote a lengthy letter to Münzer, but the letter never reached its goal, and Münzer, who was captured and executed, 1525, probably never heard of Grebel. Münzer's program of violence was entirely unacceptable to the nonresistant Swiss Brethren. Grebel wrote to Münzer as follows, "[Christians] use neither the worldly sword nor engage in war, since among them taking human life has ceased entirely. . . . " Swiss Anabaptism had no connections with Münzer's peasant revolt of 1524-25.

The theory that Anabaptism was a social-economic movement has been supported by such Socialist writers as Karl Kautsky, 1854-1938, and by sociologists like H. Richard Niebuhr, 1894-, yet this theory breaks down under the load of the evidence to the contrary. The chief founder of the Swiss Brethren was the university-trained son of a rich patrician family. The founders of Swiss Anabaptism preached not social revolt, but repentance, faith, and holiness.

Albrecht Ritschl, 1822-99, a liberal German writer, advanced the theory of a monastic origin for the Anabaptist vision. It is indeed true that such Catholic orders as the Franciscans sought to recapture the spirit of apostolic Christianity. It is also true that the reproduction of the apostolic church was the vision which the Anabaptists earnestly sought to realize. But as a matter of fact, the Swiss Brethren set up their church because Zwingli did not go far enough in his deviation from Catholicism. Anabaptism was vigorously opposed to Catholicism and the Catholic orders. It drew its inspiration from the Scriptures, not from anything Catholic.

Some Baptist writers used to try to hold to the theory of apostolic succession. According to this theory one could trace a line of Biblical faith and practice through various groups outside the Catholic Church all the way back to the apostles of Christ. Montanists, Novatians, Catharists, Donatists, Paulicians, Albigenses, Waldenses, and many other groups, were thought to have wholly, or in part, preserved the true faith through the long centuries of spiritual darkness when Catholicism was the reigning ecclesiastical organization. As early as 1897 Albert Henry Newman, 1852-1933, a Baptist historian, demonstrated the unreliable character of the theory of apostolic succession. Yet a Mennonite Church history of 1905 taught the older apostolic succession theory. As a matter of fact, all the founders of the Anabaptist movement were originally members of the Roman Catholic Church, many being even priests.

A German writer, Ludwig Keller, 1849-1915, attempted to connect the Anabaptists with the Waldenses and similar groups whom he labeled "the old evangelical brotherhoods." But an investigation of the actual founding of the Swiss Brethren, as well as the Dutch Obbenites, reveals the false character of Keller's hypothesis. The Waldenses disappeared in Switzerland a hundred years before the Swiss Brethren arose. When the Obbenites arose in the Netherlands, that area was otherwise almost wholly Roman Catholic.

Rufus M. Jones, the well-known Quaker mystic, is inclined to interpret Anabaptism in terms of mysticism. But the Anabaptists objected vigorously to the mysticism of their day; they were Biblicists, not mystics. Pilgram Marpeck, Anabaptist elder (bishop) of south Germany, opposed the mystical Schwenckfeld, insisting upon the Christian's obligation to obey the written Word of God, and the Dutch Mennonite elder, Dirck Philips, opposed Sebastian Franck who had attempted to depreciate the external observance of the ordinances. The Anabaptists were not mystics, but Bible literalists.

(2) *The Founder of Anabaptism*

The founder of Anabaptism was a young patrician and scholar named Conrad Grebel. His parents were Jacob and Dorothea Fries Grebel. The Grebel family had originally settled in Zurich in 1386 and was always prominent in the affairs of the city. Jacob was one of the most outstanding of the Grebels, being a wealthy iron merchant and leading citizen. He was elected to the Zurich city council in 1494, and was made magistrate or ruler (*Vogt*) of the township of Grueningen, just east of the city, in 1499. Conrad was born in the city of Zurich about 1498. His boyhood was undoubtedly spent in the castle at Grueningen. He probably spent six or seven years in the Latin school at the Great Minster in Zurich. This school was called Carolina in honor of the man who was supposed to have founded it, Carl the Great or Charlemagne. In the Carolina his courses would have been Latin grammar, Latin literature, Latin church hymns or liturgies, and dialectic or debating. Jacob and Dorothea Fries Grebel were the parents of at least six children: Barbara, Euphrosine, Conrad, Andrew, Martha, and Dorothea.

In October 1514 Conrad Grebel enrolled in the University of Basle, Switzerland, for a winter's study. The custom of the day required groups of students to live in houses, each of which was called a *Bursa*. They studied under the supervision of a teacher who held the master's degree. The typical Bursa had a group of about fifteen youths. Grebel's teacher was the best in Basle, a scholar named Henry Loriti, but usually called Glarean after his Swiss home in Glarus. Glarean probably taught Latin, Greek, Hebrew, and mathematics. The rules of the Bursa were strict; for example, the young men had to be in their rooms by eight o'clock in the evening. Grebel's stay at the University of Basle was from October, 1514, to May, 1515.

In the fall of 1515 Grebel did not return to Basle. For one thing, his beloved Glarean had gone to Italy for further study. Also, Jacob Grebel had secured from Emperor Maximilian a stipend for Conrad to study at the University of Vienna. Young Grebel studied at Vienna from September, 1515, until June, 1518. He was a pupil there of the famous Joachim von Watt, of St. Gall, Switzerland, popularly known as Vadian. By 1516 Vadian had doctors' degrees in both philosophy and medicine. A warm friendship developed between Vadian and Grebel. Each spoke of the other in the highest terms. Fourteen years after Grebel's death Vadian referred to him as "endowed with great gifts." Vadian married Conrad's younger sister, Martha, in 1519.

During his years in Vienna, Grebel grew intellectually. When he left in 1518, as a young man of about twenty, he was richly talented, a youth with great ambitions and with the marks of a coming leader of men. But in personal piety he was deficient. As a Catholic university student, he was not particularly concerned to lead a good life. Perhaps, as a result of his loose living, he suffered with ill health during the remainder of his short life.

Grebel reached his Swiss home in the middle of July, 1518. That summer, in the company of Vadian and a friend, named Myconius, Grebel went to Lucerne where the party got permission to climb Peak Pilatus. This interesting expedition has been called the first scientific ascent of Pilatus. The leader was a Lucerne canon named John Zimmerman.

After returning from Lucerne, Grebel went to Baden to try to regain his health. While there he also visited his older sister Barbara, wife of Leonard Karli.

On September 30, 1518, Conrad Grebel left Zurich for Paris, where he arrived, October 20. There he entered the Bursa of his former teacher, Glarean. He also attended lectures at the University of Paris. His study in Paris was made possible by a royal grant which Jacob Grebel had secured from the king of France. Grebel's life as a student in Paris was not very fruitful. He quarreled with Glarean and left his house. He fled Paris for six months because of an epidemic of the plague. Further, his moral life was lacking in self-control and holiness. For him, God and Christianity were not closely related with life. Perhaps the most hopeful thing about him was his growing sense of discontent and personal unhappiness. He was gradually to find out that nothing but God, through Christ, can satisfy the soul. When he returned to Zurich early in July, 1520, without securing a doctor's degree, he was ripe for the Gospel. He was sick and unhappy, longing for peace and real joy.

The first year or so of Grebel's life back in Zurich was a period of continued unhappiness. Perhaps his chief pleasure was obtained in the meetings of a learned circle which were held in 1521 for the study of Greek literature. In November of that year he reported to a friend that he was reading the writings of Plato with Zwingli and two other scholars. He also planned to continue his studies at the University of Pisa in Italy, and with this end in view his father secured another stipend for him, this time a papal grant. But the plan was never carried out. Grebel remained in Switzerland.

In the year 1521 Grebel fell madly in love with a girl named Barbara; his *Holokosme* (*Whole World*) he called her. She was apparently not of high social standing like the Grebels, and Conrad's family firmly opposed the match. But he was determined to have his *Barbarity,* as he once jokingly referred to her. He went to the city of Basle and worked as a proofreader in the shop of the famous printer, Cratander, from August until October, 1521. He then returned to Zurich where, in spite of parental opposition, he and Barbara were married on February 6, 1522. Conrad and Barbara were the parents of three children. Theophilus was born in 1522 and died in 1541 at the age of nineteen. Joshua was born about August 11, 1523. On June 21, 1549, Joshua was married to Catherine Steiner. Their son, Conrad, became the Zurich city treasurer in 1624. A grandson of this Conrad, also named Conrad Grebel, 1615-74, became burgomaster of Zurich in 1669. In 1936 Dr. Hans von Grebel, a direct descendant of the founder of Swiss Anabaptism, was president of the supreme court of Zurich. The third and last child of Conrad and Barbara Grebel was Rachel, born January 6, 1525. She apparently died in infancy. Grebel himself died in 1526, and on December 5, 1527, his widow, Barbara, married a man named Jacob Ziegler, undoubtedly a member of the Reformed Church, for Barbara did not stand by her first husband during his trying months as leader of the Swiss Brethren. Relatives of the Reformed faith reared Theophilus and Joshua. Therefore, none of the descendants of the founder of Anabaptism are found in the Mennonite Church today.

2. The Lutheran Reformation

In order to understand the background of the Swiss Brethren movement it will be necessary to survey briefly both the Lutheran and Zwinglian reform movements. Martin Luther and his work came first in point of time and influence.

The founder of the Sixteenth Century Reformation was a German theologian named Martin Luther, 1483-1546. Luther entered a Catholic monastery in 1505. He was painfully conscious of his sins and struggled for a long time, trying to achieve peace with God. He fasted, prayed, and did all kinds of good works, but in vain. "How," he cried, "can I obtain a gracious God?" In the year 1512 Luther received the degree, Doctor of Theology. About the same time, he finally was delivered from his agony of soul by seeing that man did not have to achieve for himself his peace with God. It is Christ that has reconciled man to God. This He did by His atoning death on Calvary. The verse which helped Luther in a special way was Romans 1:17. In this grand passage Paul indicates that the way to become righteous in God's sight, to have a perfect standing before Him, is simply to exercise personal faith in Christ. "The just man," Paul quotes from Habakkuk 2:4, "shall live by his faith." God reckons the righteousness of Christ to every Christian believer. This doctrine of justification by faith was the glorious truth which changed the fearful priest into a lionhearted reformer. His Catholic friend, John von Staupitz, helped Luther to this truth. At the very beginning the Reformation was therefore purely religious in origin.

At this time, 1512, Luther had not the slightest intention of leaving the Roman Catholic Church. Even five years later, when John Tetzel went through Germany selling indulgences, Luther still thought of himself as a loyal Catholic. But the sensitive soul of Luther was shocked at the practice of Tetzel. His sense of justice was outraged, and he resolved to protest. On October 31, 1517, a memorable day for all Protestants, Luther tacked his ninety-five theses on the church door at Wittenberg. In this town Luther was serving as priest and theology professor, and was preaching frequently, sometimes daily. The theses of Luther challenged the Catholic doctrine of indulgences. They were soon translated from Latin into German and broadcast over Germany. Luther was attempting an enormous task in challenging the Catholic Church, but he had the support and protection of Frederick the Wise, the Elector of Saxony.

In 1520 Luther went still further; he published three reform booklets. On June 15 of that year the pope at Rome finally acted. He issued a formal threat of excommunication, and excommunication was regarded by Catholics as excluding one from salvation until restoration to fellowship in the Catholic Church was made. But Luther did not base his salvation on the sacramental doctrine of the Catholics. He stood on the Pauline doctrine of justifying faith. He therefore defied the pope by publicly throwing the papal document into a bonfire at nine o'clock in the morning on December 10, 1520. Into the fire also went the papal decretals, the canon law, and some other Catholic books—this in reply to the papal order for Luther's books to be burned. The struggle between the Wittenberg doctor, still a Catholic in intention, and the Roman pope, was on in dead earnest.

The next year Luther was summoned to the diet (or parliament) which convened in the German city of Worms. And there, on April 18, 1521, he refused to make the recantation which the Catholic Church demanded of him. On his return journey his friends, at the instance of Elector Frederick, "kidnaped" him and hid him in a castle in Wartburg. There he let his beard grow and lived under the name of Knight George. "George" spent one of the most profitable years of his life (almost eleven months, to be exact) in this castle, for in that period he translated the Greek New Testament into German. His translation was in good, living German; it made Jesus and the apostles "talk German"; it was a great achievement.

In March, 1522, Luther returned to Wittenberg and undid some of the work of the earnest reformer, Andrew Bodenstein, called after his home town, Carlstadt, by restoring certain Catholic practices which Carlstadt had abolished. Luther himself returned to his monastery and observed the Catholic fasts. But he did not restore the most objectionable passage from the Latin mass which had been omitted by Carlstadt.

During the next few years Luther worked hard for Catholic reform. He also took some drastic steps for a priest. On June 13, 1525, he renounced Catholic asceticism by taking to wife, Catharine von Bora, a former nun. In October, 1525, he introduced (at Wittenberg only, apparently) his evangelical worship service which he published the next year in the book, *Deutsche Messe* (German Mass). The Diet of Spires, in the summer of 1526, conferred upon the evangelically minded princes and city rulers the right, they thought, to reorganize the worship service and the organization of the church. Evangelical worship was finally established in all of Saxony in 1526; there was then actually a Lutheran state (provincial) church. Other German provinces did likewise, with the princes serving as the heads of the church. Ultimately, with some regional differences, Lutheranism covered a huge portion of the German Empire, an area roughly in the shape of a triangle, with its base running along the Baltic Sea from the Netherlands to East Prussia, and with its apex reaching to Switzerland. The Lutheran churches of Northern Germany, also those of Scandinavia, adopted the order of Wittenberg, while those of southern Germany had a simpler service. Luther attempted to remove the more grievous abuses of Catholic worship, but permitted the use of vestments, altars, candles, crucifixes, pictures, organs, and church bells. It should be noted that in 1526 and the following years an entire population, priests and laity alike, were forcibly changed from Catholics to Lutherans by the decision of the anti-Romish princes. The civil rulers were responsible for the "conversion" of the population from Catholicism to Protestantism. In fact, whole populations sometimes changed faiths more than once on orders from their ruler. It is little wonder that such a reformation was not highly successful in producing holiness of life. Luther decided not to abolish infant baptism, even if babes have not conscious faith. What Luther did was to emphasize justification by faith while retaining a state church, infant baptism, and a modified form of the mass. The Augsburg Confession of 1530 says expressly that the mass was still retained by the Lutherans, though certain abuses, such as withholding the cup from the laity, were removed (Article XXIV).

Luther was a great man, a powerful leader, a talented personality. He was reformer, theologian, preacher, writer, poet, and musician. He wrote hymns as widely different as the militant song, "A Mighty Fortress is Our God," and the tender Christmas hymn, "Away in a Manger." His family life was a model of Christian joy and piety. Yet, in controversy Luther was violently abusive. The title of his book against the Anabaptists was, *Of Sneaks and Hedge Preachers,* 1532. In fact, he went so far as to defend the right of the state to execute Anabaptists (1531). Also in the Peasants' Revolt of 1524-25, Luther encouraged the magistrates to "stab, kill, and strangle" the peasants like mad dogs. Luther's language was always direct and vigorous. For example, he said that he married to please his father, to tease the pope, and to vex the devil. Again, his three rules on preaching were: Walk up briskly; open your mouth; stop quickly. He said that Tetzel, the seller of indulgences, dealt with the Bible "like a pig with the meal bag." It is regrettable that a man so richly endowed of God as was Luther should have taken some of the attitudes he did. It is even more regrettable that the Lutheran Reformation lowered, rather than raised, the moral level of the people. And for this moral declension some of Luther's careless statements were surely partially responsible. He emphasized justification by faith so vigorously that many people thought a sinful way of life was of no consequence. Menno Simons lamented this "Protestant" attitude and quoted the popular couplet, "The bond is broken, and we are free."

Martin Luther did a great work in inaugurating the Reformation, but he did not go all the way in simple obedience to the New Testament. Rather, he retained a state church, infant baptism, an elaborate ritual in worship, and an ineffective emphasis on holiness of life. He did not believe in religious toleration, freedom of conscience, Biblical nonresistance, or separation of church and state. The Swiss Brethren must have been bitterly disappointed in Luther, in his execution of a program of reform by using civil princes as "emergency bishops," in the content of his teaching and religious practice, and in the fruits of his reformation.

3. The Zwinglian Reformation

The influence of Martin Luther was not confined to Germany. The Catholics of German-speaking Switzerland were early influenced by his reform literature. The most influential priest in the Swiss reform was a leader in Zurich named Huldrych (Ulrich) Zwingli, 1484-1531. Temperamentally Zwingli and Luther were quite different. Luther was impulsive, a man of powerful passions. Ultimately he had an overwhelming sense of the love and grace of God. Zwingli was, by nature, cool and practical, with no profound sense of sin. Yet he, too, was an earnest reformer.

Zwingli was educated in the Latin schools of Basle and Berne and at the Universities of Vienna and Basle. He secured his Master of Arts degree from the University of Basle. In 1506, at the age of twenty-two, he became priest at Glarus, Switzerland. In 1513 he took up the study of Greek in order to understand better the New Testament. In 1516 he transferred to Einsiedeln, Switzerland, where his preaching was marked by its Biblical content and emphasis.

Einsiedeln was a place to which Catholic pilgrimages were made. More than a hundred thousand people are said to have visited annually the shrine of the black image of the virgin Mary at Einsiedeln. Against this Catholic superstitious practice Zwingli preached. He was, above all, a devoted student of the Greek New Testament. With his own hand he copied the epistles of Paul in Greek, that he might have them conveniently available for study and memorization. Yet he did not live a morally chaste life.

In 1518 Zwingli opposed another Catholic practice. A seller of indulgences, named Bernard Samson, appeared in Switzerland. Zwingli and others preached against him, and he was driven away. The pope advised Samson to leave the country. In December of that year Zwingli was called to the post of priest and preacher in the Great Minster of Zurich, the leading church of the city. In the pulpit Zwingli acquitted himself ably. As a speaker he thrilled his audiences. One man declared that when Zwingli preached it seemed that he held him by the hair of his head. Zwingli abolished prescribed Scripture lessons and preached in regular order through entire books of the Bible, Matthew's Gospel for instance. This was quite new to the people. They heard portions of the Bible which were entirely new to them.

Late in the year 1519 Zwingli began to read Luther's writings, and their impression on him was profound. Zwingli's debt to Luther was great, although he was later unwilling to admit it. Another experience of 1519 helped to ripen Zwingli as a reformer. An epidemic of the plague broke out in Zurich, and Zwingli was one of the victims. In the severity of his illness, when death seemed near, Zwingli made a surrender to God, more profound than any he had ever made before. But never in his life did he approach Luther's consciousness of the grace of God.

Following this deepening of his Christian experience Zwingli went forward in his reform work. By 1520 he was preaching against tithes, fasting, monasticism, the intercession of deceased saints, and belief in purgatory. The monks accused him of being a follower of Luther. This he denied, but he did defend the writings of Luther. In 1520, to stop the agitation of the monks, the city council ordered the clergy to confine their preaching to what could be substantiated from the Scriptures. In 1522 Zwingli defended some Zurich citizens who ate meat during Lent. In August of that year he published a book, *Archeteles,* which denounced tradition and upheld the Word of God alone as the norm of authority in religion. In July 1522 he entered into a secret union with a widow, named Anna Reinhart. He made a public announcement of this marriage relationship in 1524.

Zwingli held three disputations on Catholicism. The first one convened in the city hall of Zurich on January 29, 1523. In sixty-seven articles Zwingli opposed almost all that was distinctively Catholic: the mass, fasts, pilgrimages, indulgences, purgatory, saint worship, auricular confession, clerical celibacy, monasticism, and popery. He even questioned the propriety of infant baptism. The city council supported him, but the chief result was a change in public sentiment. The monasteries were soon deserted and the priests and nuns married, but the observance of the mass and of infant baptism went on largely as before. A second disputation was held, October 26-28, 1523, but no representative of traditional Catholicism appeared. Once again the sole authority of the Scriptures was recognized, but no action, such as abolishing the mass, was decided upon. Following the third disputation on January 20, 1524, there was action, however. That spring, all works of art, all "holy" relics, all altars, candles, and crucifixes, were removed from the church buildings of Zurich. The inside walls were whitewashed to cover the pictures. The buildings were to be meetinghouses for the proclamation of God's Word, not "holy" temples. Yet, Catholic mass continued to be said until Passion Week, 1525. On April 13, 1525, a Thursday, the first Swiss Reformed communion service was held in Zurich's Great Minster. The people sat along both sides of a long table, which had been placed in the aisle, to eat the unleavened bread and to drink the wine.

The Zwinglian Reformation spread to other cities and cantons of Switzerland and South Germany. The chief centers were Basle, Berne, Schaffhausen, St. Gall, and the Alsatian Strasburg. Zwingli went far beyond Luther in his reformation. Luther rejected only those doctrines and practices which conflicted with the Bible, while Zwingli aimed to discard every teaching and ceremony which lacked Biblical support.

The Catholic cantons of Switzerland formed a military alliance against the Zwinglian Reformation, but war was averted only at the last moment by the peace of Cappel (1529). In 1531 armed conflict broke out, however. Zwingli himself participated in a small skirmish with the Catholics, the so-called Battle of Cappel, in the fall of 1531, and was killed on the field of battle on October 11. His body was cut in pieces by the Catholics and burned. Zwingli's forebodings were realized. Halley's comet in August and September, 1531, had been interpreted by Zwingli as a token of disaster to his cause and as a sign that his own death would occur. But Zwingli took the sword, and by the sword he perished. More than four years before his death he had decided to wipe out the Swiss Brethren faith by persecution unto the death, if necessary. Jacob Grebel, minority leader in the city council and father of Conrad Grebel, Zwingli had caused to be beheaded in 1526, ostensibly on a charge of receiving money illegally from abroad, but actually because, although himself not an Anabaptist, he had favored dealing mildly with the Swiss Brethren. Zurich put the first Swiss Brethren in prison early in 1525, and put their first martyr (Felix Manz) to death on January 5, 1527. Zwingli had decided to employ force in the establishment of his reformation and he himself came to a tragic end on the battlefield of a "religious" war. Yet to Ulrich Zwingli goes the chief credit for inaugurating the Swiss Reformation and for the conversion to evangelical faith of the men who, in turn, became the founders of the Swiss Brethren Church.

4. The Swiss Brethren

Conrad Grebel was won for the evangelical cause by Ulrich Zwingli. During the year 1522 Grebel made the change, and a thorough conversion it was. It was undoubtedly the preaching of Zwingli which led to Grebel's conversion. Grebel himself stated that he got "on this way" through Zwingli. No account of Grebel's conversion has been preserved, however. Indeed, Grebel wrote very little, and not even all of what he wrote is extant. We have three short poems, a petition to the Zurich Council, and sixty-nine of his letters, 1517-25. Most of the letters, however, were written during his student days; therefore, they antedate his conversion. Unfortunately, his letters do not cover the period of his inner change. No letter from Grebel has been preserved for a nine-month period in 1522, the very time when he underwent his conversion experience. His spiritual renewal probably took place in the spring or early summer of 1522. And how different are his letters thereafter! Now he writes no more of his discouragement, ill health, and other troubles. Now he is a man on fire for God. He has an intense desire to know the will of God, and to do His will at any cost. He is determined to make the Scriptures the norm of his thinking, his rule of faith, and his guide in life. Everything must be substantiated by the Scripture. Catholic traditions which lack Scriptural support must be rooted up and abolished forever. Grebel was filled with indescribable joy to be at the side of the great reformer, Zwingli. And Zwingli was highly pleased with the young patrician and scholar, son of one of Zurich's leading citizens. Both Jacob Grebel and Conrad Grebel were significant supporters of Zwingli in the early years of his reform work. A contemporary chronicler says, "Jacob Grebel aggressively assisted Zwingli in all his endeavors." One of Zwingli's friends in Solothurn wrote to Zwingli on October 5, 1522, expressing his joy because Conrad Grebel had become "a distinguished patron of the Gospel." According to Bullinger, who was Zwingli's successor in Zurich, Zwingli promised to recommend Conrad Grebel and Felix Manz for the positions of Greek and Hebrew teachers in the theological school which was planned for Zurich.

In July, 1522, Conrad Grebel, Nicholas Hottinger and Henry Aberli were notified by the Zurich Council no longer to speak against the monks from the pulpit; further, they were to stop disputing and discussing these [religious] things. Evidently, Grebel was already an enthusiastic Zwinglian.

As a loyal follower of Zwingli, Grebel took a stand against taking usury. He also was in vigorous agreement with Zwingli in his condemnation of requiring tithes of Christians. It should be emphasized that Grebel held this position in full agreement with Zwingli and on the basis of their understanding of Scripture. It should also be noted that the Swiss Brethren, in testimony given in 1532, differentiated sharply between charging interest and paying interest; the latter they considered a Christian obligation.

During the year 1523 a tinge of disappointment began to color the attitude of Grebel and his colleagues toward Zwingli. During that summer Simon Stumpf, priest in Hoengg, near Zurich, went to Zwingli and laid before him a plan for a new Christian church. He was followed by Grebel. Both men felt that Zwingli was going too slowly and too mildly in his reformation. Greater earnestness was required, they thought, than Zwingli was manifesting. They longed to see Zwingli lead out in setting up a church of converted believers, abolishing the state church system, and disentangling the disposition of church questions from any connection with the civil authorities.

They were especially distressed at the continued observance of the Catholic mass. Zwingli was not willing to follow their plan, however.

The issues which Grebel and Stumpf raised came to a head in the second disputation in October, 1523. On the afternoon of the last day (October 28) Grebel and Zwingli came to an open break. The dispute centered around the Lord's Supper. Grebel raised a number of points. He thought leavened bread ought to be used, since the (Latin) Bible says *panis,* the word for ordinary bread. Zwingli considered this unimportant. Grebel then objected to the mixing of wine with water because we are to follow the Bible simply without addition or subtraction, and the Bible says nothing of adding water. To this Zwingli agreed. Grebel then objected to the priest's inserting the wafer into the communicant's mouth—as if he had no hands. Zwingli did not agree with Grebel on this, however. Grebel then made several points concerning the time of day when mass is observed, stressing especially the fact that Jesus instituted the Supper at the evening meal. Zwingli replied that if Grebel wanted to be so scrupulous about the exact reproduction of the Lord's Supper he would have to observe it at the same time as Christ did, and in the same clothing, and each would have to wash the other's feet beforehand [!].

At this second disputation Grebel declared: "The one thing necessary before all else is the abolition of the mass. Much has been said about the mass but none of the priests is willing to forsake this great abomination." Now the interesting point is that this had been the very thing which Zwingli had planned to ask for. But Zwingli, as a shrewd statesman, was interested in making only such changes as he could bring about with the approval of the city council. And he saw that the city fathers were not ready for the change. So he replied to Grebel: "The council will decide concerning the mass." At that, Simon Stumpf cried out. "Master Ulrich, you have not the right to leave the decision of this question to the council. The matter is already decided; the Spirit of God [through the Scripture] decides it." These words were again in exact agreement with what Zwingli had written in his book, *Of Divine Righteousness,* the previous June: "One must not ask the government in such matters, for the civil authorities are not ordained to rule over the Word of God and Christian liberty, but only over things that are of a secular nature...." Stumpf himself did proceed to quit saying mass in Hoengg, and on November 3 of that year he was ordered out of town by the council, and on November 20 he was exiled from the Canton of Zurich.

Zwingli had held, for a time, to the view that it were better not to baptize infants, but to let them first come to years of understanding. Zwingli admitted this in print in 1525, and his followers constantly insisted on the fact. Dr. Balthasar Hubmaier said that he had discussed infant baptism with Zwingli in May, 1523, and that Zwingli had conceded that children ought not to be baptized before they are instructed in the faith. John Hottinger complained of Zwingli: "Today he preaches one thing; tomorrow he recalls it; to wit, he preached years ago that one ought not to baptize the children, but now otherwise again."

One of the men who early took his stand for reformation and who also taught the principles of believers' baptism was a priest named William Reublin, who began to preach against various Catholic traditions at the St. Alban Catholic Church in Basle. Great crowds attended his services. A contemporary reported that he "interpreted the Scriptures so well that the like had never been heard before." In a religious procession of June 13, 1522, instead of bearing some "holy" relics, Reublin carried an open Bible, saying, "This is the true, sacred thing; the other is only dead men's bones." On June 28 he was banished by the Basle Council for abetting the violation of a church fast on Palm Sunday. He went to Zurich and was appointed priest in the near-by Wytikon. In August, 1523, Reublin was publicly married—the first Swiss priest to take this step. In 1524 he began to advocate the position which Zwingli had even earlier upheld, that it would be better to wait with baptism until a child was old enough to choose its baptismal sponsors. Many parents accepted this counsel and delayed to baptize their children. This was true not only in Wytikon, but also in near-by Zollikon where John Broetli was a priest. Because of his having occasioned this parental postponement of baptism, Reublin was arrested on August 11, 1524 and spent some time in prison.

In 1524 Grebel began to reach out for other contacts. He was bitterly disappointed at the program of Zwingli, determined and modified as it was by political considerations and expediency. Grebel wrote a long letter and a lengthy postscript, or second letter, to Thomas Münzer. He lamented the attitude of the "evangelical" preachers, cautioned Münzer not to do anything which he could not substantiate by the clear Word of God, and remonstrated with him for various unscriptural practices. The first letter was signed by "Konrad Grebel, Andreas Castelberg, Felix Manz, Hans Oggenfuss, Barthelemae Pur, Heinrich Aberli, und andere Deine Brueder." The letter was actually written by Grebel, in the name of them all. The second letter, or extended postscript, was written in the time made possible by the delayed starting of the letter bearer, due to rain. The second part was signed by "Conrad Grebel, Andreas Castelberger, Felix Manz, Heinrich Aberli, Johannes Pannicellus, Hans Oggenfus, Hans Huiuf, Dein Landsmann von Hall. . . ." This second letter contains the information that there were not twenty in Zurich who believed God's Word (as did Grebel and his friends).

Grebel also wrote to Luther, appealing to him to cease desisting from following God's Word on the pretext of sparing the "weak" [who thought they needed the unscriptural Catholic practices]. Grebel received no letter from Luther, but a common friend named Erhard Hegenwald reported in a letter to Grebel that he had called on Luther and "Martinus" had asked him to send his greeting so that he would not think that he was unkindly disposed toward him, but he said he did not know how to reply to Grebel's letter. As a matter of fact Luther was leading his reform movement in the same manner as Zwingli; he was moving slowly enough to carry along the civil authorities who, in turn, were to compel the masses to abandon certain Roman Catholic practices. Little wonder that Luther knew not how to reply to Grebel!

Andrew Castelberger wrote to Carlstadt (July, 1524), but this led to no permanently significant or fruitful contact.

Conrad Grebel and his fellows were a source of embarrassment to Zwingli all during 1524. It was not merely that there were differences between Grebel and Zwingli. The awkwardness of the situation was due to the fact that Grebel was developing and insisting upon the very principles which Zwingli had earlier taught him. That was particularly the case with infant baptism. Zwingli finally saw himself compelled to act. And the Brethren were also demanding reasons for Zwingli's stand; they petitioned the council to ask Zwingli to overcome them *with Scripture*. About the middle of December, 1524, Zwingli and his supporters met the Brethren for a debate, but only one of the Brethren was permitted to participate. Another debate between Zwingli and the Brethren was held on January 10, 1525.

Both parties claimed the victory. The council issued a mandate that "all who held the error that infants should not be baptized," should appear before the council in the city hall the morning of Tuesday, January 17, 1525, to give reasons "from divine Scripture" for their position. This opportunity was, of course, seized. The speakers for the Brethren were Conrad Grebel, Felix Manz, and William Reublin. Bullinger, who was present at the memorable disputation, gives the following summary of the position taken by the Brethren:

"Infants cannot believe nor can they understand the meaning of baptism. Baptism should be administered to believers to whom the Gospel has been preached, who have understood it and of their own accord desire baptism, and who are willing to mortify the old man and lead a new life. Of all this the infants know nothing whatever, therefore baptism is not intended for them." Here they cited the Scriptures on baptism from the Gospels and the Acts of the Apostles, and showed that the apostles did not baptize infants, but only those who had come to an age of understanding; therefore the same should now be done. And infant baptism, being not administered in accord with the Scripture, was invalid, and it was necessary to be baptized anew.

Bullinger, though a bitter opponent of the Brethren, has undoubtedly given a reliable account of this disputation. The Zurich Council, in reporting to the Schaffhausen authorities, claimed modestly that Zwingli had shown that infant baptism was "nothing wrong" (*nichts unrechtes*).

The next day, January 18, the council issued a decree that all who failed to baptize their infants before the age of eight days were to be exiled.

On January 21 the council issued a mandate to restrain Conrad Grebel and Felix Manz from holding further meetings. These meetings had been held for several years prior to 1525, in various places in Switzerland, under the leadership of men called *readers*. The meetings were called *Bible schools*. The leaders read and expounded the Word of God. In St. Gall, for instance, John Kessler was a reader. Those who participated in the St. Gall meetings called one another *brethren*. (Kessler finally ceased being a reader at the request of the St. Gall Council. His place as a reader was taken by Wolfgang Schorant, called Ulimann.) In Zurich Andrew Castelberger, called *Andrew-on-the Crutches*, originally of the

Grisons, a bookseller, held Bible meetings as early as 1522. He gave expositions of the Epistles to the Romans, and taught Biblical nonresistance. Conrad Grebel and Felix Manz also held meetings, Grebel expounding Matthew's Gospel from the original Greek, and Manz teaching from a Hebrew Old Testament. These *schools* were the nuclei out of which the Swiss Brethren members were recruited.

What would have been the natural thing for the Zurich Brethren to do in view of the council's mandate of January 21, 1525? They probably met together to discuss their plight. In any case it is known that "a few days" after the debate of January 17 the Brethren met together, apparently in Zollikon, near Zurich, and inaugurated believers' baptism. Conrad Grebel was the recognized leader of the Zurich Brethren and he it was who took the momentous step of founding Anabaptism, on or about January 21, 1525.

An interesting account of this memorable occasion, apparently as seen through the eyes of George Blaurock, a participant, has been preserved in *The Oldest Chronicle of the Hutterian Brethren* (translated), Zieglschmid edition, 1943, pages 46 to 49:

> At this time it came to pass that a person came to them [to Grebel and Manz] from Chur, namely a priest [a monk from the St. Lucius monastery of Chur, the Grisons] named George of the House of Jacob. He was also called *Blaurock* [Bluecoat] because one time when they were having a discussion of matters of faith in a meeting, George of the House of Jacob presented his understanding [of the matter] also. Someone asked who it was who had just spoken. Thereupon someone answered: The person in the blue coat spoke. Thus he got the name *Blaurock* [Bluecoat] after that. . . .
>
> This one first came to Zwingli and discussed matters of faith with him at length, but accomplished nothing. Then he was told that there were other men there who were more zealous than Zwingli. These men he inquired for diligently and found them, namely, Conrad Grebel and Felix Manz. With them he spoke and talked through matters of faith. They came to one mind in these things, and in the pure fear of God they recognized that a person must learn from the divine Word and preaching a true faith which manifests itself in love, and receive the true Christian baptism on the basis of the recognized and confessed faith, in the union with God of a good conscience, and henceforth serve God in a holy Christian life with all godliness; also to be steadfast in affliction [persecution] to the end.
>
> And it came to pass that they were together until anxious fear came upon them, yea, they were moved in their hearts. Then they began to bow their knees to the Most High God in heaven, and called upon Him the Knower of hearts, imploring Him to enable them to do His divine will, and to manifest His mercy to them. For flesh and blood and human forwardness did not motivate them, since they well knew what they would have to bear and suffer on account of it.
>
> After the prayer George of the House of Jacob arose and asked Conrad Grebel to baptize him, for God's sake, with the true Christian baptism upon

his faith and knowledge. And when he knelt down with that request and desire, Conrad baptized him, since at that time there was no ordained minister to perform such work. After that was done the others similarly desired George to baptize them, which he also did upon their request. Thus they together gave themselves to the Name of the Lord in the high fear of God. Each ordained the other to the ministry of the Gospel, and they began to teach and keep the faith. Therewith began separation from the world and its evil works. . . .

Therefore it [Anabaptism] spread through persecution and much affliction; the church increased daily, and the Lord's people grew in numbers. This the enemy of the divine truth could not endure. He used Zwingli as an instrument, and he began to write diligently and to preach from the pulpit that the baptism of believers and adults was not right and should not be tolerated—contrary to his own confession which he had previously written and taught, namely, that infant baptism cannot be demonstrated or proved with a single clear word from God. But now, since he wished rather to please men than God, he contended against the true Christian baptism; he also stirred up the government to act on Imperial authorization and behead as Anabaptists those who had properly given themselves to God, and with a good understanding had made the covenant of a good conscience with God.

Finally it reached the point that over twenty men, widows, pregnant wives, and virgins were cast miserably into dark towers, sentenced never again to see either sun or moon as long as they lived, to end their days on bread and water, and thus in the dark towers to remain together, the living and the dead, until none remained alive—there to die, to stink, and to rot. Some among them did not eat a mouthful of bread in three days, just so that others might have to eat.

Soon also there was issued a stern mandate at the instigation of Zwingli that if any more people in the Zurich territory should accept [re]baptism they should immediately, without further trial, hearing, or sentence, be thrust into the water and drowned. Here one sees which spirit's child Zwingli was, and those of his party still are.

Conrad Grebel was led to evangelical faith by Zwingli. But once Grebel began to read God's Word with an earnest determination to follow God in everything, he simply had to come to a break with the Roman priest, Zwingli. There was no choice. God had to be obeyed at the cost of liberty, yea, of life itself. The Brethren saw the issues; they knew what the consequences of their decision would be; they did what they knew God required of them. And thus was Swiss Anabaptism born. God Himself kindled the light that has shone, though at times rather weakly, for more than four centuries. To Him be all the glory.

READINGS

Bender, H. S.: "Conrad Grebel, The Founder of Swiss Anabaptism," *Church History,* 7:157-178, June 1938.

Bender, H. S.: "Conrad Grebel, the First Leader of the Swiss Brethren (Anabaptists)," *The Mennonite Quarterly Review,* I, 10:5-45, Ja. 1936; II, 10:91-137, Ap. 1936; III, 10:151-160, Jl. 1936 [IV] 15:67-82, Ap. 1941.

Bender, H. S.: "The Theology of Conrad Grebel," *The Mennonite Quarterly Review*, 12:27-54, Ja. 1938; II, 12:114-134, Ap. 1938.

Bender, H. S.: "The Anabaptist Vision," *The Mennonite Quarterly Review*, 18:67-88, Ap. 1944.

Bender, H. S.: *Mennonite Origins in Europe*, M.C.C., Akron, Pennsylvania, 1942, 8-18.

Bergmann, Cornelius: *Die Täuferbewegung im Kanton Zürich Bis 1660*, Verlag von M. Heinsius Nachfolger, Leipzig, 1916, 1-170.

Burckhardt, Paul: *Die Basler Täufer*, R. Reich, Basel, 1898, 6-125.

Fisher, G. P.: *History of the Christian Church*, Charles Scribner's Sons, New York, 1916, 287-318.

Heussi Karl: *Kompendium der Kirchengeschichte*, Mohr Verlag, Tübingen, 1933, 244-276.

Horsch, John: "The Rise and Early History of the Swiss Brethren Church," *The Mennonite Quarterly Review*, 6:169-191, Jl. 1932; 6:227-249, O. 1932.

Horsch, John: "The Struggle Between Zwingli and the Swiss Brethren in Zurich," *The Mennonite Quarterly Review*, 7:142-161, Jl. 1933.

Horsch, John: "The Faith of the Swiss Brethren," *The Mennonite Quarterly Review*, 4:241-266, O. 1930; 5:7-27, Ja. 1931; 5:128-147, Ap. 1931; 5, 245-259, O. 1931.

Horsch, John: "An Inquiry into the Truth of Accusations of Fanaticism and Crime Against the Early Swiss Brethren," *The Mennonite Quarterly Review*, 8:18-31, Ja. 1934; 8:73-89, Ap. 1934.

Horsch, John: "The Swiss Brethren in St. Gall and Appenzell," *The Mennonite Quarterly Review*, 7:205-226, O. 1933.

Horsch, John: "The Character of the Evangelical Anabaptists as Reported by Contemporary Reformation Writers," *The Mennonite Quarterly Review*, 8:123-135, Jl. 1934.

Horsch, John: "The Persecution of the Evangelical Anabaptists," *The Mennonite Quarterly Review*, 12:3-26, Ja. 1938.

Horsch, John: *Mennonites in Europe*, Scottdale, Pennsylvania, 1942, 21-69.

McGlothlin, W. J.: *The Course of Christian History*, The Macmillan Company, New York, 1918, 102-117.

Neff, Christian: "Konrad Grebel, Sein Leben und Wirken," *Gedenkschrift Zum 400 Jährigen Jubiläum der Mennoniten oder Taufgesinnten, 1525-1925*, Ludwigshafen a. Rh., 1925, 65-133.

Neff, Christian: "Grebel, Konrad," *Mennonitisches Lexikon*, Herausgegeben von Christian Hege, Frankfurt am Main, und Christian Neff, Weierhof (Pfalz), Zweiter Band, 1937, 163-169.

Newman, A. H.: *A Manual of Church History*, Volume II, American Baptist Publication Society, Philadelphia, [1903], 40-200.

Newman, A. H.: *A History of Anti-Pedobaptism . . .*, American Baptist Publication Society, Philadelphia, 1897, 62-76, 88-119.

Nichols, R. H.: *The Growth of the Christian Church*, Volume II, *Modern Christianity*, The Westminster Press, Philadelphia, 1939, 23-49.

Qualben, Lars P.: *A History of the Christian Church*, Thomas Nelson and Sons, New York, 1933, 205-248.

Schaff, Philip: *History of the Christian Church*, Volume VI, *Modern Christianity*, Charles Scribner's Sons, 1908, 105-549.

Smith, C. Henry: *The Story of the Mennonites*, Mennonite Book Concern, Berne, Indiana, (1941), 9-74.

Smithson, R. J.: *The Anabaptists: Their Contribution to Our Protestant Heritage*, James Clarke & Co., Ltd., London, [1935], 35-55, 141-143.

CHAPTER III

The Swiss Brethren and Their Leaders

It should be of interest to present brief biographical sketches of a few of the more outstanding leaders of the Swiss Brethren. Sketches will be given only of those who were recognized as in full fellowship with the Swiss Brethren and who subscribed to all their teaching. Men like Hans Denck, who had his own mystical brand of Anabaptism, and Balthasar Hubmaier who led a group of Anabaptists who rejected nonresistance(the so-called (*Schwertler*) will not be discussed.

1. Felix Manz, c. 1480-1527

Felix Manz was born about 1480, the son of a Catholic canon (cathedral clergyman) of Zurich. A well educated man, he had a knowledge of Latin, Greek, and Hebrew. Manz, like Grebel, was an enthusiastic follower of Zwingli in the early years of his reform work. And, like Grebel, Manz broke with Zwingli on the issue of a speedy abolition of the mass, the introduction of believers' baptism, and the separation of church and state. Manz participated in the first disputation with Zwingli on January 17, 1525, and he was undoubtedly present a few days later when Grebel inaugurated adult baptism.

Following the second disputation with Zwingli, held March 20, 1525, Manz, along with twenty other Swiss Brethren (fourteen men in all, and seven women) was imprisoned in the "Witch Tower" on the *Prediger-Kirchhof* of Zurich. In April they escaped from their imprisonment. Soon they were again seized and examined as to their faith. In the examination Manz stated that he never rejected the government, nor *Zinsen, and tithes.* (The meaning of *Zinsen* is not entirely clear. Used alone, the term meant interest or usury. Used in conjunction with tithes it apparently referred to a sort of church tax. The income from *Zinsen* and tithes was used in the support of Catholic clergymen, as Conrad Grebel indicated in his letter to Münzer.) At his hearing Manz further stated that he rejected both capital punishment and the use of the sword. However, he did not teach the community of goods; he taught only that Christians should be ready to share with the needy. He admitted that he had performed baptisms at Embrach fourteen days after his escape from the Witch Tower,—and he would do so again!

Following his release, Manz worked in the Zurich *Oberland* (Highland), especially in Grüningen. By the middle of May, however, he was in the canton of the Grisons. On July 18 he was forcibly returned by the authorities from Chur to Zurich where he was imprisoned in the Wellenberg prison until October 7, 1525. The next day he and Grebel were participating in an Anabaptist meeting which the local ruler (*Landvogt*) suddenly took by surprise. Grebel was caught, but Manz escaped and was not captured until October 31.

On November 6-8, 1525, a third disputation was held. As in March, Grebel, Manz, and Blaurock stood against Zwingli on baptism. But the November meetings, begun in the city hall and completed in the Great Minster, were more nearly a real debate than the March sessions. In March Zwingli simply called in the Swiss Brethren leaders one by one, and asked them certain questions. But even in the November disputation Zwingli decided which questions should be discussed. The outcome was that on November 18 the three Brethren were sentenced to imprisonment on a diet of bread, gruel, and water. But soon the Brethren were free and worked in the Zurich Highland until they were once more arrested. On March 7, 1526, Grebel, Manz, and Blaurock together with fifteen other Swiss Brethren, including six women, were sentenced to live on beds of straw in the New Tower, on a diet of bread and water, until they should die and rot. Yet the leaders were out of prison the next month. It appears that there were friends of the Brethren in high places.

On December 3, 1526 Manz and Blaurock (Grebel had died of the plague the previous summer) were seized in a meeting of the Brethren in a Grüningen forest and were shortly thereafter brought to Zurich and imprisoned for the last time in the Wellenberg prison. Manz was sentenced to die on January 5, 1527,

> because he accepted the teaching of rebaptism contrary to Christian order and practice, accepted the same [was rebaptized], taught it to others and was especially a chief leader and instigator of these things; because he admitted having said that he and others like him who accepted Christ and intended to follow Him wished to come together and unite themselves through rebaptism, and leave the others [undisturbed] in their faith; that he and his adherents wished to separate themselves from the Christian Church, and intended to raise up and mobilize a peculiar, self-initiated sect under the pretense and

appearance of a Christian meeting and church; because he rejected capital punishment; and for the sake of greater success boasted of certain revelations from the epistles of the apostle Paul. But since such teachings are detrimental to the uniform practice of all of Christendom, and since they lead to scandal, rebellion, and riot against the government, to the ruin of the general peace, of brotherly love and of civil concord, and to every calamity, therefore Manz shall be delivered over to the executioner who shall bind his hands, put him in a boat, lead him to the lower hut, and at the lower hut place his bound hands over his knees and thrust a stick between his legs and arms, and throw him bound in that way into the water, and leave him in the water to die and to perish. Thus shall he pay the price to law and justice.

This dreadful sentence was carried out at three o'clock in the afternoon. Past the fish-market Manz was led as he praised God with a loud voice. From the other side of the Limmat River his mother called to her son to be steadfast. Before Manz was thrown into the water, he cried out in Latin with a loud voice, "Into Thy hands, O Lord, I commend my spirit." His body was laid to rest in St. Jacob's cemetery, Zurich.

Felix Manz was the author of hymn number six in the *Ausbund,* the Swiss Brethren hymnbook of 1564. The hymn begins, "With pleasure will I sing; My heart doth joy in God," and closes with the words, "With Christ will I remain, Who all my need doth know."

2. George Blaurock, c. 1480-1529

George of the House of Jacob was born in the Swiss canton of the Grisons, in a town called Bonaduz. He secured his academic training in the schools of Chur, and near Chur he entered the St. Lucius Monastery. He came to Zurich in time to be present at the memorable meeting when Conrad Grebel founded Swiss Anabaptism, January, 1525. It is claimed that when George came to Zurich he was already a married man. He was described as a "tall, powerful figure with fiery eyes, black hair and a small bald spot." Because of his great energy and zeal he was called "Strong George." Two incidents will illustrate the zeal of Blaurock and Manz.

On the first Sunday in February, 1525, Blaurock and a group of his adherents appeared in the Zollikon Church and asked the priest, who was about to ascend to the pulpit, what he wished to do. "Preach the Word of God," replied the priest, a follower of Zwingli. "You were not sent to preach; it was I," declared Strong George, and he proceeded to the pulpit and preached. On February 7, Manz, Blaurock and twenty-two others were imprisoned in the Augustinian Monastery in Zurich. Soon all but Manz and Blaurock were released again, however.

The following story illustrates the methods of Blaurock and Manz. It rests on the testimony of Rüedi Thomann of Zollikon, an eye-witness and participant (the events described took place in his home):

> After much conversation and reading, Hans Bruggbach stood up weeping and crying out that he was a great sinner and asking that they pray God for him. Then Blaurock asked him whether he desired the grace of God. He said he did. Then Manz rose and said, "Who will forbid that I should baptize him?" Blaurock answered, "No one." Then Manz took a dipper with water and baptized him in the name of the Father, Son, and Holy Spirit. Then stood up Jacob Hottinger. Him also Manz baptized. Then the others all went away and Manz and Blaurock remained with him over night. They rose early the next morning. Then Blaurock said to his son-in-law: "Marx, you have hitherto been a gay young man. You must make a change. You must put away the old Adam and put on a new. Marx answered that he would do his best. Then Blaurock asked whether he desired the grace of God, and when he said that he did, Blaurock said: "Come hither and I will baptize you also." Then Marx went to him and was baptized. Then Blaurock said to him (Rüedi Thomann), that he was an old man and near to death and that he should amend his life, and said that if he desired the grace of God he would baptize him too. And when he said that he did, Blaurock baptized him. After this Blaurock would have no rest until he had baptized the whole household. . . . They had a loaf upon the table and Blaurock said: "Whoever believes that God has redeemed him with His death and His rose-colored blood, let him come and eat with me of the bread and drink with me of this wine." Then they ate and drank (Newman).

As soon as Blaurock was released from prison he returned to Zollikon and in Jacob Hottinger's house baptized Henry Aberli with a "handful of water." He also preached to an assembly of over one hundred and fifty people in the forenoon and afternoon, baptizing both men and women. The meetings were held in John Maurer's house.

In April 1525, Blaurock was imprisoned in the Witch Tower in Zurich, but that same month he, along with Grebel, Manz, eleven other Brethren and seven women made their escape. Manz and Blaurock then worked first in the Zurich Highland, then in Chur, Blaurock's former home. There they were arrested in July. Manz was returned to Zurich but Blaurock had friends who succeeded in having him released. Thereupon he worked in Appenzell for a time, after which he returned to the Zurich Highland.

On October 8, 1525, Blaurock entered a church at Hinwyl where over two hundred worshipers were assembled. He went up into the pulpit and began to preach. The pastor of the church entered the building and heard Blaurock preaching. He listened quietly until Blaurock got on the subject of baptism. Then he interrupted him and a tumult arose. So the pastor left the church and ran to the ruler of Grüningen for help. When the ruler arrived, Blaurock was still in the pulpit preaching. He was promptly arrested, placed on a horse, and taken away, singing as he went. This arrest at Hinwyl, together with other things, led to the third Anabaptist disputation after which Blaurock and others were sentenced to live out their days in the New Tower on a diet of bread, water, and gruel.

Soon Grebel, Manz, and Blaurock were again free, however, and were working in the Zurich Highland. Once more they were arrested. Blaurock then had a three-hour discussion with Zwingli and his coworker, Leo Judae. Nothing came of the argument, of course, for neither Zwingli nor Blaurock would budge an inch. On March 7, 1526, the three leaders, and fifteen more of the Swiss Brethren faith (nine men and six women) were sentenced to "die and rot" in the New Tower. But somehow they did not die in jail. There were evidently powerful friends of the Brethren who managed to thwart the plans of Zwingli. One of these was Jacob Grebel whose influence ended only when he was beheaded on October 30, 1526.

Blaurock promised to leave Zurich territory for good. But, as Dr. Neff observes, his love for the Brethren and for his life work was stronger than his sense of obligation to a promise made under duress. So he returned to Grüningen and on December 3, 1526, he was once more arrested, this time in a meeting of the Brethren in a forest. On the day of Manz's martyrdom, Blaurock, not being a Zurich citizen, was not executed but was stripped to the waist and severely beaten with rods as he went from the fish-market to the lower city gate. There, after first protesting, he is said to have sworn never to return to Zurich. As he left the city he shook the dust off his clothing against it.

Blaurock now moved about a great deal. In January, 1528, he appeared in Berne, Switzerland, where he and seven other Brethren had a disputation with Zwingli and an assistant named Smith. One of the eight Brethren was persuaded to unite with Zwinglians, not Blaurock to be sure! Blaurock then went to Biel in the Canton of Berne. Later he appeared in Appenzell. In May, 1529, he was in the Tirol, where he spent the remainder of his days. And very active days they were. Blaurock "went everywhere, preaching the Word": Vels, Tiers, Breitenberg, ab-Penon, Clausen.

Finally Blaurock and a fellow minister named John Langegger were arrested and imprisoned in August 1529. On the twenty-fourth day of the month they were horribly tortured. On September 6, 1529, Blaurock and Langegger, a weaver, were burned to death as heretics. A. H. Newman estimates that during the four and a half years of his career as a Swiss Brethren leader, Blaurock baptized a thousand or more converts. But at last he died a martyr's death. At last he won a martyr's crown. In one of his hymns, Blaurock had written:

As He Himself our sufferings bore,
When hanging on the accursed tree,
So there is suffering still in store,
O pious heart, for you and me.

3. Michael Sattler, c. 1495-1527

Michael Sattler was born in the town of Staufen in Breisgau, then Austrian territory, the latter part of the fifteenth century. Staufen is not far from the German city of Freiburg. It is supposed that Sattler studied in the University of Freiburg, for he was described as "a highly educated man, well versed in several languages and in the holy Scriptures, a true lover of God."

As a young man he decided to consecrate his life to the service of the Roman Catholic Church. He entered St. Peter's Monastery near Freiburg, and in time occupied a position of trust and responsibility. He himself speaks of having been a "lord according to the flesh." But the lord of the monks was not content to continue in the monastery. He studied the word of God—he mentions the Pauline epistles in particular—and being nauseated with the carnality of the monks and priests, he left his order and married a wife. In 1525 he was in Zurich, Switzerland, where he associated himself with the Swiss Brethren. But his work in the canton of Zurich was destined to be of short duration. On November 18, 1525 he was banished as an Anabaptist.

His next major place of residence was in Strasburg in Alsace. There Wolfgang Capito (1478-1541), the official head of the Strasburg clergy, received Sattler into his home. Following the martyrdom of Sattler, Capito paid him this tribute: "He ever exhibited an excellent zeal for the honor of God and the Church of Christ, a church which he demanded be pious and honorable, pure from calumny and inoffensive . . ." The leading reformer of Strasburg, Martin Butzer

(1491-1551), was of the opinion that out of love the Anabaptists ought to unite with the state church regardless of their differences in Christian doctrine and practice. Early in 1527 Sattler submitted a statement of his views to Capito and Butzer, a statement consisting of twenty articles. The essential difference between Sattler and the Strasburg clergy lay in their respective doctrines of the church. The clergy thought of the church as a people's church in which all infants were gathered into the fold by infant baptism; a church whose members undertook the necessary duties of earthly citizenship. Sattler and his Swiss Brethren fellow believers insisted that the church was composed only of those who were personally united to Christ in saving faith and whose lives were lived in strict obedience to Christ. The earmark of true Christians is their carrying out of Christ's teachings in their lives. The citizenship of Christ's followers is in heaven, not on earth. Indeed they have a feeling of inner estrangement from the "world." When a person becomes a believer he is to be inducted into Christ's body by water baptism, not baptized as an infant.

Sattler soon left Strasburg and settled for a time in the area of Horb, a small town on the Neckar River, in the south German province of Württemberg. In Horb Sattler had good success in his ministry. Thirty-five families were represented in the list of accessions to the Swiss Brethren congregation there.

On February 24, 1527 Sattler presided over a conference of Swiss Brethren held in the Swiss village of Schleitheim. He was the author of the confession of faith which the group adopted unanimously. (See pages 206-213 of this book.)

Soon after the Schleitheim conference Sattler was arrested and thrown into prison at Binzdorf. There he lay for over eleven weeks. in the company of some of his followers. From the prison he wrote a long letter to his congregation at Horb. This letter is printed in the *Martyrs' Mirror* (1938 edition, 418-420). "I cannot forget you," he wrote, "though I am not present with the body." "Dear brethren and sisters, you well know with what ardent love I admonished you the last time I was with you. . . ." "The brethren have doubtless informed you that some of us are in prison; and afterwards when the brethren at Horb had also been apprehended, they brought us to Binzdorf. At this time we met with various designs of our adversaries. Once they threatened us with bonds: then with fire, and afterwards with the sword. In this peril I completely surrendered myself into the will of the Lord, and together with all my fellow brethren and my wife, prepared myself even for death for His testimony. . . ." Apparently with the Schleitheim conference in mind he wrote: "Remember our assembly, and strictly follow that which was resolved on therein. . . . Be liberal towards all that are in want among you, but especially towards those who labor among you in the Word, and are driven about, and cannot eat their bread in peace and quietness." ". . . If I be offered up to the Lord, do for my wife what you would for me."

About the middle of May, 1527 Sattler was taken from the Binzdorf Tower and transferred to Rottenburg, another city on the Neckar, where he stood trial for the "heresy" of Anabaptism. The court preferred nine charges against him.

> First, that he and his adherents have acted contrary to the mandate of the Emperor.
> Secondly, he has taught, held and believed that the body and blood of Christ are not present in the sacrament.
> Thirdly, he has taught and believed that infant baptism does not conduce to salvation.
> Fourthly, they have rejected the sacrament of extreme unction.
> Fifthly, they have despised and condemned the mother of God and the saints.
> Sixthly, he has declared that men are not to swear before the authorities.
> Seventhly, he has commenced a new and unheard of custom in regard to the Lord's Supper, placing the bread and wine on a plate, and eating and drinking the same.
> Eighthly, he has left the order, and married a wife.
> Ninthly, he has said that if the Turks should invade the country, no resistance ought to be offered them; and if it were right to wage war, he would rather take the field against the Christians than against the Turks . . .

Sattler requested the privilege of conferring with his "brethren and sisters," which was granted. In a short time he fearlessly made his reply to eight of the nine charges; he omitted the seventh. The first charge he denied, claiming that the Imperial Mandate required fidelity to the Gospel and to God's Word, not to Lutheranism. Secondly, he admitted denying the doctrine of transubstantiation. Thirdly, he admitted holding to the belief that faith alone, not infant baptism, can save. Fourthly, he stated that the "pope's oil" (extreme unction) is not what James mentions (5:14). Fifthly, he denied the form of the charges relating to Mary and the saints, but he did state that Mary was not a mediatress, and that we believing Christians are the "saints." Sixthly, he based his nonswearing of oaths on the direct words of Christ (Matt. 5:34). To the eighth charge he replied that the great carnality of the celibate clergy, together with God's command, had led him to marry a wife. On the last charge he admitted teaching that Christians should not resist evil men but should earnestly cry to God for divine protection. On the charge of preferring to fight at the side of the Turks he explained that the Turks, not being Christians, do not know better than to kill believers; but the professing Christians who persecute Christ's pious witnesses are "Turks after the spirit." In conclusion, Sattler pleaded for the privilege of discussing the Word of God with the judges, but at the conclusion of his speech the judges indulged in laughter. Sattler was also abused by a town clerk who was present. The clerk, in his "godly" zeal, declared: "You desperate villain and arch-heretic, I tell you if there were no hangman here, I would hang you myself, and think that I had done God service." The abuse continued after the judges had retired to determine the sentence. After an hour and a half they returned and the sentence was read:

> In the case of the Governor of His imperial Majesty *versus* Michael Sattler, judgment is passed, that Michael Sattler shall be delivered to the executioner, who shall lead him to the place of execution, and cut out his tongue; then throw him upon a wagon, and there tear his body twice with red hot tongs; and after he has been brought without the gate, he shall be pinched five times in the same manner. Thereupon he shall burn his body to ashes as a heretic.

This dreadful sentence was carried out May 21, 1527; he was burned to ashes as a good witness of Jesus Christ. While in the fire he help up his hands as a token of his faith, a sign which he had previously given to his followers. His wife showed the same constancy as her noble husband and won the martyr's crown by being drowned for her faith, in the Neckar river.

4. Pilgram Marpeck, c. 1495-1556

Conrad Grebel died in 1526 of the plague. Felix Manz was put to death by drowning in 1527. Michael Sattler was burned to death the same year. George Blaurock was also burned to death, in 1529 in the Tirol. The only outstanding Swiss Brethren leader who was permitted a normal life span and a natural death was the Tirolese, Pilgram Marpeck.

Pilgram—a form of *Pilger* (Pilgrim)—was born at Rattenberg in the Inn valley of the Tirol the latter part of the fifteenth century, probably within the last decade. Judging by the Latin flavor in Marpeck's language, he must have attended the Latin school of Rattenberg as a youth.

By the year 1520 Marpeck was getting a start in the world. On February 26 of that year he and his wife Anna were received into the mining guild at Rattenberg. Three years later he became a member of the lower city council, and by 1525 he was a member of the upper council.

In April 1525 he was appointed as a mine magistrate at Rattenberg and granted an annual salary of sixty-five pounds. But this position he did not hold very long. By the close of 1527 Marpeck had made the spiritual journey from Catholicism to Lutheranism to Anabaptism. On January 28, 1528 he lost his position as mine magistrate. His property was confiscated under the pretense of raising funds for the rearing of the three orphans he had taken into his home.

Pilgram, his wife Anna, and their daughter fled the country early in 1528. Before the close of the year he was participating in Anabaptist meetings in Strasburg in Alsace. There he received employment as an engineer to construct waterways for floating lumber to the city. It was not long until Marpeck succeeded William Reublin as leader of the Strasburg Anabaptists. By 1531 Marpeck was baptizing converts, in spite of the disfavor with which Anabaptism was regarded in the city. On October 23, 1531, Martin Butzer wrote: "Pilgram will not desist from baptizing and persuading people that swearing and defense by force are not right; I fear he will be exiled." It was also in the year 1531 that the Strasburg censors suppressed two booklets of Marpeck which defended believer's baptism. Marpeck also lost his freedom, and was punished for giving pastoral aid to his fellow prisoners. In December 1531 and January 1532 Marpeck had three disputations with Martin Butzer but neither man would yield to the other. Pilgram was expelled from the city for opposing infant baptism, insisting on rebaptism, establishing a "separatist" church, opposing the civil oath, and rejecting defense by force. Where Marpeck settled in 1532—if he had a settled residence—is not clear. Some clues point to a possible return to the Inn valley in the Tirol. In 1540 he visited Moravia, also in the Grisons, now a Swiss canton. In 1542 Marpeck was in Ulm, Württemberg, South Germany. From 1544 until his death in 1556 Marpeck lived in the city of Augsburg in Bavarian Swabia.

Marpeck was active as a Swiss Brethren writer. Early in 1542 he and his collaborators issued a Treatise on Baptism and the Lord's Supper, without author's name, date, or place of publication. By August of 1542 Caspar Schwenckfeld (1489-1561) a Reformer of a mystical type, had completed a *Criticism* of the Anabaptist treatise. At Schwenckfeld's invitation, Marpeck and his friends then wrote a *Reply* to Schwenckfeld—a huge manuscript, in two parts, printed for the first time in 1929. Marpeck and his brethren also issued a book of over eight hundred pages entitled *Testament Explanation.* These three volumes are the most extensive source of sixteenth century Swiss Brethren doctrine which is available.

Marpeck's first task as an engineer in Augsburg was the improvement of the city aqueducts, the building of waterways for floating lumber, and similar assignments. From 1546 until his death the city paid him 150 florins annually for his services as the *Stadt-Werkmeister.* Only one thing marred his relations with the city fathers, that was his activity as an Anabaptist. The mayor of the city sent him a warning in 1545. Five years later the city council was calling him to account for being charged with having written an Anabaptist book. In 1553 he was sent another warning. And a year later he was told that since he was still propagating his error, he should earn his shekels elsewhere. Nevertheless he managed to retain his position until his death.

Marpeck will never be rated as a great theologian, but he has furnished us with a good statement of Swiss Brethren doctrine, and he was the leading minister in the Swiss Brethren Church for twenty-five years.

5. Four Centuries of Swiss Brethren History

The Brethren in Switzerland never thrived numerically. One of the reasons was the heavy hand of persecution. Eberli Bolt, a minister, was burned to death by the Catholics on May 29, 1525, the first known Swiss Brethren martyr. William Reublin left Switzerland, spent some time in Strasburg and later was active in Moravia after which he disappears from the records. John Brötli of Zollikon on Lake Zurich was martyred in 1528, as was John Langenmantel of Augsburg, Germany. Langenmantel wrote hymn Number 37 in the Ausbund.

1. *Zurich*

The last known Swiss Mennonite to be executed (1614) was John Landis, "a tall stately person, with a long black and grey beard, and a manful voice." When Landis, a minister of the Brethren, was standing at the place of execution, his wife and children approached him to bid him a final farewell, but he requested them to depart lest their weeping disturb his tranquility. A Zurich clergyman who was present described Landis as "cheerful and of good courage." The executioner, Paul Volmar by name, dropped the rope by which he was leading Landis, raised both hands to heaven and entreated Landis for God's sake to forgive him. It was the opinion of the people that the dropping of the rope was to permit Landis to escape. But this he made no attempt to do. Rather he comforted Volmar, assuring him of his forgiveness. Having commended his soul to God, Landis was quickly beheaded. Landis had earlier been sentenced to galley slavery, but had escaped with the aid of some brethren. (Read the full story in the *Martyrs' Mirror*, 1103-5.)

The last struggle of Zurich with the Brethren began in 1635. (See the *Martyrs' Mirror*, 1938 edition, 1108 ff.) The persecution was especially severe from 1637 to 1639. The harshness of the Swiss so excited the sympathy of the Dutch government that the Lords States General of Holland addressed letters to the Zurich and Bernese governments. Following are extracts from the letter to Zurich:

THE STATES

TO THE CITY OF ZURICH IN SWITZERLAND:

Noble, very respectable, wise, prudent lords, especially good friends and neighbors. From the complaints of divers persons delegated by their respective churches who here in this land are called Mennonists, citizens and inhabitants of the cities of Dortrecht, Harlem, Leyden, Amsterdam, Goude, and Rotterdam, all situated in the province of Holland, we have learned that their fellow-believers under the name of Anabaptists have suffered great persecution in your dominion by virture of very rigorous edicts enacted against them, and that they have thereby been compelled to leave everything and to remove to other countries to their great inconvenience and total ruin.

All this has moved us to Christian compassion, and we could therefore not forbear, but on the contrary deemed it good hereby to request you very kindly and neighborly, also most earnestly, that you according to the good example of the magistrates of the city of Schaffhausen release the property of the fellow believers of the supplicants, which you have now for several years had managed by directors appointed over them, and drawn the fruits thereof, and deliver them to be sold within a certain sufficient time and turned into money for their benefit. . . .

We will rest confident, that you will defer to our well-meant friendly and neighborly intercession, as much as the justice of the matter demands, and as we expect from your usual wisdom and discretion. . . .

This accords with the minutes preserved in the records of their High Mightinesses.

J. Spronssen

In spite of severe persecution it is claimed that remnants of the Swiss Brethren held out in the Canton of Zurich until about the year 1735.

2. *Berne*

The Swiss Brethren faith was carried from the Canton of Zurich to the Canton of Berne the very year of the founding of the church, 1525, and for three hundred years there was more or less tension between the Swiss authorities and the Brethren. For the first century there were numerous martyrs—such as Hans Seckler, 1528; Conrad Eicher, two believers from Bix, a tinker from the Emme valley, Ulrich Schneider, a young lad from Wallis, and a martyr named Hagerly, 1529; Moritz Losenegger, 1536; Bernard Waelty, John Schweitzer, Juerg Hoffser, Ulrich Bichsel, Barbeli Willher, Barbeli zur Studen, Catharina Friedli Imhoff, Verena Issoli and Ulrich of Ruegsau, 1537; Cunas Seidenkohen, Peter Stucki, Ulrich Huben, John Willer, Elizabeth Kuepfer, two other women, Peter Wessenmiller, Stephen Ruegsegger, one from Siegnau, one from Summiswald and Rudolph Isolly, 1538; Lorenz Aeberly and John Schumacher, 1539. Perhaps the most famous of the Bernese Swiss Brethren martyrs was John (Hans) Haslibacher who was beheaded December 20, 1571. (The account of his martyrdom is found in the last hymn of the Swiss Brethren hymnal, the *Ausbund.* An English translation of this hymn of 32 stanzas is found in the *Martyrs' Mirror,* 1128f. In many cases no records were kept by the Bernese authorities of their executions of Swiss Brethren victims. But in the treasurer's books will be found an occasional notation: "For burying an Anabaptist" or "For burying two Anabaptists."

Many disputations were held between the Swiss Brethren ministers and the Reformed Church clergy. The two most important disputations were those held at Zofingen in canton Berne July 1-9, 1532 and the 1538 disputation at Berne. A printed record of the 1532 sessions has been preserved and unprinted minutes of the 1538 discussions are still extant.

Not only were disputations held, however. Many mandates against the Brethren were issued from 1525 until 1743. The Berne mandate of 1659, for example, contains the following declarations:

> But to those who accept no reminding, instruction or admonition but continue disobedient and stubborn, neither will renounce or depart from their error, the penalty of banishment imposed upon them shall be announced, and their immovable obstinacy and reprobacy be made known to the directors appointed by us over the affairs of the Anabaptists, that our further orders with regard to it may be expected.
>
> And when such obstinate, erring persons upon the above-mentioned report have been sentenced by the court, it is our meaning, intention and command that they under a safe escort be conducted to the boundary and by a promise in place of an oath (since they do not swear an oath) be utterly banished from our country and dominion until their apparent conversion; and if they, notwithstanding the banishment, return unconverted and are apprehended and still do not recant but obstinately persevere in their error as before, they shall as often as this occurs be publicly scourged with rods, branded, and again as before expelled and banished from the country. . . . (The full text of this mandate is found in *Martyrs' Mirror,* 1938 edition, 1130, 1131.)

In 1659 Berne created a department of government called the "Anabaptist Commission," the purpose of which was to suppress the Swiss Brethren church life. It was therefore a godsend for the Brethren when in 1664 the Count Palatine opened up his country, the Palatinate, to the Swiss Anabaptists. And when Berne initiated another wave of persecution against the Brethren in 1671, the offer of the Count Palatine, qualified as it was, appeared most attractive to the Swiss. In 1671 the Bernese magistrates also sold six Brethren into galley slavery on the Mediterranean, to row ships from Milan to Malta; one of the six was the father of nine children. Indeed the Bernese council actually decided on a policy of sending the younger men to the galleys and of either banishing the older men or sentencing them to life imprisonment for their "heresy." Consequently about seven hundred Bernese Mennonites fled down the Rhine, and with Dutch Mennonite aid, established themselves in the Palatinate. (Cf. *Martyrs' Mirror,* 1125-1127.)

Another source of misery for the Bernese Brethren was the creation of special constables called *Täufer-Jäger* (Anabaptist-hunters) to apprehend the Brethren.

In 1709 there was a fresh outbreak of persecution for the Mennonites living in Berne and another flight of Swiss refugees occurred. This time they settled not only in the Palatinate, but also in Holland and North America. Again the Dutch Mennonites were of great assistance financially. As late as 1714 Berne sentenced a number of Brethren to the galleys. And as recently as 1811 twenty-seven Mennonite children were baptized by force by the Reformed clergy at Langnau in the Emme valley.

Persecution and immigration kept the number of Swiss Mennonites small. In 1823 Berne ordered a census of all its Anabaptists, together with the time and place of their meetings. In that year the Brethren numbered 1,365. During the first half of the nineteenth century many Bernese Mennonites settled in Wayne County, Ohio, and Adams County, Indiana, where strong congregations soon developed.

At last, in the year 1815, Berne finally decided to allow its Mennonites to purchase military freedom. The matter was discussed in the Berne senate in 1835. One senator declared, "If we wished to compel the Anabaptists to do military service, we would make them martyrs of their faith. For not a single Anabaptist will allow himself to be forced to take up arms."

The last known Swiss Mennonite to be imprisoned for his faith was Elder (bishop) Ulrich Steiner (1806-77). The charge against him was "proselyting."

In 1874 two significant changes were made in the Bernese law regarding the Mennonites: (1) they were at last given full religious freedom; (2) they lost the military exemption which had been granted them in 1815. The only provision made for their scruples against military training and service was that they were permitted to do noncombatant service such as that in the sanitation department of the army. At first the Mennonites objected strenuously, particularly to the compulsory wearing of the uniform, but in the end they submitted. Today many Swiss Mennonites accept full military training, and some have even become officers in the Swiss army.

Most of the Swiss Mennonites still live in the canton of Berne; a few are found in Basle and elsewhere. Altogether they number something like a thousand baptized members, comprising fourteen small congregations. All the Swiss Mennonites could therefore be seated in one of the larger meetinghouses of the American Mennonites. Incidentally the Swiss Mennonites built their first church building in 1888, the "Kehr" meetinghouse near Langnau in the Emme valley, canton Berne. The Emme valley congregation with three hundred baptized members is the largest of the Swiss Mennonite churches.

6. Schisms in Berne

(1) *The Amish,* 1693

Only one major division took place in the entire four centuries of Swiss Brethren history. The trouble started when a young elder named Jacob Ammann began to hold the communion service twice a year instead of annually as had earlier been the Swiss Brethren practice. (It is still held annually in most of the Franconia Conference congregations in Pennsylvania.) In connection with the discussion of the communion matter, Ammann, who was a man of profound opinions and a bit rash, demanded to know the opinion of an older bishop, John Reist, on the subject of avoidance or shunning. (Avoidance means the breaking of social fellowship between the brotherhood and an excommunicated person. Prior to this time—that is, from 1525 until 1693—the Swiss Brethren had not placed a very strict interpretation on such Scriptures as I Corinthians 5:11, "with such an one no not to eat." Indeed, the Swiss had never applied this particular Scripture to anything but the Lord's Supper, and even the Alsatian Brethren who in 1660 had adopted the Dutch Dordrecht Confession of Faith of 1632, article 17 of which teaches avoidance, did not practice shunning in a strict manner at all.) Reist did not favor Ammann's views on avoidance.

Ammann also took it upon himself to raise the level of Mennonite Church life in Switzerland to what he thought it should be. He went about from place to place demanding that the ministers take a stand on avoidance. Reist wrote a letter which rejected Ammann's emphasis on avoidance and which also urged the readers not to pay too much attention to the young man Ammann. Ammann called a meeting which Reist did not attend and "expelled" Reist and several other ministers. In fact he expelled Swiss Brethren ministers not only in Berne but also in Alsace. However the following Alsatian ministers stood by Ammann: Jacob Kleiner, Jacob Kauffman, John Moyer, Peter Zimmerman, John Bachman, John Newhouser, Felix Hager, Nicholas Augspurger, Henry Gerei, Christian Steiner, Ulrich Oswald, and Ulrich Ammann. The following is a partial list of the Swiss ministers who sided with Reist: Peter Habegger, Ulrich Falb, Nicholas Baltzli, Peter Geiger, Dursch Rohrer, Jacob Swartz, Daniel Grimmstettler and Ulrich Baltzley. The following Palatine ministers also stood by Reist: Jacob Good, John Good, Peter Zolfinger, Christian Holi, Benedict Mellinger, John Henry

Baer and John Rudy Naegeli. Ammann finally had placed ministers from Switzerland, Alsace, and the Palatinate, some of whom he had never seen, under the ban.

Ammann's point of view was that the Reist party was too lenient, both on avoidance and on other things. The other items were chiefly three: (1) Ammann was critical of Reist for failing to excommunicate a woman who was said to have told an untruth; (2) Ammann wanted the stand of the church to be clear that the "true hearted" were not saved (the "true hearted" or "half-Anabaptists" were members of the state church who were kindly disposed toward the Brethren, believing that theirs was indeed the true faith, aiding them in every possible way even if it jeopardized their own safety, but failing to leave the state church and unite with the Brethren); (3) Ammann also insisted on a more detailed regulation of the clothing of the Brethren than had been the case with the Swiss Brethren in the past. This latter point was a matter of concern to the well known North German elder, Gerrit Roosen (1612-1711), who wrote to the Brethren in Alsace, protesting against the attitude of those who think highly of themselves and "make laws about things which are not treated of in the Gospel." Roosen objected in particular to Ammann's making regulations on headgear, clothing, stockings, shoes and the manner of cutting the hair of the men. But the central item of controversy was avoidance, not clothing regulations.

Efforts were made by the Reist and Ammann parties to effect a reconciliation, but in vain. One of the first was in 1694, but the Reist party refused the only terms under which the "Amish" would consider a union, namely that the united brotherhood practice avoidance.

About the year 1700 the Amish made an effort to return to the Brethren, going so far as to admit that they had done wrong, asking for patience, and entreating the Brethren to pray for them. But the desired reconciliation was not achieved. The Reist brethren could not bring themselves to adopt the practice of avoidance, and the Amish could not with good conscience discontinue the practice.

(2) *The Froehlich Schism,* 1835

A minor disturbance among the Swiss Mennonites was caused by a man named Samuel H. Froehlich (1803-57) in the years 1832-35. Froehlich, a non-Mennonite, had studied theology at Zurich and had been expelled from the Reformed ministerial association of Aargau.

At this time the Langnau congregation in the Emme valley was not too strong. For a long time the Swiss Brethren congregations of the Emme valley had been served by ministers from the Jura mountains, —in the canton of Berne since 1815. In 1809 Alsatian and Palatine ministers and elders came to the Emme valley and ordained Peter Pfister and Michael Kipfer to the ministry. In 1821 Christian Gerber was added to the ministry and Ulrich Kipfer was ordained as a deacon. When Michael Kipfer died in 1825 the Jura elders came down to the Emmental (Emme valley) to ordain an elder. The lot fell on Peter Pfister. At the same time Christian Baumgartner and Ulrich Kipfer were ordained as ministers. The older minister, Christian Gerber, was an energetic and gifted preacher. He introduced various innovations into the life of the church. He was also critical of the other ministers for being "lukewarm" and not sufficiently alert.

In 1832 Froehlich came to Langnau and created somewhat of a sensation by his earnestness and oratory. He preached for the Brethren in their services. Soon a group of the Brethren withdrew from the others and met separately to hear Froehlich. The Froehlich group demanded that communion services be held almost every week in an effort to return to the apostolic pattern. About Christmas, 1834, Gerber and Baumgartner, two Froehlich disciples, began to hold communion services separately with their own followers only. In January 1835, four leaders from the Jura came to Langnau to straighten out the difficulty if possible: David Baumgartner, Hans Zingg, Jacob Nussbaumer and Ulrich Lehman. But nothing was accomplished. Froehlich, who had been forced to leave the Emme valley, then sent a young man of twenty-one, George Steiger by name, to Langnau. Steiger pronounced as "dead" all those who remained in the old church and refused immersion. The outcome was that the Froehlich group started out as a new denomination with about one hundred twenty members—half of which were former Brethren and half, Reformed.

The Froehlich group emphasized emotional conversions and baptism by immersion, while the Brethren were less demonstrative, rather emphasizing religious training and indoctrination, and baptizing converts by pouring. Both groups believed in thorough conversions, sincere repentance and true faith.

The Froehlich group was extremely exclusive, refusing spiritual fellowship with all other Christian bodies, not allowing their members to hear sermons by any but their own ministers. In Switzerland the denomination is commonly known as Neu-Täufer (New Anabaptists), while in America they are referred to as "New Amish." Their correct name is "Apostolic Christian Church." Their first members emigrated to North America in 1846. Since 1877 their membership in America has increased from less than one hundred to several thousand members. Their chief congregations are in the state of Illinois.

READINGS

Ausbund, das ist: Etliche schöne Christliche Lieder, Wie sie in dem Gefängnis Zu Passau in dem Schloss von den Schweizer-Brüder . . . gedichtet worden . . ., Verlag von den Amischen Gemeinden in Lancaster County, Pa., 1935. [See hymns number 5 (Blaurock), 6 (Manz), 7 (Sattler), 132 (John Landis), 140 (Haslibacher).]

Bender, H. S.: *Mennonite Origins in Europe,* MCC, Akron, Pennsylvania, 1942, 19-24, 51-53.

Correll, Ernst H.: *Das schweizerische Täufer-Mennonitentum, Ein Sociologischer Bericht,* Tübingen, 1925.

Gascho, Milton: "The Amish Division of 1693-1697 in Switzerland and Alsace," *The Mennonite Quarterly Review,* Goshen, Indiana, XI, 4 (October 1937), 235-266.

Gedenkschrift zum 400 Jährigen Jubiläum der Mennoniten oder Taufgesinnten, 1525-1925, Ludwigshaven a. Rh., 1925.

Geiser, Samuel: "The Mennonites of Switzerland and France," *The Mennonite Quarterly Review,* XI, 1 (January 1937), 44-60.

Geiser, Samuel, *et. al: Die Taufgesinnten-Gemeinden,* Karlsruhe (Baden), [1931], 126-490.

Hege, Christian, & Neff, Christian: *Mennonitisches Lexikon,* Frankfurt a. M. & Weierhof (Pfalz), Band I, 1913-1924, articles *Amman, Jakob; Basel; Bern; Blaurock, Georg; Emmental;* Band II, 1937, *Fröhlich, Samuel; Jura;* Band III, *Manz, Felix; Marbeck, Pilgram.*

Horsch, John: *Mennonites in Europe,* Mennonite Publishing House, Scottdale, Pennsylvania, 1942, 52-123, 132-137.

Horsch, John: "The Debate in Zofingen in 1532," *Christian Monitor,* Scottdale, Pennsylvania, June 1932, 165-167.

Käser, Hans: *Aus der Täufergeschichte: Ausserkirchliche Christlich Versammlungen im Unteremmental in früherer Zeit,* Newton, Kansas, 1928, 1-45.

Köhler, Walther: *Brüderlich vereinigung etzlicher Kinder Gottes sieben Artikel betreffend . . . ,* Verlag von Rudolf Haupt, Leipzig, 1908.

Kurzgefasstes Glaubensbekenntnis der Altevangelischen Taufgesinnten-Gemeinde im Emmental, Joh. Kipfer, Kehr, Langnau, 1937, 3-20.

Müller, Ernst: *Geschichte der bernischen Täufer,* Frauenfeld, 1895.

Newman, A. H.: *A History of Anti-Pedobaptism from the Rise of Pedobaptism to A.D.* 1609, American Baptist Publication Society, 1897, 120-152.

Smith, C. H.: *The Story of the Mennonites,* Mennonite Book Concern, Berne, Indiana, [1941], 9-38, 125-168.

Smithson, R. J.: *The Anabaptists: Their Contribution to Our Protestant Heritage,* James Clarke & Co., Ltd., London, [1935], 35-55, 154-159.

Van Braght, T. J.: *The Bloody Theater or Martyrs Mirror . . .* , Mennonite Publishing House, Scottdale, Pennsylvania, 1938 [Manz, 415, Sattler, 416-420; Blaurock, 430-432; Landis, 1103-05].

Von Muralt, Leonhard: *Glaube und Lehre der Schweizerischen Wiedertäufer in der Reformationszeit,* Beer & Co., Zürich, 1938, 3-49.

Weber, Harry F.: *Centennial History of the Mennonites of Illinois,* The Mennonite Historical Society, Goshen, Indiana, 1931; [The "New Amish," 34-36]

Wenger, J. C.: "The Life and Work of Pilgram Marpeck," *The Mennonite Quarterly Review,* Goshen, Indiana, XII, 3 (July 1938), 137-166.

Wenger, J. C.: "Pilgram Marpeck, Tyrolese Engineer and Anabaptist Elder," *Church History,* March 1940, 24-36.

CHAPTER IV

Swiss Brethren in Other Lands

1. Alsace

In the early years of the movement the Swiss Brethren center of Alsace was the city of Strasburg. William Reublin and Michael Sattler were in Strasburg as early as 1526. Sattler's stay was brief, and in a few years Reublin too was gone, being succeeded as leader of the Brethren by Pilgram Marpeck. The Swiss Brethren actually flourished for a time in Strasburg. In the spring of 1529 one hundred Anabaptists were there who had been exiled from the city of Augsburg in Bavarian Swabia. Not that Strasburg welcomed the Anabaptists! On the contrary, every few years the city issued a fresh mandate against them, or renewed an old one: 1527, 1530, 1535, 1538, 1540. But strange as it may seem, Strasburg never executed a single Anabaptist; it merely imprisoned or banished them. In spite of thirty years of persecution, the Swiss Brethren congregation in Strasburg numbered about one hundred members in 1556. One of their members at that time, Peter Novesianus, a *Gymnasium* (senior high school and junior college) professor, was banished from the city. A number of Brethren left the city with him. The congregation survived the years of persecution only to die ultimately of inner weakness in 1875.

With Strasburg as a center, the movement spread over Alsace. Soon there were Brethren in Eckolsheim, Lingelsheim, St. Oswald, Schnakenloch, Ruprechtsau, Schiltigheim, Benfeld, Schlettstadt. Little is known of them. One of their elders (bishops) was a basket-maker named Sebastian von Dingelen. In 1538 twenty-five members were arrested in a forest near Epfig. A state clergyman reported that there had been an assembly of three hundred Anabaptists in a forest. In 1540 sixty-nine were arrested at one time near Illkirch. At Ensisheim in Alsace, a city in the district of Gebweiler, the Austrians executed six hundred, according to Sebastian Franck. In 1643 a Catholic priest described the services of a Brethren congregation in the Schlettstadt area. He reported that they held their German services in a barn in a forest. They sang their Psalms from the Lobwasser translation. For baptisms and weddings someone came from Switzerland. The priest, Jean le Bachelle by name, said that he himself had seen such a man, "clothed according to the Swiss manner."

King Ferdinand of Austria issued a severe mandate against the Brethren in 1529. This was reaffirmed in 1535 and 1544. In 1561 he issued another mandate, lamenting the laxity with which the earlier mandates had been carried out, demanding the most severe persecution of the Anabaptists. The elders (*Vorsteher*) especially were to be executed according to the Imperial Law of 1529. The Count of Rappoltstein, an Alsatian principality, added his own further instructions when he issued Ferdinand's mandate, threatening to take proper measures against the civil officers should they manifest negligence in enforcing the sanctions of the mandate. But the Brethren were "stiffnecked" in their views. In 1572 a village called Ingersheim near Colmar contained thirty men and women who were "infected" with Anabaptism.

In the seventeenth century (e.g., in 1641) Brethren from Zurich and Berne, because of the stern measures of the Swiss rulers, migrated to Alsace and settled in the mountainous areas of the Vosges. There they reared large families (eight or nine children), and excelled in animal husbandry, on the farms which they rented. The immigration from Berne was especially strong from 1671 until 1711. In that period the Brethren secured military exemption, locally at least, by the payment of a sum of money. In 1704 a local census, signed by John Zimmerman and Jacob Ammann, contained such names as Lugenbühl, Bachmann, Yoder, Hochstettler, Rupp, Maurer, Gerig, Gerber, Müller and Roth.

In 1712 the secretary of King Louis XIV of France informed an Alsatian official that the King was not minded to tolerate the Mennonites in Alsace. They should be banished from the country, he said. The official, Pelletier de la Houssaye, thereupon gave orders that the Mennonites should be driven out of Alsace. Many of them left, especially from the principality of Rappoltstein, settling in Montbeliard (prior to the French Revolution a part of Wurttemberg), in Breisgau (a territory in what is now South Germany), in Zweibrücken (a duchy adjoining both Alsace-Lorraine and the Palatinate) and in the Palatinate itself.

In the eighteenth century the bishopric of Strasburg continued as somewhat of a Mennonite center. The Brethren held meetings in Baldenheim, Ohnenheim, Jebsheim and Markirch. Ohnenheim will be remembered as the place in Rappoltstein where the Alsatian ministers subscribed to the Dordrecht Confession of Faith in 1660.

In 1728 the king of France issued through one of his ministers another harsh directive against the Mennonites. The Duke of Zweibrücken who was then the ruler of Rappoltstein made a plea to the French court in behalf of the Mennonites. He pointed out that they had settled in Rappoltstein more than a century before its union with France. They had brought a large area of land into a high state of cultivation. He called special attention to the valley of St. Marie which had been devastated by the Swedes and then transformed into a fruitful land by the Mennonites. He also mentioned their excellence in animal husbandry: on one occasion they had saved many cattle from infection during an outbreak of a cattle plague. He therefore asked whether it were not advisable to keep a fixed number of Mennonites in the St. Marie Valley. How much good his plea did is not known. In any case the Mennonites stayed.

The Brethren were often in difficult circumstances because they refused to swear an oath. They requested exemption from the requirement to swear the usual oath in court. This appeal was directed to Count de Choiseul. He turned down their request completely in his reply of April 6, 1766. Indeed, in a second communication that same year he threatened them with total banishment should they dare to make any further complaints. Three years later a Mennonite named Jacob Frey refused to swear an oath when called into court as a witness. He was fined and banished from Alsace for life. It is probable, says Dr. Christian Neff in his thorough article on *Elsass* in the *Mennonitisches Lexikon,* that the republican government of France excused the Mennonites from the swearing of oaths. In any case they are known to have received this privilege by French law in 1812. This exemption was confirmed by the French Supreme Court at Strasburg in 1881 and by a county court at Colmar, capital of Upper Alsace, in 1882.

The other issue which caused the Mennonites of Alsace great concern was the demand of the state that they perform military service, an obligation which they felt was impossible for them because of New Testament teaching. On this question also the Republican government of France showed kindness. On December 14, 1790, the "Anabaptists" were granted exemption from the universal obligation of French citizens to sign up for service in the national guard. In 1793 in response to a petition the Mennonites were also excused from the bearing of arms, and given opportunity to choose such service in the army as digging trenches, building roads, or providing transportation—or even simply to pay for such service. This order was signed by Robespierre and five other officials. But after Napoleon became emperor of France this military exemption was no longer in force. In vain did the Brethren petition the emperor. On June 19, 1808, the Alsatian Mennonites met in conference at Bildhäuserhof near Schlettstadt to consider the military problem. Twenty-two ministers representing nine congregations were present. It was decided to send two brethren, who could speak French, to Paris to do whatever they could about securing military exemption. January 29, 1809, was appointed as a day of prayer in behalf of their mission. The cost of the trip was borne by the congregations; financial help came even from a few congregations in the Palatinate, and in Rhenish Hesse. Nothing was accomplished in Paris, however. This occasioned two special conferences in the year 1811. But the galling situation remained unchanged: "No one may refuse military service because of his faith." Only these alternatives then confronted the Mennonites: (1) Give up nonresistance, or (2) emigrate. Many chose to emigrate. During the nineteenth century many Alsatian Mennonites migrated to North America, settling chiefly in Ohio, Illinois, and Iowa. Those who remained behind were forced to do military service regardless of any scruples the brotherhood may have had on the matter.

An author named A. Frölich wrote a description of the Brethren in Alsace and Lorraine in a book published in 1889. He reported that most of them lived in the districts of Saargemünd, Saarburg, Mühlhausen, Altkirch, Gebweiler, Weissenburg, and Schlettstadt. There were, he said, two kinds of Mennonites: the *Häftler* who wore hooks-and-eyes and were strict, exclusive, and conservative, and the *Knöpfler* who wore buttons and were more progressive. He reported that the Mennonites were generally "tranquil, quiet, reserved, industrious, peace-loving, faithful, temperate, well-mannered, benevolent, kind, and pious." He stated that they avoided lawsuits, and settled their disputes within the church.

The Alsatian Mennonite ministers participated in several great conferences. Two of these met in the eighteenth century, the first at Steinselz in 1752, the second at Essingen in the Palatinate in 1779. Among other things both conferences condemned the use of tobacco.

In the year 1896 the Amish Mennonites of Alsace-Lorraine once more held a conference and decided to convene annually.

The Swiss Brethren in other areas will be presented only briefly, for Alsace has served as a type of the lot of "The Swiss Brethren in Other Lands."

2. Lorraine

When Louis XIV of France ordered the Mennonites to leave Alsace in 1712 many of them settled in Lorraine. They settled in the Saar Valley and spread out over the land as far as Zweibrücken. In the nineteenth century the Lorraine Mennonites migrated westward and established a number of new congregations. These new congregations are French-speaking, whereas the older congregations speak the German language.

3. Montbeliard

The French city of Montbeliard lies some twenty miles west of the northwest tip of the Swiss canton of Berne. The city was formerly the capital of the principality (county) of Montebeliard which belonged to the province of Wurttemberg from 1397 until the time of the French Revolution in the latter years of the eighteenth century. Mennonites from Berne fled across the frontier soon after 1700 and settled in the principality of Montbeliard. Many Mennonites from Rappoltstein in Alsace, especially from the Markirch Valley, also settled in Montbeliard when Louis XIV banished them from Alsace in 1712. They settled on the farms of Count Leopold who was happy to see first-class farmers settle on his lands. Here the Mennonites secured permission to have their own cemetery and to organize a school for their children, and they were granted exemption from the obligation to swear oaths.

In 1790 minister Samuel Stoll and elder Christian Känel (Kennel) migrated to Poland. How many followed them is not known.

A list of the members at Montbeliard was drawn up in 1793. It contained thirty-six family names and a total of 250 souls. The present figure is only slightly larger (300). The congregation has lost members from various causes including immigration to North America.

When Montbeliard became a part of France the Mennonites became subject to military service in the national guard and to the requirement to swear oaths. They protested for conscience' sake and were given some consideration by the French government.

Many members of the Montbeliard congregation are Swiss citizens. As such they are not involved in any wars in which France participates.

One of the elders at Montbeliard, Pierre Sommer, the leading minister of the French Mennonites, wrote about 1936:

> Not many Mennonites are living today in France and all of them are in the northeast of the country. About one thousand live in Alsace-Lorraine, which as is well known was German territory from 1871 to 1918. This group has retained the German language, whereas those who have lived in French territory continuously since their first arrival at the beginning of the eighteenth century, have become French and have lost the German language almost entirely. Our families all came from Switzerland and long held fast to the German language. Here in Montbeliard we still occasionally had German meetings until a few years ago. The congregations in France are for the most part small, the members are widely scattered, they could not have their own schools, and so could not retain their language. Spiritual life had also sadly deteriorated. Thanks be to God, the last thirty years has witnessed new life and today we have many who have an assurance of salvation through the blood of Christ and who are endeavoring to be true witnesses for the Lord. The congregations in France are organized into a conference which meets twice yearly, once in the spring and once in the fall. The French-speaking congregations have their own annual conference in the French language even though they also belong to the official conference.

The Mennonites of France still have an untrained ministry. Converts are usually baptized between the ages of twelve and fifteen. The two chief factors which are hindering the growth of the French congregations are the customs of marrying outside of the church, and of having small families. Many French congregations also retained the use of the German language too long. In 1906 a church periodical, *Christ Seul* (Christ Only), was established and continued until the time of the first World War; its publication was resumed in 1926. The Mennonites of France are divided into two groups: the French-speaking congregations, which were organized into a conference in 1908 and which today have about 1,000 baptized members; and the German-speaking congregations, about a dozen in number, with possibly 800 baptized members.

4. The Palatinate

Within a year or two after the founding of the Swiss Brethren church in Zurich there were Anabaptists in the Palatinate. On January 8, 1528 John Dobneck, best known as Cochlaeus, wrote a letter to Erasmus reporting that in the prison in Alzey there had been for some time (*schon lange*) eighteen Anabaptists. He requested Erasmus to write immediately a small book against the Anabaptists, a task which he could perform in three days (!). Cochlaeus tried to impress Erasmus with the urgency of the task: Germany was in desperate straits and souls were in danger; eighteen thousand people had already become Anabaptists. But Erasmus did nothing about the plight of the Fatherland. It was the executioner who was called upon to silence the voice of Anabaptism. According to refugees from the Palatinate about three hundred fifty Palatines were known to have been executed as Anabaptists within a few years. Among the early Palatine prisoners were the Brethren Philip Rupp and "Henner" Schuhmacher.

The Brethren would have had a difficult time to keep in the good graces of the Palatine Elector had they had any desire to do so, for the faith of the throne changed five times in fifty years. The order was as follows: Catholic (Frederick II, 1544-56), Lutheran (Otto Henry, 1556-59), Reformed (Frederick III, 1559-76), Lutheran (Ludwig VI, 1576-83), and Reformed (John Kasimir, 1583-92).

All during the sixteenth century, church and state wearied themselves trying to "convert" the "sectarian" Brethren. In 1557 the Lutherans and the Swiss Brethren in the Palatinate held a disputation at Pfeddersheim near Worms. Five questions were discussed: Infant baptism, civil government, the oath, reasons for withdrawal from the state church, and the ban (church discipline). The lot of the Brethren was made worse rather than better following the disputation. In 1571 Frederick III decided to have the Reformed theologians try their hand at convincing the Brethren. A disputation was held from May 28 to June 19. At the close of the disputation the Reformed spokesman, Peter Dathenus, informed the Brethren: "So long as you do not become converted we cannot hold that you are a part of the true church of Christ." But this verdict was but the least of the burdens the brotherhood had to bear. By the middle of the seventeenth century the congregations of the Brethren in the Palatinate had been reduced to mere remnants. But about that time refugees from Switzerland began to come down the Rhine to find a more livable existence in the Palatinate. But conditions were still far from comfortable there. In 1661 fifty persons were arrested in a private dwelling near Sinsheim where they had assembled for a communion service. They were given an extremely heavy fine. In fact the government of the Palatinate ruled on January 4, 1662 that a poll tax was to be levied on every attendant at the services of the Brethren. The Mennonites appealed to the government for relief. Perhaps even more significant was the influence of a letter written by an English Quaker, W. P. Hilley, to the Palatine Elector in June 1664. On August 4, 1664 Elector Karl Ludwig issued a *Concession* granting the *Menisten* limited toleration. This toleration was to be granted the "Mennists" (he avoided the term Anabaptist because of the Imperial laws against them) because of the way his country had been devastated by war; the Mennonites could help rebuild it. Also, no *Aufruhr* (riot or rebellion) was to be feared from them. They were to be allowed to hold divine services but not more than twenty persons could assemble at one time. The Mennonites were to pay six florins per family per year as a toleration-fee. Persons of other confessions were not to be admitted to membership in the *Mennist* brotherhood by rebaptism nor were they even to be admitted to the services of the group.

Although the above conditions seem harsh today they looked rosy to the Brethren in Switzerland who at that time were being whipped and sold as galley slaves on Mediterranean ships. Jacob Everling, a Palatine Mennonite minister, reported on November 2, 1671, that thus far two hundred refugees had reached the Palatinate: cripples, aged persons seventy to ninety years old, families of eight or ten children—all arrived destitute, carrying bundles on their backs. By January 1672 Everling reported that there were 215 refugees on the west side of the Rhine and 428 on the east side. The Dutch Mennonites carried on a splendid relief ministry among the miserable Swiss immigrants in the Palatinate.

Soon new trouble arose. In 1680 Elector Karl Ludwig died and was succeeded by his son Karl. To him the Mennonites turned, requesting confirmation of the Concession of 1664, and particularly pleading not to be required to swear oaths. His answer was only partly satisfactory. In 1681 he gave notice that in Alzey and Mosbach, districts in which the Mennonites were strongly represented, the religious privileges granted them would not apply to new settlers. Furthermore, both the state churchmen and the government exerted themselves to win the *Mennists* for the Reformed Church.

In 1685 Elector Karl died and in his place came the Catholic ruler, Philip William. The next year he confirmed the Concession to the Mennonites. But other trouble came. Louis XIV had his armies ravage the Palatinate in 1689. The French destroyed Heidelberg, Manheim, and other cities. The Mennonites suffered severely. The Elector fled to Vienna where he died in 1690. Once again the Mennonites appealed to his successor for a confirmation of their Concession. In fact, the weary tension between the government and the downtrodden Mennonites continued for more than another century. It was not until the years 1799 that religious toleration came to the Palatinate.

Since many eighteenth century Mennonite emigrants came from the Palatinate the conditions obtaining in that era are of special interest. On March 3, 1717 the Mennonites addressed another petition to the new Elector, Karl Philip, for a confirmation of their privileges. The advisers of the Elector succeeded in having him hesitate to grant it. By this time the Mennonites were about worn out by the everlasting vicissitudes and constant irritations. As early as April 1717 three hundred Palatine Mennonites were in Rotterdam, expecting with Dutch Mennonite aid to settle at last in the Land of Liberty, the earthly Paradise, America. Anna Brons asserts that by 1732 three thousand Mennonites had emigrated from the Palatinate to America. This figure is certainly too large, but it is true that a wave of emigrants crossed the Atlantic in the eighteenth century. Meanwhile conditions in the Palatinate made the lot of the *Mennists* more unpleasant. Dr. C. Henry Smith states:

> Throughout the eighteenth century they were forced to pay tribute money for such toleration as they enjoyed. They were denied residence in the cities, they could not engage in trade, nor were their children admitted to apprenticeship in the trade guilds. . .
>
> The exemption and protection money was doubled. The marriage of young people was made extremely difficult, being permitted only with the consent of the central government. [This sometimes required a year.] . . .
>
> The acquisition of land was made difficult and uncertain by the revival [in 1726] of an ancient right called *Ius Retractus* which stipulated that land which had once been in the possession of a member of one of the three tolerated religions, and in the meantime had been bought by a Mennonite, could at any time later again be reclaimed by the original owner upon the payment of the first purchase price. . . (*The Story of the Mennonites,* 313f.)

The *Ius Retractus* (Law of Retraction) was in force from 1726 until 1801, although in 1739 after a number of Palatine Mennonites had left the land the right of repurchase for the sale price was limited to a period of three years from date of sale.

The lot of the Palatine Mennonites in the eighteenth century is exemplified by the case of two orphans from an Amish Mennonite home. As children they were taken by force to a Catholic institution where they were indoctrinated as Catholics. Years later, about 1780, they decided to leave the Catholic Church and unite with the church of their parents. An elder named John Nafziger of Essingen baptized them and received them into the church. A Catholic body adjudged the girls to be worthy of death, but the Palatine Elector commuted the sentence to one year in prison and subsequent banishment from the land. The elder was fined five hundred florins and was also banished.

Such were the conditions the Palatine Mennonites endured for several generations before seeking the haven of William Penn in the New World.

A truly remarkable Palatine Mennonite farmer was David Möllinger, 1709-86. He was born at Dühren near Sinsheim in Baden. His wife's name was Mary Kindig. They lived first at Mutterstadt in the Palatinate. In 1732 they settled at Cronau near Mutterstadt, and in 1744 at Monsheim near Worms. Möllinger was a pioneer in the improvement of farming practices. He excelled in the production of crops and devised a splendid crop rotation system. By raising clover and spreading gypsum on his land, he greatly enriched the soil. From his vinegar factory and brewery he obtained a mash with which he fattened cattle. His crop rotation system was generally adopted in the Palatinate, the growing of clover improved the soil of the country, and the number of cattle was tripled. "For all this," wrote J. N. von Schwerz in 1816, "the Palatinate may thank a single man, a Mennonite." Möllinger is known as "The Father of Palatine Agriculture."

Today there are in the Palatinate and in Hesse about a dozen and a half Mennonite congregations with a total of approximately nineteen hundred members.

5. Baden to Galicia

Evangelical Anabaptists were found in Baden, the south German province on the east side of the Rhine, soon after the establishment of Anabaptism in Zurich in 1525. The Hutterian chronicles report that in Baden thirty-six Anabaptists were martyred. Before the passing of a decade there were meetings of the Brethren attended by two or three hundred worshipers. Services were sometimes held in the forest, sometimes in isolated houses. Among the ministers of the Brethren were Philip Weber, Julius Lober, Wendel Metzger, and John Gentner. Within about thirty years, however, the heavy hand of persecution silenced the witness of the Brethren.

About a century later (1652) Brethren refugees from Switzerland were settling in Kraichgau in the *Unterland* of Baden. Early in the eighteenth century they were appearing in various places. Their history somewhat resembles that of the Brethren in Alsace and the Palatinate. They had to pay "protection" money, and they were harassed on the matters of the oath and military service. In one era it was the oath; in another, military service. Many families migrated to America to preserve the faith and practice of the New Testament, as understood by Mennonites, for future generations. Today there are in Baden eleven congregations with a total membership of less than six hundred baptized members. The adjoining Wurttemberg has four congregations with less than two hundred members.

In Bavaria the persecution of the Brethren four centuries ago was especially severe. From 1527 to 1581 it is known that 223 Anabaptists were martyred for their faith. It was the policy of the ruling dukes, William IV and Ludwig, to execute every Anabaptist who was apprehended. "He who recants shall be beheaded; he who does not recant shall be burned up." By the close of the sixteenth century the Brethren in Bavaria seem to have been annihilated. About two centuries later a number of Mennonite families settled in Bavaria. The first of the "new" congregations were Bildhausen and Mönchshof which were established by Mennonite families who came from Baden and Wurttemberg about 1770. In 1802 eight Palatine *Mennist* families settled near Ingolstadt and founded the Maxweiler congregation. In 1855 the bulk of the congregation emigrated to America. Today there remain in Bavaria some seven congregations with about five hundred members.

About 1784 twenty-eight Mennonite families, chiefly from the Palatinate, settled in the vicinity of Lemberg (Polish Lwow) in the area called Galicia. The territory of Galicia had been taken from Poland and annexed to Austria in 1772. Kaiser Joseph II welcomed German settlers into Galicia—and 3,300 families responded. The handful of *Mennists* prospered for a time. They were granted religious freedom in Galicia, including military exemption. But before long about half the Mennonite families—more exactly Amish Mennonites—sold their holdings and moved eastward across the frontier into South Russia, locating eventually in Volhynia (Russian Volyn) (Their descendants almost all settled in North America later.) In 1800 the Galicia Mennonites numbered about one hundred souls, counting children. By 1868, the total had reached four hundred.

In the years 1878 to 1883 the poorer half of the colony—seventy-five families—emigrated to Minnesota and Kansas. The present Mennonite population amounts to about six hundred souls, living in a hundred Polish villages—for former Galicia was returned to Poland after the first World War.

In 1858 an Amish Mennonite family named Oesch migrated from Lorraine to Luxembourg and settled in that tiny country. In 1870 a Schertz family arrived, and in 1892 a Nafziger family. Today the Luxembourg Mennonites constitute a small congregation comparable with those in South Germany.

"The Swiss Brethren in Other Lands" forms a sad picture. Misunderstanding and misrepresentation, oppression and persecution, imprisonment and martyrdom, discouragement and defeat, quiet endurance and victory, a moving about for conscience' sake and emigration to America—all these enter into the picture. The staunchest believers in nonresistance seem in many cases to have fled to America. Today there are about eighty little congregations of Mennonites in France, the Palatinate, Luxembourg, Hesse, Baden, Switzerland, Wurttemberg, Bavaria, and Southern Poland, totaling about five thousand baptized members—an average of about sixty per congregation.

6. The Hutterian Brethren, 1528

Shortly after the founding of Anabaptism by Conrad Grebel Swiss Brethren refugees from various parts of South Germany and the Tirol found their way to Moravia. It was their belief that in Moravia they would enjoy religious toleration, but they were destined to experience partial disappointment. At Nikolsburg a group of two or three hundred Brethren under the leadership of one Jacob Wiedemann was told to leave the place unless they were willing to attend the services of the recognized pastors. In the spring of 1528 they left. At their first place of encampment they chose "ministers of temporal needs" (deacons), and these stewards "spread a cloak before the people, and everyone laid down on it his earthly possessions unconstrainedly and with a willing mind according to the teaching of the prophets and apostles." (The New Testament pattern was, of course, the Jerusalem church, Acts 4:34f.) Thus was born the Christian communism of the Wiedemann group. It is evident that the straits in which the migrating Brethren found themselves almost made imperative a total sharing of their assets, a "communism of consumption." Even before the departure from Nikolsburg the group had had to care for so many refugees that it had practiced a partial communism of consumption. Now that the group was making a trek in search of toleration they pooled fully their resources. Upon the invitation of the Lords von Kaunitz the Brethren proceeded to Austerlitz, another location in Moravia.

In 1529 a Swiss Brethren minister named Jacob Huter from the Tirol was sent by his people to visit the brotherhood in Moravia. He united with the Wiedemann group in Austerlitz. After the departure of Huter a division occurred in the church at Austerlitz. In 1531 the stricter party removed to another village called Auspitz where they established a common household, an estate for communal living—in German, a *Bruderhof*. In 1533 Huter, who had come to the Auspitz group was chosen as its pastor. He introduced strict discipline, particularly in reference to the "community of goods," the distinguishing feature of the Hutterian Anabaptists. Huter was burned at the stake in his native Tirol on February 26, 1536. Wiedemann was martyred about the same time.

In contrast with the horrible persecution of the Swiss Brethren in other lands, (it is estimated that a thousand were martyred in the Tirol and Gorizia by 1531) the Hutterian Brethren after a time thrived in Moravia; the Brethren Chronicle calls the period 1564-92 their "golden age." About 1618 they were estimated by a traveler and cartographer named Martin Zeiller at seventy thousand.

In the year 1622 another wave of persecution set in and Hutterian Brethren in great numbers (one estimate is twenty thousand) were driven from Moravia. Some settled in Hungary, some in Transylvania, and some scattered. By 1631 they were reduced to a membership of about two thousand. In 1665 they sent two delegates to the Netherlands to solicit help from the Dutch Mennonites. They received large contributions.

Time and again the Jesuits tried to "convert" the Hutterians to the Roman Catholic faith. In the eighteenth century the congregations in Hungary were totally destroyed by the Jesuits. Most of the people remained, but when the Jesuits were through with them they were Catholics—not Hutterians. From Transylvania and Hungary a pitiful remnant of sixty-seven souls fled to Wallachia in modern Roumania. Those Catholicized Hutterians who remained in Hungary —they are still there—are called *Habaner*. One theory is that the name comes from a Hungarian word *Haban* (ball) ; on one occasion one of the Hutterian ministers is said to have appealed to his people to be steadfast in faith even though the vicissitudes through which they had passed had tossed them about like a *Haban* in the hand of a boy. But the persecution of the Jesuits proved too much for the Brethren in Hungary. It was in 1759 that Empress Maria Theresa had granted permission to the Jesuits to "convert" the Hutterians.

In 1781 an edict of toleration was issued. The *Habaner* supposed that this would permit them to return to their former faith. But in this they were mistaken. Thereupon fifty of them migrated to Russia where the ruler, Catherine the Great, granted exemption from military service to nonresistant Christians. In Russia the first *Bruderhof* was built in 1857. Each *Bruderhof* is an estate on which are the buildings where the group lives. Each group is an economic unit in itself with the group owning everything and the individual owning nothing—a genuine Christian communism.

Fear of possible compulsory military service moved the Hutterian Brethren in Russia to migrate to North America, 1874-75. Three groups came: (1) The *Smith* Group, led by Michael Waldner, a smith; (2) The *Darius* Group, led by Darius Walter; (3) The *Teacher* Group, led by two teachers, Jacob Wipf and Peter Hofer. In America the Hutterian Brethren prospered, now having about fifty *Bruderhofs*.

They suffered for the principle of nonresistance during the first World War, however. Four of their young men were abused most unmercifully because they refused to wear the army uniform, etc. In Alcatraz, a federal prison in California, they were stripped of almost all clothing, forced to sleep on a cold concrete floor, given a ration of one-half glass of water per day for four and one-half days, beaten until one of them lost consciousness, and kept in solitary confinement for four months, being permitted one hour of exercise per week. In November 1918 they were taken to the federal prison at Leavenworth, Kansas, in chains, and further maltreated. Two of them, Joseph and Michael Hofer, finally were delivered from further "justice" by death. Because of their ill-treatment in the United States, most of the Hutterians migrated to Canada. Today they number only about four hundred in the United States while in Canada they are approaching six thousand.

The Hutterian *Chronicle* after giving a regional census of the number of Anabaptist martyrs in various parts of Europe—an (in complete) total of 2,173 persons—commented:

. . . Many were dealt with in wonderful ways, rare and unheard-of, often by day and by night, with great craftiness and roguery; also with many sweet and smooth words, by monks and priests, by doctors of theology, with much false teaching and testimony, with many threats and menaces, with insults and abuse, yea, with lies and dreadful slanders, but they did not make them despondent.

As some of them lay in grievous imprisonment they sang hymns of praise to God, as those who are in great joy. Some did likewise as they were being led out to death and the place of execution; as those going to meet the bridegroom at a wedding they sang out joyfully with uplifted voice that it rang out loudly. Many maidens, when they were to go to the place of execution, adorned themselves, dressing up and making themselves attractive, with the delight of a day of rejoicing, and of those who have experienced a heavenly joy—yea as those who are to pass through the gates of everlasting joy. Others stepped up with a smile on their lips, praising God that they were accounted worthy of dying the death of sincere and Christian heroes, and would not have wished to die [a natural death] in bed. Others exhorted the spectators most earnestly to repentance and amendment of life. Others who were cut short and had not received water baptism hastened nevertheless to the baptism of blood, to be baptized therewith for the sake of God's truth, on their living faith—some whom we could name, but of that there is no need. Yea, many who never came to the congregation, and never saw it, but who had merely heard the truth and understood and believed it, remained steadfast therein, so that they were taken away. They did not allow themselves to be terrified or moved by fire, water, sword or executioner. No human being and nothing on earth could take anything from their hearts, such zealous lovers of God were they. The fire of God burned within them. They preferred to die the bitterest death, yea ten deaths, rather than forsake the truth they had come to know. They would accept nothing as the price of their faith in Christ, no glory, no principality, no kingdom, yea not all the pleasure and wealth of the world, for they had a foundation and an assurance in their faith.

From the shedding of this innocent blood arose Christians everywhere, and fellow believers in all those places here and there; it was not without fruit. Many were moved thereby to serious thought and to order their life, their thinking and striving, in preparation for the future. Finally the executions were carried on in many places at night, as in the county of the Tirol; the executions were done in secret and at night, so that not many people would see, hear, or know of them. They were also done elsewhere than at the customary places of execution because they killed them illegally, condemning the innocent, sometimes murderously without a sentence.

In some places they filled the prisons and jails with them, as did the Count Palatine on the Rhine, supposing they could dampen and extinguish the fire of God. But in prison they sang and were joyful; nothing was of any avail; the enemies outside, who thought that the prisoners in jail should be fearful, themselves became much more afraid and did not know what to do with them. For they became aware for the most part of their innocence. Many lay in jails and prisons, some for a shorter and some for a longer time, some for many years. They endured all sorts of torture and pain. Some had holes burned through their cheeks after which they were released. A portion of them got out in an upright manner through the help of God, some through wonderful and special means and providences of God, and thereafter persevered in the faith unwaveringly until God took them.

* * *

Everywhere much slander and evil was spoken of them, that they had goats-feet and ox-hoofs, and that when they gave people to drink out of a little flask, thereafter they had to do like they. They also lied about them that they had their wives in common. . . ; that they slew and ate their children. . . .

* * *

But when our Lord Jesus Christ will come in flaming fire, with many thousands of angels, to hold the judgment on His great Day, everything will again come forth. The earth will bring out the blood which it drank in, and will not hide its slain. The sea shall give up its dead which are therein, which have been burned to dust and ashes, and they shall arise and come forth. That will be a different judgment from that which the world now holds. . . .

But the holy martyrs of God who are now in every distress will enter upon and receive a beautiful crown, a glorious kingdom, a great joy, a heavenly rest, an eternal life, an everlasting salvation, an eternal and immeasurably weighty and excellent glory. The suffering of this present time is not worthy of that glory which no eye has seen, nor ear heard, nor has it entered into any human heart, nor is any tongue so eloquent as to be able to speak what God has prepared for those who love Him. This blessedness and glory shall have no[temporal] place and no end but shall endure from eternity to eternity for ever and ever. (Zieglschmid edition of the *Chronicle*, 1943, 237-241.)

7. The Society of Brothers, 1920

Within the present generation a man named Eberhard Arnold established in Germany what could appropriately be called Neo-Hutterianism. Dr. Arnold, 1883-1935, was the son of Carl Franklin Arnold, professor of church history at the University of Breslau. At the age of sixteen young Eberhard experienced a deep religious awakening through the activity of the Salvation Army and similar groups. He studied theology but finally discontinued his membership in the German Protestant Church. He received a Doctor of Philosophy degree in 1909 at the University of Erlangen. Shortly thereafter he married Emy von Hollander, daughter of a Professor of Law at the University of Halle. They became the parents of five children, all of whom became Neo-Hutterians.

Arnold was apparently filled with a longing to escape from the competitive and capitalistic society of the modern world. In 1920 he and his family removed from Berlin to the village of Sannerz, about sixty miles northeast of Frankfort-on-the-Main. There he established a colony of like-minded people. By 1922 he had a community of forty adults. But an anticlimax followed—all but seven quit. But in time a gradual growth enlarged the community to the point where they had to find larger quarters. In 1926 they purchased eighty acres about eight miles to the northeast of Sannerz. Later they added two more farms and adopted the name RHOENBRUDERHOF. In 1930 Dr. Arnold came to North America and visited the Hutterian Brethren in Alberta. On December 9, 1930 he was received into their fellowship. Ten days later they ordained him to the ministry. Thereupon he returned to his *Bruderhof* in Germany. His community engaged in agriculture, bookbinding, printing, etc.

In the course of time Germany became national socialist and the *Rhoenbruderhof* became obnoxious to the party in power. For one thing the colony held to the doctrine of nonresistance which was regarded as a doctrine of weakness by Hitler Germany. On April 14, 1937 German police raided the colony and arrested and imprisoned the leaders. Some of the members fled to Lichtenstein, the tiny country on the eastern frontier of Switzerland, and many escaped to England with Dutch Mennonite aid. Fortunately two American Hutterian Brethren were in the colony when the raid occurred; they have given the world a printed account of the unhappy event.

Before the dissolution of the *Rhoenbruderhof* two new colonies had been established: the *Almbruderhof* in Lichtenstein, 1934 (abandoned 1938), and the Cotswold *Bruderhof* in Wiltshire, England, 1936. The Oaksey *Bruderhof,* about five miles from Cotswold, was established in 1938. In England the Hutterians took the name *Society of Brothers.*

In 1939 Great Britain and Germany became involved in a state of war. The nonresistant German Hutterians were then not altogether welcome in England. Plans were therefore made for the English Society of Brothers to leave the British Isles and settle in Paraguay, South America. In October 1940 the group left. A few brothers stayed behind to close up the establishments. But interestingly enough, the simple nonresistant way of life had not been without influence. It had attracted the favorable attention of some earnest Christians. People came and desired to unite with the Society of Brothers. So the witness of the Neo-Hutterians is continuing in England beyond the close of the second World War.

Some people are still willing to renounce all personal property in order to share in the quiet and peace of a small, closed Christian community which seeks to pattern itself after the Jerusalem Church of the long ago.

READINGS

Bach, Marcus: "Experiment in Contentment," [American Hutterites], *Coronet,* Vol. 20, No. 2 (June 1946), 135-139.

Beck, J. V.: *Die Geschichtsbücher der Wiedertäufer . . .* 1526-1785, Wien, 1883.

Bender, H. S.: *Mennonite Origins in Europe,* M.C.C. Akron, Pennsylvania, 1942, 48-58.

Bender, H. S., "Palatinate Mennonite Census Lists," *The Mennonite Quarterly Review,* Goshen, Indiana, XIV (1940) Jan., 5-40; April, 67-89; Jl, 170-186; Oct., 224-248; XV (1941) Jan., 46-63.

Bossert, G.: *Quellen Zur Geschichte der Wiedertäufer. I. Band, Herzogtum Württemberg,* Leipzig, 1930.

Friesen, J. J.: *An Outline of Mennonite History,* Herald Publishing Co., Newton, Kansas, 1944, 9-32.

Friedmann, Robert: *Die Habaner in der Slowakei,* Wien, 1927.

Geiser, Samuel: "The Mennonites of Switzerland and France," *The Mennonite Quarterly Review,* Goshen, Indiana, XI, 1 (January 1937), 44-60.

Geiser, Samuel, *et. al: Die Taufgesinnten-Gemeinden,* Karlsruhe, (Germany), [1931], 126-273.

Gerbert, Camille: *Geschichte der Strassburger Sectenbewegung . . .*, Strassburg, 1889.

Hege, Christian: *Die Täufer in der Kurpfalz,* Hermann Minjon Verlag, Frankfurt am Main, 1908, 1-178.

Hege, Christian & Neff, Christian: *Mennonitisches Lexikon,* Frankfurt am Main und Weierhof (Pfalz), I. Band, 1913-24; II. Band, 1937. Articles: *Augsburger Täufergemeinde, Baden, Bayern, Colmar, Deutsches Reich, Durlach, Elsass, Frankenthaler Religionsgespräch, Frankreich, Galizien, Hessen, Hessen-Nassau, Ibersheim, Ibersheimer Beschlüsse, Klein-Polen, Kraichgau, Kurpfalz, Lemberg, Lothringen, Montbeliard,* and the "Literature" cited at the close of the several articles.

Hofer, David: *Die Auflösung des Rhönbruderhofes in Deutschland,* Pflug-Verlag des Cotswold-Bruderhofes, Ashton Keynes, Wiltshire, England, 1938, 2-8.

Horsch, John: *Mennonites in Europe,* Mennonite Publishing House, Scottdale, Pennsylvania, 1938, 124-155, 259-270.

Horsch, M.: *Die Auflösung des Eingetragenen Vereins "Neuwerk Bruderhof,"* Post Neuhof, Kreis Fulda, [c. 1937], 5-32.

Hruby, Frantisek: *Die Wiedertäufer in Mähren,* Leipzig, 1935.

Hulshof, A.: *Geschiedenis van de Doopsgezinden te Straatsburg van 1525 tot 1557,* Amsterdam, 1905.

Kraus, Frantisek: *Nove Prispenky K Dejinam Habanov Na Slovensku,* 1937. [Illustrated with several Habaner pictures: people, dwellings, churches and ceramics.]

Loserth, J.: "Reichsgesetze gegen die 'Wiedertäufer,'" *Mennonitische Geschichtsblätter,* I. Jahrgang, Nr. 1/2 1936, 27-29.

Mathiot, Ch.: *Recherches Historiques sur les Anabaptistes,* Belfort, 1922.

Müller, Lydia: *Glaubenszeugnisse oberdeutscher Taufgesinnter,* Heinsius Nachfolger, Leipzig, 1938.

Müller, Lydia: *Der Kommunismus der Mährischen Wiedertäufer,* Leipzig, 1928.

Neff, Christian: "The Mennonites of Germany, Including Danzig and Poland," *The Mennonite Quarterly Review,* XI, 1 (Jan. 1937) 34-43.

Nestler, Hermann: *Die Wiedertäufer-bewegung in Regensburg,* Joseph Habbel, Regensburg, 1926.
Newman, A. H.: *A History of Anti-Pedobaptism from the Rise of Pedobaptism to A.D. 1509.* American Baptist Publication Society, Philadelphia, 1897, 159-172, 188-253.
Schornbaum, Karl: *Quellen zur Geschichte der Wiedertäufer: Markgraftum Brandenburg,* M. Heinsius Nachfolger, Leipzig, 1934.
Schowalter, Paul: "Die Essinger Konferenzen 1759 und 1779," *Mennonitischer Geschichtsblätter,* 3 Jahrgang, Nr. ½, 1938, 49-55.
Smith, C. H.: *The Story of the Mennonites,* Mennonite Book Concern, Berne, Indiana, [1941], 296 315.
Smithson, R. J.: *The Anabapists: Their Contribution to Our Protestant Heritage,* James Clarke & Co., Ltd., London, [c. 1935], 56-79.
Sommer, Pierre: "The Present Situation of the French-speaking Mennonites," *The Mennonite Quarterly Review,* Goshen, Indiana, II, 4 (October 1928), 268-274.
Wappler, Paul: *Die Täuferbewegung in Thüringen von* 1526-1584, G. Fisher Verlag, Jena, 1913.
Wenger, J. C.: "German Mennonites," *Gospel Herald,* Nov. 17, 1937, 706f.
Wolkan, R.: *Die Lieder der Wiedertäufer,* Berlin, 1903.
Zieglschmid, A. J. F.: *Die älteste Chronik der Hutterischen Brüder,* Carl Schurz Memorial Foundation, 1943.

CHAPTER V

Spiritual Babel in the North

1. *The Melchiorites*

The Melchiorites derived their name from a man named Melchior Hofmann, c. 1495—c. 1543, a native of a place called Hall in Swabia, South Germany. Hofmann had a strange and tragic life. He was successively Lutheran, Zwinglian, and some sort of an Anabaptist. He was eloquent, filled with a knowledge of the letter of the Bible, and able to make an appeal to the masses. In June 1525 Luther had licensed Hofmann to preach—but later regretted having done so, of course.

In 1526 Hofmann went to Sweden where he published a treatise on Daniel 12. He taught that the elements of the Lord's Supper were but symbols, the Zwinglian view. On the other hand only non-Christians were to take part in the magistracy, the Anabaptist view. Like the Anabaptists he also opposed the swearing of oaths. In addition to holding these views, Hofmann held fanatical notions in the realm of prophecy. He taught that Christ's second coming would take place in 1533. In 1527 Hofmann was in Lübeck in North Germany, but by June 1529 he was in Strasburg in Alsace. It is claimed that in 1530 he received rebaptism in Strasburg. Certain it is however that he did not unite with the Swiss Brethren for they later declared: "Hofmann is not named a brother by us, but we oppose him with all earnestness, and consider his opinion, as we have heard it from himself and others of his party, an error" (Berne Disputation, 1538). In 1530 Hofmann was teaching his peculiar view of the incarnation. It was his interpretation that Christ inherited nothing from Mary, a view which was later held among the Dutch Mennonites for some time. Hofmann was also becoming visionary. For example, he allowed a "prophetess" to teach upon the basis of a vision which she thought she had seen that Hofmann was the Elijah of Old Testament prophecy. Other Melchiorites had other "revelations."

Hofmann traveled about considerably. In 1530 he organized a congregation at Emden, East Friesland, now a part of Hannover in northwestern Germany. After a time he was back in Strasburg, only to appear in the Netherlands early in 1531. At Emden, Hofmann left a man named John Volkertszoon or Trijpmaker (slipper-maker) in charge of his flock. In November 1530, Trijpmaker went to Amsterdam and in December 1531 was beheaded in the Hague. Hofmann once more returned to Strasburg where he was imprisoned, May 1533. It is reported that he rejoiced at being arrested for he thought Christ would shortly come and set up an earthly kingdom at Strasburg. When Christ comes all God's enemies were to be destroyed, said Hofmann. But the saints in the meantime before Christ returns, were to wait patiently and be obedient to the governments of this world. Hofmann waited and waited, but Christ did not come. Finally, a sick and broken man, Hofmann died in prison about the close of 1543.

In Holland the followers of Hofmann were called Melchiorites or Covenanters (*Bontgenooten*), and constituted a party within the Roman Catholic Church. Trijpmaker was baptized by Hofmann in 1530; he in turn baptized a man named John Matthys. About the end of the year 1533 two "apostles" of Matthys, Bartholomew Bookbinder and Dirck Kuiper (Cooper), baptized a number of converts to Melchiorism in the Friesian town of Leeuwarden. One of the converts was a barber and surgeon named Obbe Philips. A week later Peter Woodsawer, another Matthys "apostle" baptized Obbe's brother, Dirck Philips, a former Franciscan Monk. The Philips brothers later had great significance in Dutch Mennonite history. At this point they were still under the spell of Melchiorism however. One of the interesting items of Melchiorite belief was that during the years 1532 and 1533 the Melchiorites should form circles of secret believers in Hofmann's brand of Anabaptism and continue outwardly as members of the state church—in the Netherlands the Roman Catholic Church.

2. *The Münsterites*

The city which became the scene of a major tragedy caused by religious fanaticism was Münster in Westphalia, in northwestern Germany. On January 7, 1532 the Catholic Bishop of Münster, Franz von Waldeck, silenced a priest named Bernt Rothmann for teaching unsound doctrine. But a month later, on Feburary 18, an influential citizen named Herman Knipperdolling secured permission for Rothmann to resume his ministry. Rothmann preached in St. Lambert's Church. Something over a year later, May 1533, Rothmann began to preach against infant baptism.

In the course of time John Matthys, a Haarlem baker and Melchiorite leader, himself more radical than Hofmann, decided to send "apostles" to Münster, the Zion of God. The men who went, January 1534, were Gerrit Tom Kloster and John Bockelson, also called John of Leiden. John Matthys himself arrived in "Zion" the next month. On February 23, 1534 Herman Knipperdolling was elected as the civil head of the city. Two days later Matthys gave evidence of his mental, ethical, and spiritual imbalance by announcing that all the "godless" (those resisting his ideas) would be executed. Fortunately he proclaimed a "Day of Grace" (permitting flight from the city), the same to end on March 2.

The Bishop of Münster now became alarmed. He assembled his army and laid siege to the city. At Easter, 1534, Matthys, obsessed with the delusion that he would be a second Gideon, sallied forth rashly against the Bishop's troops. He was quickly slain.

At this point John Bockelson, a carnal opportunist, became the prophet-ruler of "Zion." John thought of himself as God's vicar ruling over the Theocracy of Münster. In May 1534 he claimed to have been told, while in a trance, to become the ruler of the city. And he was able to command the support of his deluded and perhaps somewhat intimidated subjects. On May 25 the Bishop's army attacked the city, but John's forces repulsed it.

The summer of 1534 John decided that since he was God's ruler he might as well exercise regal prerogatives. Accordingly he introduced the practice of polygamy among his subjects. Forty-nine men who objected were promptly executed. John himself set an example by taking numerous wives, being careful to give Old Testament support for every move. It was not until September 1544 that a "prophet" anointed John as king. Because of the scarcity of food, King John set up a sort of communism, taking charge of all the stores of food which could be located. While people starved to death, King John lived in a riotous manner, all the while exhorting the people to wait for "God's salvation." By the spring of 1535 conditions in the city were horrifying. The subjects of King John ate cats, dogs, mice, rats, grass, moss, old shoes—following the usual pattern of starving people, including the consumption of human flesh. Finally on the night of June 24-25, 1535 the city was betrayed over to the armed forces of the Bishop. Knipperdolling, King John, and Bernard Krechting, city chancellor, were in due time executed (January 22, 1536). Before his execution King John acknowledged the awfulness of his error. The bodies of the three men were placed in iron cages on the tower of St. Lambert's Church. Visitors in Münster are still shown the iron cages, silent witnesses to the folly of John Matthys, John of Leiden, and their deluded followers. Needless to say, Münster reverted to Roman Catholicism.

It should not be necessary to remark that the Münsterites had almost nothing in common with the Swiss Brethren or with the Dutch Anabaptists (Obbenites and Mennonites). Both the Swiss and Dutch Anabaptists placed chief emphasis on the New Testament while the Münsterites appealed to the Old Testament in support of their strange doctrine and practice. Unfortunately however the Münster tragedy has often been interpreted as the logical outcome of Anabaptism. The injustice of this is apparent when it is remembered that Anabaptism arose in Zurich as a sane Biblical movement, the left wing of the Protestant Reformation, and is represented today by several hundred thousand Mennonites. The Münster episode on the other hand was the result of the fanaticism and the carnality of a few ungodly men. Obbe Philips, whose break with Melchiorism took place in 1534, placed the "ban" on all those who were infected with the Münsterite error and insisted that they be avoided ("shunned"). Indeed this was the origin of shunning among the Dutch Anabaptists.

Even Melchior Hofmann cannot be held entirely responsible for Münsterism. He would certainly have restrained Matthys and Bockelson had it been in his power. Yet it must be admitted that by his fanatical and fanciful views of prophecy and of special revelations Hofmann planted the seed which grew into a noxious plant in the impure mental soil of the Münsterite leaders.

3. *Davidians and Batenburgers*

David Joris was born in the Netherlands about 1501 or 1502. He learned the trade of glass-painting. He first identified himself with the Lutherans, later with the Obbenites (to be described shortly), and was ordained to the ministry by Obbe Philips. He was a radical, fanatical, and visionary person, and in a few years it was evident that he was not spiritually attuned to the Obbenites. In August 1536 he made the ridiculous attempt to unite Obbenites, Melchiorites, and Batenburgers—the latter being the radicals who attempted to keep Münsterism alive in the world. Joris himself began to get visions.

He depreciated the letter of the Scriptures and gloried in his "spiritual" insight, while his life and teaching took a serious turn toward antinomianism. It is claimed that he taught the impossibility of a Christian really sinning. One should confess his "sins" until no shame is any longer felt. Menno Simons roundly condemned him as a false prophet. Joris in turn hurled a verbal blast at Menno, asking him who counseled him "to rise up so proudly against the Lord." The essential differences between Menno and David concerned their respective attitudes toward the Bible. Menno took the Bible—that means the words of the Bible—as the sole norm of faith and life, while David Joris regarded such an attitude as a "dead-letter faith."

The civil authorities soon began to try to crush out the Davidians. Over fifty of them were executed at Delft, 1538-39, including David's own mother. Joris was not minded to become a martyr however. He decided on a policy of hypocrisy to escape persecution. The plan was to participate in the state church services just as if there was full agreement with the state church. Joris himself set an amazing example of such deception.

On April 1, 1544 a distinguished looking man arrived in Basle, Switzerland, giving his name as John of Bruges. "John" reported that he was a persecuted Zwinglian and asked permission to settle in the Zwinglian city. His fellow-Zwinglians of course welcomed him to their fellowship. On August 25, 1544 he moved to Basle with his family and retinue of servants. He attended state church services and gave alms as a solid Zwinglian citizen. His children married into prominent families of the city. On August 25, 1556 he died and was properly buried for a man of his station in life. But some two years later the fraud was discovered. In their zeal for orthodoxy the Baslers exhumed the body of David Joris and duly burned it as that of a heretic! But the "'corrupt sect" of the Davidians was still in existence in Holstein in the seventeenth century.

Even more radical than the Davidians and the Münsterites were the Batenbergers, followers of John Batenburg. John was born in 1495 and before his conversion to the "corrupt sects" was burgomaster of a Dutch town called Steenwijk. He attempted to carry on the doctrines of Münsterism and thereby won the name *Schwertgeister* (sword-spirits) for his followers. He taught the desirability of plundering churches, of practicing polygyny, and of "having all things common"—quite a mixed program. He taught that the sword should be used to set up the kingdom of God (hence the name, "Sword-spirits"), only the time had not yet come. Batenburg was executed in 1538, and his party seems not to have survived him for very many years. Batenburg had thought to escape persecution by teaching his followers to outwardly profess loyalty to the state church. Consequently they attended Roman Catholic services, biding their time to erect God's kingdom by force.

Menno Simons, about the year 1537, wrote as follows concerning the "corrupt sects":

> Through the false, misguided teachers, Satan has perverted the spiritual sense of the Scriptures into carnality. He has preached the use of the sword and weapons of destruction, and thereby has engendered a spirit of revenge against all the world. He has moreover, without any scriptural foundation, cloaked and palliated shameful adultery [Menno means polygyny] with the example of the Jewish patriarchs, also a literal kingdom and king and other ungodly errors at which a true Christian is stricken with terror.

READINGS

Cornelius, C. A.: *Geschichte des Münsterischen Aufruhrs,* Leipzig, 1860.

Hege, Christian and Neff, Christian: *Mennonitisches Lexikon,* Frankfurt a.M. und Weierhof (Pfalz), I. Band, 1913-24; II Band, 1937, articles: *Batenburg, Johann; Blesdijk, Nikolaus Meynertsz; Bockelson, Johann; Hofmann, Melchior; Joris, David; Ketel, Jurjen; Knipperdolling, Bernard; Krechting; Matthys, Jan; Münsterische Wiedertäufer.*

Horsch, John: "The Rise and Fall of the Anabaptists of Muenster," *The Mennonite Quarterly Review,* IX, 2 (April 1935), 92-103; IX, 3 (July 1935) 129-143.

Horsch, John: "Menno Simons' Attitude Toward the Anabaptists of Muenster," *The Mennonite Quarterly Review,* X, 1 (Jan. 1936), 55-72.

Horsch, John: *Mennonites in Europe,* Scottdale, Pennsylvania, 1942, 169-173, 219-226.

Kühn, Johannes: *Toleranz und Offenbarung,* Leipzig, 1923.

Löffler, Klemens (Ed.): *Die Wiedertäufer Zu Münster* 1534/35, Eugen Diederich, Jena, 1923.

Newman, A. H.: *A History of Anti-Pedobaptism from the Rise of Pedobaptism to A.D. 1609,* American Baptist Publication Society, Philadelphia, 1897, 254-272, 284-294.

Smith, C. Henry: *The Story of the Mennonites,* Berne, Indiana, [1941], 74-87.

Smithson, R. J.: *The Anabaptists: Their Contribution to Our Protestant Heritage,* James Clarke, London, [c. 1935], 80-87.

Zur Linden, J. O.: *Melchior Hofmann,* Haarlem, 1885.

CHAPTER VI

Menno Simons and the Obbenites

1. *The Obbenites*

In the discussion of the Melchiorites mention was made of the baptisms of Obbe Philips and of his brother Dirck by the "apostles" of the Melchiorite leader, John Matthys. Obbe himself tells the story in his CONFESSIONS, a work which was reprinted by Dr. Samuel Cramer in Volume VII of *Bibliotheca Reformatoria Neerlandica.* The translation of the Obbe quotations was made by John Horsch. Obbe wrote:

> Then there came to us at Leeuwarden [the capital of Friesland] two of those messengers, namely Bartholomew Bookbinder and Dirck Cooper. And when some of us had come together, about fourteen or fifteen persons, men and women, they sat before us and announced to us love and patience in their address. And then they declared to us the authority of their mission, namely that Jan Matthys had come to them with such signs, wonderworking, and power of the Spirit that words failed them to describe it to us. They said we should not doubt that they were endowed with power and miracle-working no less than the apostles at the day of Pentecost.
>
> They also comforted us and said, we should not be in anxiety or fear, as we had indeed long feared the great tyranny; for henceforth no blood of Christians should be shed on earth, but within a short time God would destroy all those who shed blood, all the tyrants and godless from the earth.
>
> This assertion [that God would destroy the wicked] I heard with suspicion, although I dared not contradict them, for at that time no one had the courage to contradict much, and whoever spoke against their message was denounced as one who resisted the Spirit and blasphemed. In this manner and by their threatenings of damnation they terrorized the hearts in such measure that no one had the courage to contradict them. Everyone feared that he would in some way transgress and speak against the mission and work of God. For we were all inexperienced, like children, and had no thought that we would be deceived by our own brethren who every day were with us in like danger of death and persecution.
>
> At that day we nearly all accepted baptism at their hands. [This was in December 1533.] The day following, when they were about to depart, they, after counseling with other brethren, entrusted to us the office of the ministry, by laying on of hands, namely to baptize, to teach, etc. And after they had accomplished all this among us, they at once resumed their journey on the same day.
>
> Then after eight days came Peter Woodsawer with the same mission, and baptized Dirck Philips and a few others. I was absent from the city [of

Leeuwarden] in the country to preach at that time, and did not meet Peter Woodsawer.

No sooner had this Peter Woodsawer come outside of the city walls of Leeuwarden, when all prophecy and lofty assertion proved vain; for he was immediately sought and pursued by the authorities, at first in the city and then in the villages of the country, and had a very narrow escape for the authorities used all means to pursue him.

Meanwhile I returned upon a Sunday with my brother Hans Scherder to Leeuwarden, and when we came near the city gate, about noon, we noticed that the keeper was about to close the gate. But he saw us coming and called to us, saying, if we desired to enter, we must make haste. When we heard this, we were frightened and asked the reason why the gate was closed. He said, "There are Anabaptists in the city; they are all to be seized." Then we were much more frightened and remembered the prophecies [that God would henceforth prevent the persecution of His saints.] But we, realizing the impossibility of turning back without arousing suspicion, recovered courage and went into the city about noon.

Having arrived home, I found my wife in anxiety, and she told me of the visit of Peter Woodsawer, and that some of the Melchiorites had boldly contradicted his word and his authority, which resulted in great rumor and persecution. Some had already been apprehended, and others were very earnestly sought. She entreated me by all means to go away into another house until darkness would set in.

A number of the Melchiorite ministers, "apostles" of John Matthys, decided that since there was to be no more persecution they would preach publicly. Obbe writes further:

These three men who . . . had boasted of their mission and calling as apostles and said that no blood should further be shed upon the earth were taken captive soon after that as disturbers and Anabaptists. With a number of others, sixteen or seventeen persons in all, they were taken to Haarlem and were all put to death.

Among those who were broken on the wheel at Haarlem were Peter Woodsawer who had baptized Dirck Philips, and Bartholomew Bookbinder who with Dirck Cooper had baptized Obbe. The execution took place March 26, 1534. Obbe Philips went to the place of execution but was unable to recognize any of the bodies.

The execution of the Matthys preachers was the means of disillusioning the Philips brothers. They saw clearly that they had been deceived by false prophets. Obbe himself says:

What took place was the very contrary of what they had announced to us. All that they had said would come upon the world, upon the tyrants and godless, came rather upon us, and first of all upon the messengers themselves. Alas, who is able to tell our great grief. . . . Oh how often were some of us in sadness unto death and knew not whither to turn or what to do. The whole world persecuted us to death for our faith with fire, water, sword, and all-bloody tyranny; the prophecies had deceived us; Scripture did not give us liberty to make common cause with the persecutors; the false brethren whom we reproved and contradicted swore that they would take our lives, and the love of so many hearts, who were deceived despite their good intentions, moved us to heartfelt compassion. Ofttimes my soul was sorrowful unto death

It is clear that Obbe Philips was driven to the Word of God for instruction and illumination. The Scriptures changed him from a disillusioned Melchiorite of the Matthys type (Matthys had not yet been guilty of the Münster excesses) into a sane Bible teacher, blameless in life and sound in the faith. Obbe, as a man of flesh and blood, would have gladly fled from the trying situation; but as a Christian he could not do so. He saw hungry souls who needed a shepherd and teacher. He confesses:

Had it not been for the love and pity I felt toward so many upright hearts who were daily seduced by false brethren, I should certainly have left them and with a few others withdrawn from all who were acquainted with me. For among all the teachers there was for a time no one but Dirck Philips to stand with me against the false brethren.

But Obbe and Dirck did not long stand alone. About two years after they inaugurated their evangelical program Menno Simons, a converted priest, joined their group—Obbenites was the name attached to them. And about a year after Menno's baptism by Obbe Philips, a group of fellow Obbenites waited upon him to take up the ministry. In connection with that call Menno gives a brief but significant description of the Obbenites. He says they were

of one heart and one soul with myself in their faith and life, and as far as man can judge were unblamable, and according to the testimony of the Scriptures separated from the world and subdued to the cross. They sincerely abhorred not only the sect of Münster but the anathemas and abominations of all other worldly sects. . . .

Thus, my reader, behold, I was not called to serve among the followers of Münster nor of any other seditious sect (as it is falsely reported concerning me), but I have been called, unworthily, to this office by a people who were ready to receive Christ and His Word, led a penitent life in the fear of God, served their neighbors in love, bore the cross, sought the welfare and salvation of all men, loved righteousness and truth, and abhorred wickedness and unrighteousness, which shows pointedly that they were not such perverted persons as they are slanderously reported to have been.— *Renunciation of the Church of Rome,* 1554.

It should not be necessary to point out that there was no organic connection between the Swiss Brethren in the south, founded by Conrad Grebel in 1525, and the Obbenites in the north, founded by Obbe Philips in 1534. So far as we know, Obbe at that time had never heard of the Brethren in Switzerland. Nor was the rise of the Obbenites in any way associated with the older Waldenses; there is no evidence that there had ever been Waldenses in the Netherlands at any time. The doctrine of the Obbenites and that of the Swiss Brethren were quite similar simply because both groups made a serious effort to reject tradition and to make the Scriptures the sole norm of faith and practice. On two points there was a divergence, however: (1) The Obbenites held to a strict form of shunning (see article XVII of the Dordrecht Confession of Faith) while the Swiss Brethren interpreted such Scriptures as I Corinthians 5:11 as referring to the Lord's Supper. (2) The Obbenites held to a peculiar view of the incarnation, a Melchiorite point which they failed to overcome when they broke with Melchiorism.

2. *Menno Simons, 1496-1561*

In 1496 a Dutch couple of Witmarsum in Friesland named their infant son Menno. Since the name of Menno's father was Simon the custom of the day in Holland made the child's name Menno Simonszoon—called Simons for short. As a youth Menno received training for the Catholic priesthood, perhaps in the Franciscan Monastery at Bolsward, near Witmarsum. In the monastery Menno received training in reading and writing Latin and in a study of the Church fathers, but he never read the Bible. In 1524 he was consecrated as a priest, and for seven years he served in the Pinjum parish near Witmarsum. In 1531 he was transferred to his home town where he served for five more years. His work as priest consisted in the celebration of the mass, in offering prayers for the living and the dead, in baptizing infants, in hearing confessions of sin and, unfortunately, in playing cards and drinking. Until this time Menno had feared to read the Bible, for only the Catholic Church, Menno had been taught, could infallibly interpret the Scriptures.

The story of Menno's conversion is interesting. One day in 1525, during the first year of his priesthood, while he was celebrating the mass, a doubt crept into his mind as to whether the bread and wine actually became divine. This doubt of the truth of transubstantiation was to lead to Menno's first soul-struggle. Menno first thought that this was a suggestion from the devil, and he tried by using the confessional to get it out of his system. After much worry Menno finally decided upon a course of action. He resolved to study the New Testament. This was a most important decision, for in the end it was bound to lead him from the Catholic Church; he finally had to choose between following the Word of God and following the church. For Menno this was a very hard decision.

We have already seen the part which Martin Luther played in the origin of the Swiss Brethren movement. It was Luther again who helped Menno Simons solve his problem. For Luther (through his writings) taught Menno one great truth: A violation of human commands cannot lead to eternal death. And yet Menno did not become a Lutheran; he developed his own doctrine of the Lord's Supper. But it was Martin Luther who convinced Menno that the ultimate authority in all matters of faith was the Word of God and nothing else. Menno was convinced of this about 1528, but strangely enough he went right on celebrating the mass.

In 1531 Menno Simons heard of an incident which became the occasion for his second soul-struggle. Jan Trijpmaker, a Melchiorite, had baptized a Dutchman named Sicke Freerks in 1530. Freerks was executed for his faith at Leeuwarden on March 20, 1531. Menno Simons was exceedingly astonished; the idea of a second baptism was for him completely new. To the horrified Menno now came the question: Is the Catholic Church also unbiblical as to baptism? Again Menno turned to the writings of the leading reformers. Luther said that infant baptism was justifiable because babies have "hidden faith," just as a believing adult is also a Christian even while he is asleep. Martin Butzer said that infant baptism was a pledge that the parents would give the child a godly training. Henry Bullinger, Zwingli's successor in Zurich, said that just as the Old Testament sign of the Covenant (circumcision) was performed on infants, so also the New Testament sign of the Covenant (baptism) shall be performed on infants. To Menno these arguments seemed logical enough, but he was not so much interested in logic as in the Word of God. And he could find nothing of infant baptism in the New Testament.

Through all this strain and stress Menno remained a Catholic priest. He continued baptizing infants and saying mass. In fact he even accepted promotion to become head-pastor at Witmarsum. Menno was thus living a double life. He was believing one thing and practicing another. What would it take to make Menno Simons follow the Lord in loving obedience? The answer came in 1534-35 when the Münsterites came to Holland teaching their abominable and fanatical views. Even Menno's own brother was swept along with the deluded folks, and lost his life in a little battle with the authorities on April 7, 1535.

Menno of course took up the literary fight with the Münsterites. And yet he was not a happy man. For in fighting Münsterism was he not defending Catholicism? And were not those 300 misguided souls, who perished when his own brother lost his life, more honorable than he? They gave their lives for their error; was he not willing to give anything for the truth?

About April 1535 Menno surrendered to God, crying for pardon and peace. What a decision this was for the Obbenites and for the future Mennonite Church! Strangely enough Menno apparently remained in the Catholic Church for yet another nine months, preaching evangelical doctrines from a Catholic pulpit. But this could not go on indefinitely, and in January 1536 Menno Simons renounced the Catholic Church and thus took the step which he had known for a long time was God's will for him. As was already mentioned, he was probably baptized by Obbe Philips. Before we criticize Menno for his timidity, we should remember what this step meant for him. It meant that in the eyes both of the world and of the civil authorities he was a heretic of the worst sort, even more dangerous than an ordinary criminal. While Luther and Zwingli timed and modified their programs to secure political protection, the Anabaptists went bravely ahead and organized a church which they felt was true to the teachings of the New Testament. For this step they were willing to part with possessions, friends, family, and even life itself.

Obbe Philips and the Obbenites would not allow Menno to live a private life for any length of time. It is true that for several months he evidently devoted himself to quiet meditation and study. During this time he probably preached on occasion but had no pastoral oversight. But a number of Obbenite brethren felt that Menno Simons ought to assume the duties of an elder. Consequently a deputation of brethren called on Menno and pleaded with him to accept the leadership of the brotherhood. Menno hesitated. The Brethren came a second time. This time Menno accepted the call. It was probably early in 1537 when Menno was ordained as elder (bishop). The ordination was assuredly performed by Obbe Philips, the Leeuwarden surgeon and founder of Dutch Anabaptism. Incidentally Obbe himself later lost heart, laid down his ministry, and withdrew from the church; because of this Menno called him a "Demas." Menno now took the lead in building up the brotherhood and saving it from the radical movements of the day.

From 1536 until 1543 Menno worked in Holland. Soon after becoming an Obbenite he married a woman named Gertrude; her last name is uncertain; it may have been Hoyer. Menno's family did not take first place in his life, although he no doubt did all he could for them. His great work was the proclamation of the gospel of Christ. About 1539 he called himself a "homeless man." Menno's work was richly blessed of God; many souls were won and strengthened through his ministry. One tribute to the effectiveness of his work was the opposition he received. On December 7, 1542 Emperor Charles V, ruler of Europe from the Netherlands to Austria, issued the following edict against him:

BY THE EMPEROR

To our worthy, beloved Mayors, Boards, and Counselors, etc., of our city of Leeuwarden, Greeting:

Whereas, it has come to our knowledge and we have fully ascertained that a man [named] Menno Symonss, formerly pastor at Witmarsum in our land of Friesland, being polluted with Anabaptism and other false teachings, had departed out of the said land, and we have now obtained trustworthy information that he has again secretly returned into our aforesaid land where he is now sojourning, endeavoring at night and other unseasonable times and in diverse places to seduce by his false teachings and sermons the simple people, our subjects, and to lead them away from the faith and unity of the Holy Church; and that he also has undertaken to make a few books treating on his aforesaid erroneous teachings, and to circulate and scatter the same among our aforesaid subjects, which he has no right to do, and we can not tolerate the same;

Therefore, to take appropriate steps in this matter, we ordain and command herewith, that ye everywhere in your jurisdiction, do publish, cry out, and proclaim in the places where such matters are usually brought to the knowledge of the public that every one in our aforesaid land, of whatever station he may be, should be on his guard not to receive the same man Minne Symonss into his house or on his property, or to give him shelter or food or drink, or to accord him any favor or help, or to speak or converse with him in whatever manner or place it may be, or to accept or keep in possession any of the aforesaid books published by the same man Minne, or any other books that he may publish at any future time—all on penalty of punishment on life and property, as heretics, as may be found due according to the law and our previous placards;

And further, that we have permitted and authorized every one of our subjects, whoever he may be, and permit and further authorize through decrees, that they may apprehend the same man Minne wherever they may be able to find him, no place or jurisdiction excepted, and send him captive to our court in Friesland; for which they, in case they accomplish this, shall receive for a recompense besides the expense they may have incurred in this matter, the sum of one hundred golden Karolus gulden, which shall be paid them by our General Treasurer of Friesland without any hesitancy.

To him who may undertake and accomplish this work, we decree and promise grace and pardon regarding that which he may have committed against us in the matter of Anabaptism or other heresy, or in lesser crimes, on condition, in case he was polluted by Anabaptism or other heresies, that he repent of the same and come again to the unity of the Holy Church.

In the same manner we most earnestly command, on pain of the most grievous penalties, that ye do the utmost diligence to investigate and inquire concerning the same man Minne among his followers and adherents who may be apprehended anywhere within your jurisdiction and, together with such information as ye may obtain, to send them as prisoners to our aforesaid court, that they may be dealt with according to their deserts.

We hereby also give authority and special command to you and all our subjects, in whatever jurisdiction it may be found possible to apprehend him, to be guided by the instructions above given; we bid and command every person as regards the above said capture to put forth their united efforts and render all help and assistance that may be asked of them toward that end. In doing this they will incur our pleasure.

Given, in our city of Leeuwarden under our secret seal, published as a placard, on the seventh day of December of the year 1542.

By the Emperor to his Majesty's Stadtholder, President and Counsellors in Friesland.

(Signed) Boeymer

Received on December thirteenth and published on the fourteenth of the same month. [cf. VOS: MENNO SIMONS, 235-238.]

During the years 1541-43 Menno labored in and about Amsterdam. In these years he also found time to do some writing. He published seven books and booklets from 1536 to 1543.

Menno spent a few months in East Friesland in 1543, then labored in northwest Germany for several years (until 1546). He engaged in a disputation with the noted Polish reformer, John a'Lasco, 1499-1560, on January 28-31, 1544, at Emden. The two men agreed on original sin and sanctification, but disagreed on the incarnation of Christ, baptism, and the calling of the ministry. Without securing Menno's permission a' Lasco published a statement of Menno's views. Menno then removed to the Rhineland and worked in the bishopric of Cologne for two years, 1544-46.

With his sick wife and children, Menno fled to Holstein in northern Germany, along the Baltic, in 1546. First he lived at

Wismar, later at a place called Wuestenfelde. The latter was located between Hamburg and Luebeck. In 1550 Menno wrote his *Confession of the Triune God* against Adam Pastor, a Mennonite minister who had become unsound in his view of Christ. The last years of Menno's life were spent in writing. He revised a number of his earlier productions and translated them into the dialect of the region where he was then living.

The closing years of Menno's life were also darkened by dissension within the church. The great problem was, How strictly shall the "ban" be observed? Some of the Dutch leaders were unreasonably harsh in their views, so much so that at the great Strasburg Conference of 1557 over fifty bishops dissented from the strict views of their Dutch brethren. The next year Menno wrote to Reyn Edes, his brother-in-law, "O Brother Reyn! If only I could be with you even a half day and tell you something of my sorrow, my grief and heartache, and of the heavy burden which I carry for the future of the church .... There is nothing on earth that I love so much as the church; yet just in respect to her must I suffer this great sorrow."

Menno Simons had no easy life. He was always poor in this world's goods, being forced to appeal to his brethren for financial help. Yet the Lord stood by him and preserved him from all his enemies. He died on his sickbed January 31, 1561, twenty-five years after his renunciation of Catholicism.

Menno Simons is undoubtedly the greatest figure in the history of the church which now bears his name. He had a sane and balanced program of promoting both an evangelical faith and holiness of life. He was a fearless leader who aimed at complete loyalty to the Word of God; and he was a good, practical writer. It is true that John Calvin said of him, "Nothing could be more arrogant and more impudent than this donkey," but this is just a specimen of the mud-throwing of those days.

No great monuments have ever been erected to the memory of Menno Simons. In the year 1879 a simple shaft was placed near Witmarsum, and in 1906 a granite stone containing a bronze plaque of him was dedicated at the site of Wuestenfelde. But Menno Simons' greatness cannot be measured in terms of monuments nor even by the size of the Mennonite Church. Only on that Great Day when the workers come Home, bringing their sheaves with them, will the true character of Menno's work be manifested.

READINGS

Bender, H. S. and Horsch, John: *Menno Simons' Life and Writings, A Quadricentennial Tribute,* Scottdale, Pennsylvania, 1936.

Hege, Christian and Neff, Christian: *Mennonitisches Lexikon,* Frankfurt a. M. und Weierhof (Pfalz), I. Bd., 1913-24; II. Band, 1937, articles: *Amsterdamer Taufgesinnten-Gemeinde; Friesland; Houtzager, Pieter; Leeuwarden; Menno Simons; Mennobilder; Mennodenkmal; Mennostein; Freerks, Sicke.*

Horsch, John: "Menno Simons' Attitude Toward the Anabaptists of Münster," *The Mennonite Quarterly Review,* Goshen, Indiana, X, 1 (January 1936), 55-72.

Horsch, John: "The Origin of the Mennonite Church in the Netherlands," *The Goshen College Review Supplement,* May-June 1926, 20-27.

Horsch, John: "The Rise of Mennonitism in the Netherlands," *The Mennonite Quarterly Review,* Goshen, Indiana, VIII, 4 (October 1934) 147-165.

Horsch, John: *Menno Simons, His Life, Labors, and Teachings,* Scottdale, Pennsylvania, 1916.

Horsch, John: "Is Dr. Kuehler's Conception of Early Dutch Anabaptism Historically Sound?" *The Mennonite Quarterly Review,* VII, 1 (Jan. 1933), 97-126.

Krahn, Cornelius: *Menno Simons* (1496-1561), *Ein Beitrag zur Geschichte und Theologie der Taufgesinnten,* Heinrich Schneider, Karlsruhe i. B., 1936.

Krahn, C.: *Menno Simons' Lebenswerk Kurz Dargestellt,* J. Gleijsteen, Amsterdam, 1937.

Krahn, Cornelius: "The Conversion of Menno Simons: A Quadricentennial Tribute," *The Mennonite Quarterly Review,* X, 1 (January 1936), 46-54.

Kühler, W. J.: *Geschiedenis der Nederlandsche Doopsgezinden in de Zestiende Eeuw,* H. D. Tjeenk Willink & Zoon, Haarlem, 1932, 1-244. [Note the last Horsch item, above.]

Menno Simon, The Complete Works of, John F. Funk and Brother, Elkhart, Indiana, 1871.

Newman, A. H.: *A History of Anti-Pedobaptism from the Rise of Pedobaptism to A.D. 1609,* American Baptist Publication Society, Philadelphia, 1897, 295-313.

Smith, C. H.: *The Story of the Mennonites,* Mennonite Book Concern, Berne, Indiana, [1941], 87-89, 95-124.

Smith, C. H.: *Menno Simons, Apostle of the Nonresistant Life,* Berne, Ind. [1936].

Smithson, R. J.: *The Anabaptists, Their Contribution to Our Protestant Heritage,* James Clarke, London, [1935], 80-93.

Vos, K.: *Menno Simons, 1496-1561, Zijn Leven en Werken en Zijne Reformatorische Denkbeelden,* E. J. Brill, Leiden, 1914.

Wenger, J. C.: "The Burghart Portrait of Menno," *Gospel Herald,* Jan. 27, 1938, 938f.

CHAPTER VII

Four Centuries of Dutch Mennonitism

The story has already been told of how Obbe Philips and his brother Dirck led a small group of Biblical Anabaptists in the Netherlands, beginning in 1534. With this group Menno united in 1536. Within a short time he was the outstanding leader of the Brethren, and as early as 1544 his followers were called "Mennists." In this period there were four great bishops among the Dutch and North German Mennonites: Menno Simons, Gillis of Aachen, Dirck Philips, and Leonard Bouwens. Let us look briefly at Menno's colleagues.

Dirck Philips was born at Leeuwarden, Holland, in 1504. About the close of 1533 he was baptized by an apostle of Jan Matthys, one Peter Woodsawer. Woodsawer prophesied the speedy end of persecution, but was himself executed March 26, 1534. Dirck and Obbe Philips were then disillusioned, and they bade a final farewell to the delusions of Matthys and became the leaders of a quiet type of Anabaptism, quite like that of Conrad Grebel, although independent of it in origin. The Philips brothers arrived at their views from a fresh study of the Word of God. Dirck became an author of some note, his *Enchiridion* still being cherished by the American Amish. He was described as "an old man with white hair, of medium stature, dressed in black, with a round cap, and he talked the dialect of the Brabanters." (Brabant is a Dutch province.) He was the first bishop of the Danzig Mennonite Church. He died in 1568.

Gillis of Aachen was born about 1500. Menno won Gillis for the church and ordained him as bishop in 1542 to serve the congregations in the vicinity of Cologne. Fifteen years later Gillis was arrested for his faith, near Antwerp. Losing courage he recanted but was nevertheless beheaded on July 10, 1557. Gillis had at one time been described as "a man of medium size, with a pale face, big eyes, and a pointed brown beard." In the *Martyrs' Mirror* he is frequently referred to as Jelis or Gillis of Aix-la-Chapelle (Aachen in German) one of "the heads or teachers of said sect" of the Anabaptists. (1938 edition, pages 532, 536, 538, 542, 557, 568, 575, 592, 611, 612, etc.)

Leonard Bouwens was born at Sommelsdyk in the Netherlands in 1515. As a youth he joined a club of political speakers where he no doubt developed his oratorical powers. He became a Mennonite minister in 1546 and in 1551 was ordained as elder or bishop by Menno Simons. Bouwens kept a list of the converts whom he baptized over a period of thirty years, and the list contains no less than 10,252 names. He was a good leader and a capable bishop, serving the congregations in Holland. There was some disagreement between him and Dirck Philips, and in 1565 Dirck removed him from office. After Dirck died (1568) Bouwens resumed his ministry and served faithfully until his death in 1582. Bouwens is generally referred to in the *Martyrs' Mirror as* "Leenaert" (pages 592, 593, etc.) though at least once Van Braght calls him by his full name, Leenaert Bouwens (page 737).

The first century of Dutch Mennonitism was one of severe persecution. Between the years 1531 and 1597 two thousand martyrs were put to death in the Netherlands and three-fourths of these were Mennonites. In spite of fierce persecution from without, the Dutch Mennonites still found time to strive among themselves. Even Menno Simons had to witness strife and party spirit among the brotherhood before his death. Three chief branches developed: The Waterlanders, who favored a rather mild discipline, but were, like the other two branches, evangelical in faith; the Friesians, who practiced a moderate type of discipline; and the Flemish, who were severely strict. In addition to these three groups many other divisions occurred, chiefly over trivial matters, even over personal affairs such as the sale of a house.

A healthy reaction set in, however, and efforts toward union began to be made about 1600. For example, some Friesians and Flemish united on the basis of the Dordrecht Confession of Faith in 1632. But there was a fresh division in 1664, the milder party being called "Lammists," while those of the more conservative group were called "Zonists."

By the year 1600 there was a degree of toleration for the Dutch Mennonites, but the Catholics and Calvinists continued with their petty persecution as late as the eighteenth century.

In the latter seventeenth century the Dutch Mennonites reached a high level of financial prosperity. Along with this prosperity came both a numerical increase and a spiritual decline. In 1700 the Dutch

Mennonites numbered 160,000 souls (counting unbaptized children). But soon a numerical decline also set in. To help build up the church, a seminary was established in Amsterdam in 1735 for the training of Mennonite ministers. This seminary was conducted along conservative lines for over a hundred years but was rather weakly supported by the church. By the year 1809 the Dutch Mennonites numbered only 27,000, which was about one-sixth of their 1700 census. They were also still broken up into various groups. An all-Mennonite organization, called *Allgemeene Doopsgezinde Societeit*—The General Mennonite Society, usually written "A.D.S."—was founded in 1811. Gradually almost all that was distinctive in Mennonite practice and doctrine was lost, although believers' baptism was retained. Beginning soon after 1850 the Amsterdam Seminary also became liberal in theology and gradually made the church practically Unitarian in doctrine.

The Dutch Mennonites began to carry on mission work about a century ago, founding a mission in the Dutch East Indies in 1847. This work was strongly supported by the Mennonites of Russia.

In spite of the general doctrinal decline, a small group of conservative Mennonites who believed in nonresistance remained at Balk in Holland. Under the leadership of the ministers Smit and Symensma this group of Mennonites emigrated from Holland to New Paris, Indiana, 1853-54, and some of them eventually became assimilated with the Salem Mennonite congregation. The last person who had made this journey, Jacob K. Fisher, died April 25, 1927. He had been born at Balk on July 18, 1849, and therefore crossed the ocean as a four-year-old boy.

Under English Quaker influence a more evangelical movement began among the Dutch Mennonites in 1917. It is called the *Gemeentedag* Movement, a term which cannot well be translated into English. This movement has emphasized Bible study, a deeper personal experience of Christianity, and lay activity. On the whole it has promoted a reaction against the dominant liberalism of the Dutch Mennonites. The interest in nonresistance of those affiliated with the *Gemeentheday* Movement led to the organization of a new group, the "Mennonite Committee Against War Service," which had (1940) about three hundred adherents, including quite a number of conscientious objectors.

In general it must be said that the Dutch Mennonites of today are a powerful social group, making large contributions to Dutch culture, but they are liberal in theology and have much less activity than American Mennonites. They number about 70,000 adherents, including unbaptized children; perhaps their baptized members would total 45,000. Their large congregations are located in the cities such as Leiden, Haarlem, the Hague, Rotterdam, and Amsterdam which contains 7,781 Mennonites.

READINGS

Dosker, H. E.: *The Dutch Anabaptists,* The Jordan Press, Philadelphia, etc., [1921].

Gorter, S.H.N.: "Destruction and Reconstruction in Holland," *Mennonite Life,* North Newton, Kansas, I, 1 (January 1946).

Hege, Christian and Neff, Christian: *Mennonitisches Lexikon,* I. Band, 1913-24; II. Band, 1937, articles: *Aachen, Gillis von; Algemeene Doopsgezinde Societeit; Alkmaar; Almelo; Alte Flaminger; Ameland; Amsterdamer Taufgesinnten Gemeinde; Apeldoorn; Apostool, Samuel; Balk; Bolsward; Bouwens, Leonhard; Brabant; Breda; Deknatel, Johannes; Deventer; Dokkum; Dordrecht; Dordrechter Bekenntnis; Enschede; Flaminger; Franeker; Friesische Mennoniten; Friesland; Galenus Abrahamsz de Haan; Geldern; Groningen; Gravenhage; Haarlem; Haarlemsche Vereenigung; Hochdeutsche Mennoniten; Lamm-Gemeinde; Lammerenkrijgh; Lammisten; Leeuwarden; Leeuwardener Religionsgespräch; Leiden.*

Horsch, John: *Mennonites in Europe,* Scottdale, Pennsylvania, 1942, 233-258.

Horsch, John: "The Mennonites of Holland," *Christian Monitor,* Scottdale, Pennsylvania, I. Dec. 1935, 356f.; Jan. 1936, 5ff; Feb. 1936, 38f; March 1936, 69f; April 1936, 101f.

Horsch, John: "Prominent Co-Workers of Menno Simons," *Christian Monitor,* March 1940, 69.

Ijntema, J.: "The Mennonites of the Netherlands," *The Mennonite Quarterly Review, Goshen, Indiana,* XI, 1 (January 1937), 24-33.

Krahn, C.: "The Historiography of the Mennonites of the Netherlands," *The Mennonite Quarterly Review,* XVIII, 4 (Oct. 1944), 195-224.

Kühler, W. J.: *Geschiedenis der Nederlandsche Doopsgezinden in de Zestiende Eeuw,* H. D. Tjeenk Willink & Zoon N. V., Haarlem, 1932.

Kühler, W. J.: *Geschiedenis Van de Doopsgezinden in Nederland, Tweede Deel, 1600-1735,* Willink & Zoon N. V., Haarlem, 1940.

Kühler, W. J.: "Dutch Mennonite Relief Work in the Seventeenth and Eighteenth Centuries," *The Mennonite Quarterly Review,* XVII, 2 (April 1943), 87-94.

Leendertz, J. M.: "Old Mennonite Churches in Holland," *Mennonite Year Book and Almanac, 1922,* Berne, Indiana, 39f

Miller, O. O.: "Holland Mennonites on Peace," *Gospel Herald,* Scottdale, Pennsylvania, March 7, 1935, 1030.

Newman, A. H.: *A History of Anti-Pedobaptism from the Rise of Pedobaptism to A.D. 1609,* American Baptist Publication Society, Philadelphia, 1897, 314-322.

Rues, Simeon Friederich: *Aufrichtige Nachrichten von dem Gegerwärtigen Zustande der Mennoniten oder Taufgesinnten . . . in den vereinigten Niderlanden,* Jena, 1743.

[Schurmans, N. D.]: "History of the Mennonite Mission Work in Sumatra and Java," *Mennonite Year Book and Almanac, 1895,* Berne, Indiana, 29f.

Smith, C. H.: *Menno Simons, Apostle of the Nonresistant Life,* Mennonite Book Concern, Berne, Indiana, [1936], 39-42.

Smith, C. H.: *The Story of the Mennonites,* Mennonite Book Concern, Berne, Indiana, (1941), 169-244.

Smithson, R. J.: *The Anabaptists: Their Contribution to Our Protestant Heritage,* James Clarke, London, [1935], 80-93.

Van der Zijpp: "Experiences of the Dutch Mennonites During the Last World War," *Mennonite Life,* North Newton, Kansas, I, 2 (July 1946).

Whitley, W. T.: "John Smyth and the Dutch Mennonites," *The Mennonite Quarterly Review,* Goshen, Indiana, IV, 4 (October 1930), 306f.

Menno Simons, 1496-1561; a Portrait Made in 1683

The Menno Simons Memorial Shaft, Witmarsum

Interior of a Dutch Mennonite Church, 452 Singel Street, Amsterdam

A German Mennonite Family about 1865

CHAPTER VIII

Dutch Mennonites from the Rhine to the Vistula

1. *The Lower Rhine* (*Germany*)

Anabaptists were found in various parts of what is now the Rhine province of Germany in the sixteenth century. Among the places along the Lower Rhine which contained Brethren were the duchies of Jülich and Cleve (which were united into one province in 1511) and Berg, and such cities as Aachen, Imgenbroich, Goch, Kempen, Cleve, Kreuznach, Crefeld, Eifel, Aldekerk, Gladbach and Cologne—all situated near the Rhine between the Palatinate and the Netherlands.

As early as 1533 there was a congregation of the Brethren in Aachen, the coronation city of German kings during the Middle Ages. In four edicts issued during the year 1534, the city council made Anabaptists subject to capital punishment. While this was not always strictly enforced, it was no idle threat. In 1558 six women were whipped with rods and banished from the city; at the same time a number of men were imprisoned and later executed. It is known that in 1558 John Raiffer, Henry Adams, and John Beck were burned to death as Anabaptists. The same end came to Matthew Smith and Dillman Snyder in 1559. The well-known Mennonite leader, Hans (John de Ries, spent some time in Aachen and participated in a disputation on original sin. About 1580 the Mennonite congregation in Aachen began to thrive. It had its own ministers and its own school, through the comparatively tolerant attitude of the city at that time. But in 1798 the Lutherans succeeded in having the city suppress the services of the Mennonites and banish their preachers. In 1614 six hundred Mennonites were banished from Aachen. In a town called Burtscheid, near Aachen, a small Mennonite congregation held out for another two centuries. John Hilgers served as minister in Burtscheid, 1710-46. The last resident minister was his successor Peter Stahl who served 1746-76. In 1800 but two families remained.

The city of Cologne, capital of the Rhine Province and seat of a Catholic archbishop, contained Anabaptists in the first half of the sixteenth century. Menno Simons himself lived in the archbishopric of Cologne, 1544-46; he again visited the city in 1558. Three years later the city council served notice that "the unchristian *verdampte* sect of the Anabaptists and other rebellious and seductive teaching would not be tolerated." But even before this time a Mennonite leader, Thomas of Imbroich, had been executed (March 5, 1558) at the age of twenty-five. Imbroich's Confession of Faith is printed in the *Martyrs' Mirror* (1938 edition), 367-371, and the account of his martyrdom on pages 578-582. To his wife, Imbroich had written: "Greet all the saints with the kiss of love, and all who love the Lord Jesus, and tell them to be kind; for God is the Hero and Captain who so faithfully succors in time of need. He is like a shower upon the parched earth in a dry summer. Thus He refreshes the afflicted souls that thirst for Him; He is a shadow from the heat of the sun. . . .

"Tell the brethren to take care of the novices, and to pray earnestly for me. I will also pray for them, as much as is in my power. Remember my bonds. The Lord be with your spirit. Amen."

In 1562 another Anabaptist was executed in Cologne. Two Brethren, George Friesen and William von Keppel were to be drowned for their faith. Friesen was executed according to plan, but for some unknown reason the other, a former priest, was released. Before Friesen and von Keppel were parted by death "They kissed each other with a holy kiss of love." In a farewell admonition Friesen had written: "May the King of kings to whom all things are known uphold us with His mighty hand that we may on account of no adversity depart from Him, but may faithfully adhere to His Word even unto death. Hereby I will gladly resign my life at this time, and enter this narrow way through Christ. . . . O God, that I might be so fortunate as to see the work begun in me brought to such a happy end, to the salvation of my soul and to Thy glory, and this solely through Thy power—richer or more highly exalted as a mortal I could not become! I should praise and magnify Thee for it through Christ Thy Son. Dear brethren and sisters, I have written this in my severe imprisonment, and give it to you for an admonition. I, George Friesen, have composed this in the night, while others slept; I hope that daylight will soon shine brightly. . . ."

In 1591 a large gathering of Mennonites was held in Cologne to produce unity in church practice on the part of the "High German" and Dutch congregations. The outcome was the production of a statement called the "Concept of Cologne." Congregational representatives were present from Holland, the Lower Rhine, Alsace, the Palatinate, and Breisgau in South Germany.

Undoubtedly the most significant Mennonite congregation of the Lower Rhine was Crefeld. About the year 1600 Mennonites began to settle in the city, coming from Kempen and Aldekerk. In the course of time, in spite of some adverse circumstances, the Crefeld Mennonite Church thrived. One of its leaders was Herman op den Graeff, a signer of the Dordrecht Confession of Faith in 1632. The Mennonites have played a significant role in the industrial life of Crefeld for several centuries. In the sixteenth century the von der Leyen family (Mennonites) founded the silk and textile industry which has made the city prosperous and famous. Today the Crefeld Mennonite Church has about six hundred baptized members.

It was in 1683 that the first German settlers left Crefeld and established a village, Germantown, not far from the young Quaker city of Philadelphia in Pennsylvania. Crefeld is therefore of special interest to American Mennonites, even though many of the thirteen Crefeld families of 1683 had left the Mennonite Church and united with the Friends (Quakers). Three of the family heads of the 1683 party, Abraham, Dirk, and Herman op den Graeff, were grandsons of Herman op den Graeff, 1585-1642, the first minister of the Crefeld Mennonites and the signer of the Dordrecht Confession of Faith. In 1688 Dirk and Abraham op den Graeff signed the Germantown Anti-Slavery Protest.

2. *East Friesland*

The city of Emden in East Friesland, just across the German frontier from the Dutch (West) Friesland and connected with the Ems river by a canal, was early an Obbenite and Mennonite center. It is believed that Menno's colleague, Dirck Philips, worked in Emden for a time. Menno himself was in the city briefly and seems to have spent some time in that vicinity, perhaps in the village of Oldersum. The reformer of Emden, John a'Lasco, invited Menno to a disputation which was held January 28-31, 1544 in the church of the Franciscan Monastery in Emden. They discussed the incarnation, infant baptism, original sin, sanctification; and the calling of ministers.

In 1547 Menno Simons, Dirck Philips, Francis Kuiper, Adam Pastor, Hendrik van Breden, Anthony of Cologne, and Gillis of Aachen, seven leaders of the Brethren in the North, held a conference in Emden. Kuiper and Pastor proved to be unsound in doctrine and were excommunicated soon thereafter. Pastor held an unscriptural view of the deity of Christ, while Kuiper did not hold to a Biblical doctrine of justification as well as being unsound on other points.

One of the most interesting events in East Friesland was the Emden Disputation, 1578. One hundred twenty-four sessions were held from February 25 to May 17, with the Reformed and the Mennonites setting forth their respective points of view in a rather mild manner considering the spirit of those days.

C. Henry Smith writes in *The Story of the Mennonites,* 249, 250:

> Small as the Emden group has been, however, it has given both the church and the state a long list of prominent men. In addition to the many above-mentioned church leaders who served the congregation in the sixteenth century there should be added in more recent times men and women who were prominent in affairs of both church and state—the Brons family—Anna, author of the first comprehensive history of the Mennonites in the German language, now passed through its third edition; Isaac Brons, her husband, deputy to the Frankfort Parliament in 1848, president of the East Friesland Navy League in 1861, and member of the Reichstag of the North German Confederation in 1867; and their son Bernard, leading citizen of Emden, chief magistrate for fourteen years, Swedish consul at one time for that seaport, and last but by no means least, for thirty years deacon in his home church. From the same congregation, too, there came during the late war a major general of the army, and an admiral of the navy; ample evidence that the Emden Mennonites have wandered far from the teachings of their founder on the subject of peace.

Today East Friesland contains three hundred baptized Mennonites: the Emden Mennonite Church has two hundred baptized members and one hundred unbaptized children; the Leer congregation has twenty baptized members, while Norden has eighty-one.

3. *The Hamburg Area*

Menno Simons spent the last years of his life at Wuestenfelde in Holstein, between Lübeck and Hamburg. In the latter half of the sixteenth century and the following years a number of Mennonite settlements were made in Schleswig-Holstein: Oldesloe, Steckelsdorf, Fresenburg, Glückstadt, Pinneberg, Handsbeck, Altona, Hamburg. In some places congregations developed, the most famous of these being Hamburg-Altona. The Dutch Mennonites soon changed the swampy lands of the Lower Elbe into productive farms. Some of the settlers also excelled in industry, especially as weavers. Others were fishermen. In the course of time some became well-to-do men of commerce.

Friedrichstadt, a small city on the Eider river, has had a Mennonite congregation since 1633. By the year 1703 the congregation had grown considerably, there being in that year 178 members who participated in the communion service. But as usual the other churches of the community did all they could to weaken the Mennonite congregation. In Friedrichstadt it was the Lutherans. For example, no Mennonite could marry a Lutheran without a special dispensation, and then only on condition that the children be baptized as Lutherans. Another cause of decline was the continued use of the Dutch language in church services—long after it had outlived its usefulness. By 1919 the congregation had dwindled to forty-five baptized members. In 1938 there were but seventeen.

One of the best-known and most influential Mennonite congregations of Europe has been Hamburg-Altona which, although located in both cities, constitutes but one congregation with its church building in the smaller town of Altona. The Hamburg-Altona church claims the year 1601 as its date of origin. In common with the other Mennonite settlements of Prussia, the Dutch language was used in the Altona church services for a long time—only in 1805 was German introduced at all, and the Dutch was not discontinued entirely until 1839.

Between 1640 and 1648 the congregation experienced the tribulations of a division. The issue was the proper mode of baptism. As the name indicates, the *Dompelaars* contended for immersion. Against them stood Gerhard (or Gerrit) Roosen, 1612-1711, who brought the struggling members to a final division. The *Dompelaars* died out during the following century, one of their last ministers being the gifted teacher, Jacob Denner, 1659-1746.

The pastors of the Hamburg-Altona Mennonite church during the last century have been Berend Carl Roosen (died 1904), from 1845 to 1885; Hinrich van der Smissen, from 1885 to 1928; and Otto Schowalter, 1928- .

During the first century the Hamburg-Altona congregation had *liefdepredikanten,* untrained and unsalaried ministers. But in the eighteenth century the congregation began to call trained ministers from Holland and pay them a salary. In 1764 the introduction of an organ into the church building was a further evidence of change from the old order.

Gerhard Roosen had stood for the simple Mennonite life as he knew it. He served as an unpaid minister for sixty-two years, dying an accidental death at the age of ninety-nine. He was highly regarded by all European Mennonites. He gave counsel to the brethren in the South at the time of the Amish division. Gerrit Roosen and his fellow-ministers wrote to the Mennonites of Germantown, Pennsylvania, in 1702, encouraging them to have one of their ministers proceed with the administration of baptism and communion services even though no bishop had as yet been installed in the tiny American congregation. Roosen was also the author of a much-used book among Mennonites, *Conversation on Saving Faith,* which contains the Longer Catechism of 148 questions and answers, the Shorter Catechism of 35 questions and answers, and the Eighteen Articles of Dordrecht.

4. *Danzig and Vicinity*

The strongest Mennonite congregations of Germany are those in the former free city of Danzig and in the surrounding territory of East and West Prussia. The Danzig congregation itself had in 1938 over a thousand baptized members, and seven other congregations within the territory of the free city had an additional four thousand.

According to tradition the first bishop of the Danzig congregation was Dirck Philips who lived in the nearby *Schottland* ("Scotland"). The Danzig Mennonites were from the Netherlands and had a parallel development with the Dutch congregations. The Mennonites in Danzig were divided into Friesians, somewhat mild in discipline, and the stricter Flemish, called the "Fine" or the *Klaren* (*Klarken* or *Klerken* in Plattdeutsch)—the Dutch term *Klaar* signifying *unambiguous.*

The Lutherans had tried in vain to prevent the Dutch Mennonites from settling in Danzig in the sixteenth century. A century later the Danzig Mennonites were still being fined on one charge or another. One of the most interesting events of the seventeenth century involved the Flemish minister, George Hansen. King John III of Poland directed the Catholic Bishop Stanislaus Sarnowsky to investigate the charges of doctrinal unsoundness which had been preferred against the Mennonites. On January 20, 1678, Hansen was examined for three hours in the bishop's residence and in his presence by Joachim von Hirtenberg, assisted by two Dominicans, two Franciscans, two Jesuits, and two Carmelites. Hansen was asked doctrinal questions about the Trinity, the Person of Christ, the salvation of unbaptized infants, original sin, baptism, communion, feetwashing, justification, the possibility of keeping God's law, the "intermediate state," etc. Hansen subsequently wrote a commentary on his replies which was published in the Dutch language at Amsterdam, 1696, and in German by the Mennonite Publishing Company, Elkhart, Indiana, 1893, *A Foundation-Book of the Christian Doctrine.* The outcome of the examination was that the Mennonite congregation was pronounced free of Arian and Socinian doctrines. Hansen was subsequently ordained as an elder, 1690, and died in 1703.

The Dutch language was retained in the services of the Danzig Mennonites until late in the eighteenth century.

The Danzig congregations, Flemish and Friesian, worshiped in private homes for a long time. In 1638 the Friesians built their first church building which was destroyed by the French in 1806. The Flemish erected their first meetinghouse in 1648, and according to custom built a home for the aged near by. These buildings were destroyed by the Russians in 1813. In spite of a vigorous protest by a minority, an organ had been installed in the Flemish meetinghouse in 1805. After more than two centuries of separate church life the Danzig Flemish and Friesians finally united in 1808. They worshiped in the Flemish meetinghouse until it was burned in 1813. In 1818 the Danzig congregation began to build a new church building which was dedicated September 12, 1819. A salaried ministry was introduced at Danzig in 1826. The church built a parsonage in 1884. The Danzig Mennonite church building was badly damaged during the second World War.

As early as 1608 the Bishop of Culm had complained that the whole Vistula Delta was overrun by Mennonites. But the "nest of the Mennonites," as one ruler called them, never became a major part of the population. In 1920 the population of Danzig was divided as follows: Protestants, 220,000; Catholics, 120,000; Mennonites, 6,000; and Jews, 4,000.

The chief Prussian congregations are (1939) Elbing-Ellerwald, Elbing, Königsberg, Thiensdorf-Rosengart, and Tragheimerweide.

In the territory of the former free city of Danzig are Danzig, Fürstenwerder, Neunhuben, Heubuden-Marienburg, Ladekopp, Orlofferfelde, Rosenort and Tiegenhagen. The total population of the congregations of the Danzig area is fifteen thousand souls (including children).

The country congregations of Prussia generally have an untrained and unsalaried ministry, and are more conservative than the city churches. (Sometimes the elder is educated and salaried, however.) They have held to believers' baptism, the non-swearing of oaths, the simple life, and an evangelical theology, resembling in these respects the Swiss Mennonites of South Germany. Yet it was in East Prussia that the German Mennonites manifested the greatest weakness in succumbing to the unchristian doctrines of National Socialism.

It should also be reported that a Mennonite congregation was established in Berlin in 1887. It has a baptized membership of three hundred.

5. *Poland*

In addition to the Palatine (Swiss) Mennonite settlement at Lemberg (Polish Llow) in southern Poland, two groups of Dutch Mennonite settlements are found in Poland: (1) Three former Prussian congregations are called: *Montau-Gruppe* (Polish Matawy and Grupa), established in 1568; *Schönsee* (Sosnowka), established about 1600 and now (1939) having one hundred ninety members; and *Obernessau,* established about 1530 and now a pitiful remnant of twelve souls, of which only four are voting members. (2) Three congregations in what was formerly Russian Poland are called *Deutsch-Kazun,* "below Warsaw on the left bank of the Weichsel" river, established about 1750 and now having some two hundred sixty baptized members; this congregation has suffered numerically from emigration to Russia, to America, and more recently to Paraguay; *Deutsch-Wymysle,* established since 1800 and now having two hundred forty members; and *Wola Wydezynska.*

In 1939 Germany incorporated Danzig into the Third German Reich; Montau also became German territory. But what will happen at the final peace treaty following World War II remains to be seen. In any event the Mennonites will probably have to struggle to retain anything like the main features of Menno Simons' vision.

READINGS

Bender, H. S.: *Mennonite Origins in Europe,* M.C.C., Akron, Pennsylvania, 1942, 58-61, 68-71.

A. Braun: *Christlicher Gemeinde-Kalender für das Jahr 1939; 48. Jahrgang,* Karlsruhe, 1938, 142-157.

Dollinger, R.: *Geschichte der Mennoniten in Schleswig-Holstein, Hamburg und Lübeck,* Neumünster i. H., 1930.

Ewert, Bruno: "From Danzig to Denmark," *Mennonite Life,* North Newton, Kansas, 1, 1 (January 1946).

Hege, Christian and Neff, Christian, *Mennonitisches Lexikon,* articles: *Aachen; Altona; Cleve; Danziger Mennoniten-Gemeinde; Denner, Jacob; Deutsch-Kazun; Deutsch-Michalin; Deutsch-Wymysle; Dompelaars; Elbing; Emden; Emmerich; Friedrichstadt a.d. Eider; Glückstadt; Goch; Hamburg a.d. Elbe; Hansen, Georg; Heubuden; Holstein; Imbroich, Thomas; Jülich; Leer; Montau;* and the literature cited at the close of the articles.

Horsch, John: *Mennonites in Europe,* Scottdale, Pennsylvania, 1942, 227-232.

Hunsberger, Wilson: "The Danzig Mennonite Church Buildings Today," *Mennonite Life,* IV, 3 (July, 1949), 10-12.

Mannhardt, H. G.: *Die Danziger Mennonitengemeinde, Ihre Entstehung und ihre Geschichte von 1569-1919.* Danzig, 1919.

Müller, J. P.: *Die Mennoniten in Ostfriesland vom 16. bis zum 18. Jahrhundert,* Emden und Borkum, 1887.

Neff, Christian: "The Mennonites of Germany, Including Danzig and Poland," *The Mennonite Quarterly Review,* XI, 1 (January 1937), 34-43.

Newman, A. H.: *A History of Anti-Pedobaptism from the Rise of Pedobaptism to A.D. 1609,* American Baptist Publication Society, Philadelphia, 1897, 273-276.

Rembert, Karl: *Die "Wiedertäufer" im Herzogtum Jülich,* Berlin, 1899.

Roosen, B. C.: *Geschichte der Mennoniten Gemeinde Zu Hamburg-Altona,* 1886/87.

Smith, C. H.: *The Story of the Mennonites,* Mennonite Book Concern, Berne, Indiana, [1941], 245-296.

CHAPTER IX

The Mennonites in Russia

The bulk of the Mennonites of Prussia originally came from the Netherlands, although there were also some settlements of Swiss Mennonites among them. It was the Prussian Mennoites, in turn, who colonized South Russia. The story of this colonization and of subsequent developments is a very interesting one, though it can here be told only in brief. In the late eighteenth century the ruler of Russia, Catherine II, found herself in need of settlers for sparsely settled South Russia. A Russian count had seen the Mennonites of Danzig and was favorably impressed with them. And a Russian agent who was seeking colonists, a man named George von Trappe, knew of the unfavorable conditions which the Mennonites of Danzig and Prussia had to endure. They suffered under heavy taxes, a shortage of land and other unpleasant conditions. The count and von Trappe got the Russian government to offer the Prussian Mennonites a special invitation to settle in Russia. This invitation was extended in August 1786.

Prussia was of course not at all pleased with the prospect of losing some of her best farmers, so she refused to grant the Mennonites the necessary permission to emigrate. And so the situation was solved as follows: Poland and Russia put pressure on Prussia to allow the Prussian Mennonites to emigrate to Russia!

The first Prussian Mennonite settlers, in number about nine hundred souls, reached their destination in July 1789. This settlement, the first or "Old" Colony, was located along the Dnieper River in the Ukraine, South Russia, and was called the "Chortitza" settlement. More settlers came in a few years.

The second great colony was the "Molotschna," founded in 1803, and also located in South Russia, north of the Sea of Azov, an arm of the Black Sea. More settlers arrived during the next fifteen years, and again from 1819 to 1840. In fact the trek from Prussia to Russia kept up until 1870. It has been estimated that a total of 8,000 souls made the journey.

The first decades in Russia were hard ones for these German-speaking immigrants of Dutch extraction. For one thing, the colonists were widely scattered, each colony consisting of from ten to fifty villages, stretching out over hundreds of miles. But the colonies grew rapidly. Within twenty-five years the original population had doubled; the rate of increase, it has been claimed, was second only to the Boers of South Africa. And these Prussian farmers were a thrifty and progressive people. They developed silk-growing and sheep-breeding, wheat-growing and manufacturing. Although there was increasing prosperity and wealth, there was also a certain amount of poverty. By the year 1850 one third of the Russian Mennonites had become wealthy and the remaining two thirds were landless tenants. By the time of the first World War three per cent of the population owned thirty per cent of the land.

One of the most outstanding men among the Russian Mennonites was Johann Cornies, 1789-1848. Cornies was a great farmer, breeding cattle, sheep, and horses; and promoting industry. He was also a strong force in furthering the education of youth. So prominent did he become that in 1825 he was visited by Czar Alexander I. Cornies could have been the recipient of many honors but, good Mennonite that he was, he turned them down. Only one medal did he consent to accept—and that had to be a plain one. On the one side of it was simply his name, "Johann Cornies," and on the other, in German, "Fuer Tuechtigkeit" (For Ability).

By the year 1850 there were not only riches—and poverty—among the Russian Mennonites, there was also a certain amount of "coldness" in religion. Then, under the influence of the German Baptists and of Lutheran Pietism, a great revival swept through the Russian Mennonite colonies. The leaders of the new movement stressed baptism by immersion, emotional conversions, and personal testimonies. As a result of this awakening a new Mennonite branch was formed, the Mennonite "Brueder-Gemeinde" (Mennonite Brethren), 1860. About one-third of the Russian Mennonites eventually entered the new brotherhood. This new communion strongly supported mission work.

About the year 1870 a new cloud appeared in the sky: the Russian government threatened to withdraw military exemption from the Mennonites, although it had originally been promised "forever." In the end a form of alternative service, not under the military arm of the government, was worked out. But the confidence of many people had been shaken, and about 18,000 Russian Mennonites emigrated to the prairie states and Manitoba, Canada, 1873-80.

Another group of Mennonites, the schismatic followers of one Abraham Peters, migrated eastward in 1880 under the leadership of an unbalanced man named Claas Epp (d. 1913). Some of these folks believed that Christ would soon come and that the antichrist was about to appear in the West; so to escape the antichrist and look for redemption they turned eastward and settled in Turkestan, in Asia. Epp first designated himself as Elijah, later as Melchizedek, and finally as the fourth person of the Godhead. However, the great majority of the group rejected Epp's foolish presumptions. In 1930 the baptized membership of the Turkestan Mennonite colony was about seven or eight hundred.

About the turn of the century the Russian Mennonites began to settle in Siberia. By the year 1925 it was estimated that the Siberian Mennonites numbered 30,000 souls.

In 1905 the Russian Mennonite historian, Peter M. Friesen, founded a branch known as the Evangelical Mennonite Brethren. Friesen tried to bridge the gap between the Mennonite Brethren and the parent body by including in his "Alliance" communion the truly regenerated of both groups. He wished to make one group of two, but got three.

By the time of the first World War the Russian Mennonites numbered almost 100,000 souls, including unbaptized children. The colonies were well-organized, having their own German schools, hospitals, and charitable institutions. Then came the awful Bolshevik revolution with its terror and death. Fortunately, 18,877 Russian Mennonites were able to immigrate to Canada, 1923-28; and in 1930 another 3,000 reached South America, settling in Paraguay and Brazil, where they are now having a rather hard economic struggle. But what happened to those left in Russia? Some were shot; some were exiled; some no doubt gave up their faith. The last conference of the Mennonites in the Ukraine was held at Melitopol in 1926. At that time there were still about 46,000 Mennonites (counting children) in the Ukraine. The organized life of the Mennonite Church in Russia has been broken.

The Russian Mennonites of Canada were not all satisfied with the treatment which the government gave them during the first World War. Consequently nearly 10,000 of them emigrated from Manitoba to Mexico in 1922, where they have since had some difficulties; and another group of about 1,800 migrated from Canada to

Paraguay in 1926, thus preceding by four years those who came directly from Russia.

The story of the Russian Mennonites is one of fleeing over the face of the earth for the sake of conscience, for loyalty to the Word of God as they understand it.

Before leaving Europe, mention should be made of the several district conference organizations of the Mennonites. Here are the chief ones historically: (1) Conference of the Old Evangelical *Taufgesinnten* [Baptism-Minded] Congregations (Mennonites) in Switzerland; (2) Conference of the Palatine-Hessian Mennonite Congregations; (3) Conference of South German Mennonites; (4) Conference of the Mennonites of Alsace-Lorraine; (5) Conference of the East and West Prussian Mennonite Congregations; (6) the General Mennonite Conference of Russia (last session, 1925); and (7) the (Dutch) General Mennonite Society. In recent years the Mennonites of Prussia and of South Germany have united to form (8) the Union of the German Mennonite Congregations.

READINGS

Bender, H. S.: *Mennonite Origins in Europe,* M.C.C., Akron, Pennsylvania, 1942, 62-67.

Bender, H. S.: "With the Mennonite Refugee Colonies in Brazil and Paraguay," *The Mennonite Quarterly Review,* Goshen, Indiana, XIII, 1 (Jan. 1939), 59-70.

Braun, Peter: "The Educational System of the Mennonite Colonies in South Russia," *The Mennonite Quarterly Review,* III, 3 (July 1929), 169-182.

"Document on the Mennonite Colony in Turkestan, A." *The Mennonite Quarterly Review,* IV, 4 (Oct. 1930), 302-305.

Ehrt, Adolf: *Die Mennoniten in Russland,* Langensalza, 1931.

Epp, D. H.: *Die Chortitzer Mennoniten,* Odessa, 1889.

Epp, D. H.: *Johann Cornies,* Berdjansk, 1909.

Fast, Gerhard: "Mennonites of the Ukraine Under Stalin and Hitler," *Mennonite Life,* North Newton, Kansas, II, 2 (April 1947).

Faust, J. B.: "The Mennonite Colony in Paraguay," *The Mennonite Quarterly Review,* III, 3 (July 1929), 183-189.

Friesen, P. M.: *Die Altevangelische Mennonitische Bruderschaft in Russland,* Halbstadt, 1911.

Hege, Christian and Neff, Christian: *Mennonitisches Lexikon,* I. Band, 1913-24; II. Band, 1937; articles: *Alexandertal, Allgemeine Mennonitische Bundeskonferenz in Russland, Altkirche Mennoniten, Chortitza, Malyschner Bezirk, Molotschna,* etc.

Hiebert, Waldo: "Mennonite Education in the Gran Chaco," *Mennonite Life,* II, 4 (October, 1947), 29ff.

Hildebrandt, P.: *Erste Auswanderung der Mennoniten aus dem Danziger Gebiet Nach Südrussland, Halbstadt,* 1888.

Horsch, John: *Mennonites in Europe,* Scottdale, Pennsylvania, 1942, 271-289.

Isaac, Franz: *Die Molotschnaer Mennoniten,* Halbstadt, 1908.

Janzen, Johannes: "The Mennonite Colony in Turkestan," *The Mennonite Quarterly Review,* IV, 4 (Oct. 1930), 282-289.

Klassen, C. F.: "The Mennonites of Russia, 1917-1928," *The Mennonite Quarterly Review,* VI, 2 (April 1932), 69-80.

Klassen, Peter: "The Mennonites of Brazil," *The Mennonite Quarterly Review,* XI, 2 (April 1937), 107-118.

Klaus, A.: *Unsere Kolonien,* Odessa, 1887.

Kliewer, Fritz: "The Mennonites of Paraguay," *The Mennonite Quarterly Review,* XI, 1 (Jan. 1937), 92-97.

Krahn, Cornelius: "Some Social Attitudes of the Mennonites of Russia," *The Mennonite Quarterly Review,* IX, 4 (Oct. 1935), 164-177.

Leibbrandt, Georg: "Emigration of the German Mennonites from Russia to the United States and Canada in 1873-1880," *The Mennonite Quarterly Review,* VI, 4 (October 1932), 205-226; VII, 1 (Jan. 1933), 5-41.

Rempel, D. G.: "The Mennonite Migration to New Russia (1787-1870)," *The Mennonite Quarterly Review,* IX, 2 (April 1935), 71-91; IX, 3 (July 1935), 109-128.

Smith, C. H.: *The Story of the Mennonites,* Berne, Indiana, [1941], 383-531.

Sudermann, Jacob: "The Origin of Mennonite State Service in Russia, 1870-1880," *The Mennonite Quarterly Review,* XVII, 1 (Jan. 1943), 23-46.

Unruh, B. H.: "The Mennonites of Russia," *The Mennonite Quarterly Review,* XI, 1 (Jan. 1937), 61-67.

CHAPTER X

The Mennonites in North America

1. *Immigration*

As early as the year 1644 Dutch Mennonite traders had found their way to New Amsterdam, now New York. And in 1663 a Dutchman named Cornelius Plockhoy established a colony on a small stream, the Horekill, which empties into Delaware Bay. Included in the colony were a number of Mennonites. Plockhoy was trying to create a Utopia, but he himself did not believe in full religious toleration; he excluded from his colony Catholics, Jews, "stiff-necked Quakers," and others. The English were then at war with the Dutch, and within a year or two they completely destroyed Plockhoy's "Utopia."

The first significant Mennonite settlement in North America was made at Germantown, Pennsylvania, in 1683. The Germantown settlers came from Crefeld, Germany, and arrived at Philadelphia October 6, 1683, thirty-five souls in number. These thirteen Crefeld families were in 1683 mostly members of the Quaker communion, but were all of Mennonite background and descent; some members of the group were still Mennonites. The first Mennonite minister in America, William Rittenhouse (1644-1708), served at Germantown and was probably chosen for the ministry in the year 1690. From these Mennonite and Quaker settlers of Germantown came, in 1688, the first American protest against slavery. Some of the Mennonites of Germantown were Dutch, but the Dutch element in the main branch of the American Mennonite Church today is extremely small. Throughout its history the Germantown Mennonite congregation has been numerically weak. It is now affiliated with the General Conference of the Mennonite Church of North America.

There have been four great waves of Mennonite immigration to America. The Palatine and Swiss Mennonite immigration to eastern Pennsylvania began in 1709 and continued steadily until the outbreak of the French and Indian War in 1754. It has been estimated that from three to five thousand Mennonite souls reached America by the time of the Revolutionary War (1775). Included in this first wave of immigration were several hundred Amish who settled chiefly in Berks County, Pennsylvania. Both the Mennonites and the Amish came to America to realize religious freedom and to improve their economic opportunities.

The second wave of immigration, 1815-61, began after the time of Napoleon and continued until the outbreak of the United States Civil War. In these years about three thousand souls, chiefly Alsatian Amish, but including some Swiss and South German Mennonites, came to America. These immigrants settled in western Pennsylvania, Ohio, Indiana, Illinois, and Iowa. They made the voyage to America to escape both the militarism of Europe and the difficult economic situation which followed the Napoleonic Wars.

A sample of what it meant to be an immigrant and pioneer is the case of Christian Ropp, a boy of about fourteen who emigrated with his Amish Mennonite parents from Alsace to America in 1826 and settled eventually in Illinois. (He was born in 1812, served as a bishop in the Roanoke Congregation, and died, 1896.) The story is taken from Harry F. Weber: *Centennial History of the Mennonites of Illinois,* Goshen, Indiana, 1931, pp. 83-87. Following is Ropp's account, written in 1892:

I, Christian Ropp, now an old man of nearly eighty years, at the request of my children, will attempt to write a brief account of my life. I will begin with my father. He was one of three orphan children. They had inherited a flour mill and a hemp mill, but this they lost before they grew up. Then my dear father was compelled to hire himself to strangers until he was twenty-eight years of age, when he was married to Elizabeth Eiman. His brother died, and his sister married one Zimmerman, whose Christian name I have forgotten.

My father lived in upper Alsace about six miles from Basel, and two miles from Altkirch, and five miles from Befford. And since he had heard many favorable reports of America, he thought it might be better for himself and children to emigrate to America, than to see his sons drafted into the army, for he had at that time six sons. [It is uncertain whether Befford should be Belfort.]

He lived at this time upon a small farm in upper Alsace, called "Barthel Hutte," two miles from Altkirch, two miles from Damerkirch, and five from Befford. It was in the year 1826, at a time when many people were leaving for America, that my parents decided to go also. In May, 1826, the long voyage to America began. We journeyed from Befford to Paris and Havre, where we had to wait for a number of days. We had our own horse and wagon, but here had to sell the horse.

We entered the ship, but soon most of us were seasick. My mother was seasick most of the time. We met with some stormy weather. We also caught a large fish with a hook, which pleased me very much. We were on ship forty days.

Germantown Mennonite Meetinghouse Built in 1770 and Still in Use

Reproduced from "Mennonitisches Lexikon," III, 71

Melitopol Mennonite Church, South Russia. In this building the last Russian Mennonite Conference was held in 1926

Kehr Mennonite Meetinghouse, Where the Langnau Mennonites of the Emme Valley, Switzerland, Worship

John H. Oberholtzer, 1809-95; Prominent Leader of the General Conference Mennonite Church

After we reached Philadelphia, my father hired a team to take us to Lancaster County. After we had gone thirty or thirty-five miles, we stopped over with an old Amishman by the name of Zuck [Zook]. Here we remained a number of days to arrange our affairs. Then my father bought a horse, and after setting up the wagon which we had brought with us, we started out again, for my father wished to go to Butler County, Ohio.

When we came within six miles of Lancaster, we met a Mennonite by the name of John Koenig who was plowing along the roadside. When he saw my father, he knew him by his clothing as well as his beard, for at that time no one except our people wore beards. After speaking with him, he invited him to remain over night, but my father hesitated, since there were others also with us who were on their way to Ohio. But finally my father was persuaded to remain all night, and as they were talking together during the evening, Koenig told him of Canada, and that many were now going to that place, and that each family was offered fifty acres free.

As three families were about to leave for Canada, my father decided to go with them. The names of our fellow travelers were Christian Farni, John Erb, Michael Swartz, and Zehr. After a six weeks' stay in Pennsylvania, we left with the above-mentioned for Canada.

My father bought his second horse, but after making about half of the journey, the horse became sick and had to be left behind. Then we had to do some walking. It was a long and tedious journey. The road at that time was bad. We were on the way more than three weeks, but finally in the fall we reached Waterloo Township.

We remained all night in a little village called Rumbletown, now Berlin [Kitchener]. Then my father went to Wilmot Township, where the free land was to he had, and selected a lot along the middle street. The conditions were to pay nine dollars for surveying, and to clear two rods along the street; and then the fifty acres were free. There were two hundred acres in a lot; the other hundred and fifty could be bought later for $2.50 per acre.

Then we built a little log cabin and moved into it the same fall. But now our money was all gone. We had to hire out as laborers in order to make a living, Andrew and I; but wages were very low. I received only $2.50 per month and wore out more boots and clothes than I earned.

In the spring we cleared some land and planted potatoes and garden vegetables. Then things went somewhat better, for we were supplied with food. And then each year we fared a little better. We finally cleared forty acres.

But now several of our number decided to move to Ohio, for it was too cold in Canada. These were the following: Joseph Goldschmidt, Peter Danner, Daniel Unzicker, Peter Nafziger, and several others. And since my brother Andrew had cut his foot so that he had been disabled for six months, he decided to accompany this group; so in 1831 he left for Ohio.

In 1832 we held a sale, and moved to Ohio, but I and my brother Jacob remained to collect our sale money. In 1833 my brother Andrew returned to help collect the money, for in Canada money was very scarce at that time. We then sold our property and collected about $1100.

In 1833 we left for Ohio. There were four of us, I and Andrew and Jacob, and Christian Lehman. We had a horse and covered wagon. The journey was tedious. We were on our way seventeen days, and at one time came near being robbed, but by the help of Divine Providence we escaped. We finally reached Ohio, where we found all well; and we rejoiced greatly.

But since land was high here, and hearing that land was still cheap in Illinois and that eight families from Germany had already settled there, we decided to move to Illinois. The names of those settlers were Peter Engel, David Schertz, John Schweitzer, Peter Roggy, John Auer, —— Gingerich, and Peter Beck.

In the fall of 1833 my brother Andrew journeyed to Illinois to see the land. He was well pleased and returned immediately for the rest of us. Since it was late in the year, we decided that the family should remain in Ohio until the following spring, but I and Andrew started early in January, 1834, for Illinois. We went on horseback and were thirteen days on the way, since the roads were very poor. We had to ride around many swamps and were often at a loss to know how to cross streams, for at that time there were few bridges. We arrived in Woodford County at the home of Peter Engel. Here my brother Andrew married Jacobine Wirkler. [Andrew, 1807-90, was ordained later as minister and as bishop.]

In the spring we moved over to the Mackinaw, and took up a claim, for at that time the land had not yet been put on the market. We cleared about ten acres. During this time our dear mother died in 1834 of consumption and was buried in Butler County, Ohio. But my father and the rest of the family came to us in Illinois in the spring. Christian Farni from Canada also came to us. Then we lived together until after harvest, when we were all taken sick with the "Schüttel-fieber" [ague]. Then we sold our claim for $200 to Fritz Niergarth and moved back to Metamora, to Peter Engel's.

Soon after, my brother moved to Pleasant Grove, but we moved over in the timber between Washington, Illinois, and Peoria. Here my father lived for a number of years on a claim, but it was finally taken from him. But I lived with my brother Andrew and built a blacksmith shop and worked at the trade.

In 1836 I married Magdalene Schertz and moved to Mackinaw, and hired to Christian Farni for five months for $20 per month. Then I bought eighty acres of land, and built a log cabin on it. Now I had to see that I made a livelihood, for the times were hard and money scarce. I lived on the Mackinaw for twenty-two years and passed through many experiences. Since April, 1858, we have been living in McLean County, Illinois, some thirty years, and have seen much and passed through trying experiences.

The other two waves of Mennonite immigration to North America, both from Russia, have already been described. In the years 1873-80 about 10,000 Russian Mennonites settled in the Dakotas, in Minnesota, Nebraska, and Kansas; and about 8,000 located in Manitoba in western Canada. The American Mennonites helped these Russian emigrants generously. When the Russian Mennonites tried to find a home after the first World War, of the suitable countries for settlement, only three opened their doors. Canada allowed more than 18,000 to settle in its western sections; and Brazil and Paraguay in South America took in a total of about 6,000 Mennonites.

2. *Settlements*

In the early eighteenth century there were two strong Mennonite settlements in Pennsylvania. Skippack was founded in 1702, and Pequea was established in 1710. These two original settlements became the nuclei of the Franconia and Lancaster Conference districts respectively. Franconia grew steadily and spread out somewhat but not nearly to the extent which Lancaster expanded. Franconia now has a membership of 4,600. Today the Lancaster Conference is more than fifty per cent larger than any other Mennonite district conference anywhere, having 13,300 members. Mennonites from Lancaster settled in Virginia before 1750. Ontario was colonized by Lancaster and Franconia Mennonites, beginning in 1788. By 1799 Mennonites were located in Ohio; by 1833 they were in Illinois; they were in Iowa by 1839; and in Indiana by 1843. The Mennonite settlements in Nebraska and several other western states were established since 1850.

3. District Conferences of the Mennonite Church

Accurate data is not available on the organization of the early American Mennonite conferences. It is true that a special conference attended by both Lancaster and Franconia ministers adopted the Dordrecht Confession of Faith in 1725. But this was probably a special meeting and did not lead to the organization of regional conferences. Evidently, however, the ministry of both Franconia and Lancaster were organized into district conferences about 1750. These two conferences are not yet affiliated with Mennonite General Conference. The Ontario Conference was organized about 1820, and today has a membership of 3,200. The Virginia Mennonites organized a conference as early as 1835 and today have a membership of 3,100. The Ohio Mennonite Conference was already organized in 1837—how long before is not known. The Indiana-Michigan Mennonite Conference was already organized in 1857. The Mennonite Conference of Washington County, Maryland, and Franklin County, Pennsylvania, was organized sometime prior to 1844. This conference has a membership of 1,400 and, like Franconia and Lancaster, is not affiliated with the Mennonite General Conference. The Illinois Mennonite Conference was organized in 1872. The Missouri-Iowa Mennonite Conference was organized in 1873. The Southwestern Pennsylvania Conference, a daughter of the Lancaster Conference, was organized in 1876 and now has 2,000 members. The Kansas-Nebraska Mennonite Conference was organized in 1879. The (German) Nebraska-Minnesota Conference of Russian Mennonites was organized in 1889 and was often called the Isaac Peters Conference—

after a prominent leader from Henderson, Nebraska. Another leader in this conference was Aaron Wall of Mountain Lake, Minnesota. This conference is now known as the Evangelical Mennonite Brethren and has 2,000 members. It is not affiliated with Mennonite General Conference. The Alberta-Saskatchewan Mennonite Conference was organized in 1903 and now has a membership of 600. The Pacific Coast Mennonite Conference was organized in 1907, and numbers 1,700 at present. The India Mennonite Conference was organized in 1911, and has a membership in 1923 and today has a membership of 700.

4. *Amish Mennonite Conferences*

The first conference which the Amish Mennonites founded was a general conference, organized in 1862. This annual meeting was not very long-lived, for its last meeting was held in 1878. Of the three Amish Mennonite district conferences, the first, the Indiana-Michigan Amish Mennonite, was organized in 1888. The Western District A.M. was started in 1890, and the Ohio A.M. in 1893. To this last conference Eastern Pennsylvania was added in 1897, and in 1904 the name, Eastern A.M., was adopted. The Conservative A.M. Conference was organized in 1910, and today has a membership of 4,000. It is not affiliated with Mennonite General Conference. The Ontario A. M. Conference was organized in 1924, and now numbers 2,000. It is only loosely affiliated with Mennonite General Conference.

5. *Mergers*

After the Old Order Amish had separated from the more progressive Amish Mennonites soon after the middle of the nineteenth century, the progressive Amish Mennonites and the main body of Mennonites enjoyed a constantly growing fellowship. In both groups a number of leaders began to feel that regardless of past differences there was no good reason why the two bodies should any longer maintain a separate existence. The merger finally came, beginning in the Midwest. The Indiana-Michigan Mennonite and Indiana-Michigan A. M. Conferences united in 1916, and now have a membership of 6,000. The Western District A. M. Conference merged with the various western Mennonite conferences in 1920, producing the following new alignment: Illinois, having a present membership of 3,000; South Central, formerly Missouri-Kansas, with 3,000 members today; and Iowa-Nebraska, with a present membership of 3,900. In 1926 the Ohio Mennonite and Eastern A. M. conferences merged under the name, Ohio Mennonite and Eastern A. M. Joint Conference. The present membership of this conference is 8,600. At this writing the Ontario A. M. and the Conservative A. M. conferences have not yet merged with the Mennonite Church.

6. *Mennonite General Conference*

During the latter part of the nineteenth century various Mennonite leaders urged the formation of a general conference, a meeting where the ministry from all over the country might get together for fellowship and for the discussion of church problems. A prominent promoter was John F. Funk of Elkhart, Indiana, founder of Mennonite publication work and editor of the *Herald of Truth*. A preliminary meeting of the Mennonite General Conference was finally held at the Pike Meetinghouse, Elida, Ohio, in 1897. The first formal meeting of General Conference was held the next year with Daniel Kauffman, then but thirty-three years old, serving as moderator. Regular meetings have been held every two years since 1898, except for a three-year gap between the meetings of 1902 and 1905, which makes the meeting fall on the odd year ever since 1905. The Mennonite General Conference was organized to provide church-wide fellowship; to make possible the sharing of problems on a wider scale than has previously been possible; to provide inspiration for those who attend; and above all, to help unify the church.

7. *Mennonite Schisms, 1775-1875*

The American Mennonite Church suffered a number of schisms. We are not interested in describing in detail these unfortunate events, but will list for each schism the time of the separation, the chief leader of the schism, the scene of the division, the nature of the new movement or the cause of the schism, and the present membership of the new body. About 1775 Bishop Martin Boehm of Lancaster County, Pennsylvania, separated from the Mennonite Church, struck out on a progressive path, and finally helped to found the United Brethren Church about the year 1800. In the year 1778 Bishop Christian Funk of eastern Pennsylvania separated from the Franconia Conference on various issues revolving about the question of the relation of the church to the Colonial Government of the United States; his church died out about 1850. John Herr of Lancaster County led a group of conservative followers out of the Mennonite Church in 1812; his followers now number 1,200 and are known as Reformed Mennonites. In 1846 another conservative named Jacob Stauffer led a small schism in Lancaster Conference; his group now numbers but 175. The most significant division in America took place in the Franconia Conference in 1847 when a progressive minister named John H. Oberholtzer, founded what is now known as the Eastern District Conference of the General Conference of the Mennonite Church of North America; the present membership of the Eastern District is 3,700. The Mennonite Brethren in Christ Church, often written, M. B. C., was made up of a number of Mennonite groups, led by Gehman, Hoch, Eby, and Brenneman, and one Brethren in Christ body: William Gehman of Lehigh County, Pennsylvania, seceded from John H. Oberholtzer's conference in 1857; Daniel Hoch of Ontario was a progressive leader who had led a schism already in 1847; Solomon Eby of the same province led a similar division twenty-five years later; and Daniel Brenneman of Indiana of the same type as Hoch and Eby, led still another schism, 1873-74. The present M. B. C. Church has about 13,000 members and stresses emotional conversions, the so-called "second work of grace," personal testimonies, and other points receiving little or no emphasis by Mennonites historically.

The General Conference Mennonite Church of North America and the M. B. C. Church were formed because some leaders thought that the Mennonite Church was too conservative. But a number of divisions also occurred because other leaders (besides John Herr and Jacob Stauffer) thought that the church was not sufficiently conservative. John Holdeman of Ohio, whose schism took place 1857-59, was of this latter type. His followers, called the Church of God in Christ, Mennonite, now number 4,000 members. Many members of the Russian Mennonite group known as the Kleine Gemeinde (Little Church) have united with Holdeman's group. Three other conservatives, with the years of their schisms, were Jacob Wisler of Indiana, 1871-74; Abram Martin of Ontario, 1889; and Jonas Martin of Lancaster Conference, 1893. These three bodies are known today as Old Order Mennonites, and have a combined membership of 4,800

8. Amish Mennonite Schisms

The Amish of America have also suffered several schisms. As has already been mentioned, the more progressive Amish Mennonites (now merged with the Mennonites) separated from the stricter Old Order Amish about 1850. In the years 1864-66, a man who emphasized strict discipline and progressive methods of work, Bishop Henry Egli of Adams County, Indiana, led a schism now known as the Defenseless Mennonite Church whose present membership is about 1,700. The Mission Church, under the leadership of Joseph E. Ramseyer, seceded from the Defenseless Mennonites in 1896-1898. Another Amish Mennonite schismatic was Joseph Stuckey of Illinois, a progressive leader who seceded in 1872; his followers now being known as Central Conference Mennonites and numbering 3,300. The Central Conference and the General Conference Mennonites merged, 1946. The Indiana-Michigan Conference lost some progressive members about the year 1923, but these united either with the Central or General Conference Mennonites; no new branch was formed. It is to be hoped that the American Mennonites are finally rid of the tendency exhibited in the Netherlands, in Russia, and in America which led them to divide over the exact place to draw the line in church discipline, the introduction of new methods of church work, and the like. The Mennonites of Switzerland seem to have had sufficient earnestness in the Christian life, enough love for the brethren, and ample tolerance for the differing judgments of others to have lived together for four centuries with but one division. May the Mennonites of America become their worthy sons and daughters!

READINGS

Bender, H. S.: "The Founding of the Mennonite Church in America at Germantown, 1683-1708," *The Mennonite Quarterly Review,* Goshen, Indiana, VII, 4 (October 1933), 227-250.

Bender, H. S.: "The Mennonites of the United States," *The Mennonite Quarterly Review,* XI, 1 (January 1937), 68-82.

Burkholder, L. J.: *A Brief History of the Mennonites in Ontario,* 1935.

Committee, Y.P.C.A. Historical: *Mennonite Church History of Howard and Miami Counties, Indiana,* Mennonite Publishing House, Scottdale, Pa. [c. 1917].

Fast, H. A.: "Mennonites in Paraguay," *Mennonite Life,* I, 1 (January 1946).

Gingerich, Melvin: *The Mennonites in Iowa,* State Historical Society of Iowa, Iowa City, 1939.

Grubb, N. B.: "Rev. John H. Oberholtzer," *Mennonite Year Book and Almanac,* Berne, Indiana, 1908, 34-38.

Grubb, W. H.: *History of the Mennonites of Butler County, Ohio,* Trenton, Ohio, 1916.

Hull, William I.: *William Penn and the Dutch Quaker Migration to Pennsylvania,* Swarthmore College Monographs on History, Number Two, 1935.

Indiana-Michigan Mennonite Conference, 1864-1929, Minutes of, Mennonite Publishing House, Scottdale, Pa., [c. 1929]. [Congregational histories, pp. 297-338.]

Kauffman, Daniel: "Mennonite General Conference," *Gospel Herald,* I. March 9, 1933, 1027; II. March 16, 1933, 1059; III. March 23, 1933, 1075; IV. March 30, 1933, 1090; V. April 6, 1933, 2, 3.

Kansas-Nebraska Mennonite Conference, 1876-1914, Conference Record . . . , [c. 1914]

Klassen, Peter: "Mennonites in Brazil," *Mennonite Life,* North Newton, Kansas, II, 1 (January 1947).

Lehman, Heinz: *Das Deutschtum in Westkanada,* Berlin, 1939.

Mast, C. Z. & Simpson, R. E.: *Annals of the Conestoga Valley in Lancaster, Berks, and Chester Counties, Pennsylvania,* Published by authors, 1942.

Mast, C. Z.: "Did Mennonites Ever Settle in North Carolina?" *Gospel Herald,* July 30, 1936, 394.

Mennonite General Conference, Proceedings of, Mennonite Publishing House, Scottdale, Pennsylvania, 1921. [Printed minutes issued biennially since 1923.]

"Oberholtzer, John H.," *Mennonite Year Book and Almanac,* 1896, 28, 29.

Shetler, S. G.: *Church History of the Pacific Coast Mennonite Conference District,* Scottdale, Pa. [c. 1931].

Smith, C. Henry: *The Mennonite Immigration to Pennsylvania in the Eighteenth Century,* Pennsylvania German Society, Norristown, Pa., 1929.

Smith, C. H.: *The Mennonites of America,* Goshen, Indiana, 1909.

Smith, C. H.: *The Coming of the Russian Mennonites,* Berne, Indiana, 1927.

Smith, C. H.: *Mennonites in America,* M.C.C., Akron, Pennsylvania, 1942.

Sprunger, Eva F.: *The First Hundred Years, A History of the Mennonite Church in Adams County, Indiana,* Berne, Indiana, 1938.

Toews, David: "The Mennonites of Canada," *The Mennonite Quarterly Review,* XI, 1 (January 1937), 83-91.

Minutes of the Virginia Mennonite Conference, 1939.

Schultz, F. P.: *A History of the Settlement of German Mennonites from Russia at Mountain Lake, Minnesota.* Published by the author at the University of Minnesota, [c. 1938].

Umble, John: *Ohio Mennonite Sunday Schools,* The Mennonite Historical Society, Goshen, Indiana, 1941.

Weaver, Martin G.: *Mennonites of Lancaster Conference,* Scottdale, Pennsylvania, 1931.

Weber, H. F.: *Centennial History of the Mennonites of Illinois,* Goshen, Indiana, 1931.

Wenger, J. C.: "American Conferences of the Mennonite Church," *Gospel Herald,* November 17, 1938, 722.

Wenger, J. C.: "Germantown History," *Gospel Herald,* March 17, 1938, 1082.

Wenger, J. C.: *History of the Mennonites of the Franconia Conference,* Telford, Pennsylvania, 1937.

See also the county histories of the various areas which contain Mennonite settlements.

CHAPTER XI

Conferences of American Mennonites

American Mennonites are not united in one conference but are divided into a number of separate bodies with considerable variation in religious doctrine and practice. Five groups only have more than ten thousand baptized members; one brotherhood, the Hutterian Brethren, has six thousand members; while the membership of seven other small conferences runs from about a thousand to less than five thousand each.

I. *The Mennonite Church*

The Mennonite Church is the largest body of American Mennonites, having a little over five hundred congregations with 142 bishops, 623 ministers, 320 deacons, and a total baptized membership (1945) of about sixty thousand. The membership in the United States is about 52,000; in Canada, about 5,700; and in foreign missions, India, Argentina, and Africa, about 2,300.

The background of the group is twofold, Mennonite and Amish Mennonite. The Mennonite portion of the group goes back to the Dutch and Palatine settlers who located in eastern Pennsylvania beginning feebly in 1683 and becoming much stronger in the first half of the eighteenth century when several thousand Palatine Mennonites of Swiss extraction migrated to Penn's Woods. In Pennsylvania the group thrived. Daughter colonies were established in Virginia, central and western Pennsylvania, Ontario, Ohio, Indiana, and points farther west, beginning in the eighteenth and continuing into the nineteenth century. Southeastern Pennsylvania contains in its two district conferences of the Mennonite Church—not to mention numerous Mennonite and Amish Mennonite churches of other conferences—over 140 congregations with almost 18,000 members.

The other portion of the group is the Amish Mennonite contingent. The Amish Mennonite congregations which merged with the Mennonite Church, 1916-26, are made up in part of descendants of the early eighteenth century Amish Mennonite settlers in eastern Pennsylvania and in part of descendants of the more progressive (i.e., less strict in church discipline) Amish Mennonites who left Europe in the post-Napoleonic era and settled in western Pennsylvania, Ohio, Indiana, Illinois, and Iowa.

There are certain slight differences between those congregations with a Mennonite background and those who had been Amish Mennonite. Mennonite bishops traditionally had more authority than those of the Amish Mennonites, and the latter group had less uniformity in clothing regulations than the Mennonites, particularly the Mennonites of eastern Pennsylvania. But one generation of church life and work has largely succeeded in making a united brotherhood of the two groups.

The distinguishing characteristic of the Mennonite Church is a staunch conservatism in faith and discipline coupled with a vigorous program of missions, publication, education, and mutual aid—a fraternal sharing of the financial obligations of brethren who are in need.

Those who accept Christ as their personal Saviour are baptized—either in the church building or in a stream—by pouring, on the confession of their faith. The emblems of the Lord's supper are given only to those who have been received into the group and who are in full fellowship in the congregation; the Mennonite Church believes in exercising a Scriptural discipline and practices close communion. Several days or weeks before the communion service is held the members hold another service called the Counsel Meeting in which the chief pastor, the bishop, discusses the discipline of the church and gives opportunity for the members to make any comments. The members are asked to state that they are in harmony with the standards of the church, at peace with God and with man as far as possible, and that they desire to participate in the communion service.

In conformity with its official Confession of Faith (Dordrecht, 1632,) the members of the Mennonite Church observe the ordinance of washing the saints' feet. This practice is based on John 13 and is usually observed at the close of the communion service. In connection with feet washing and on other occasions the brethren greet one another, and the sisters do likewise among themselves, with the "holy kiss" (Rom. 16:16). The church also anoints with oil those sick members who request it (Mark 6:13, James 5:14), for the healing of the body should it be God's will for them to recover.

During worship the sisters of the church wear a prayer veil as a symbol of the headship of man (I Cor. 11:2-16); in America this is usually a small white cap of a finely-woven net. In Argentina Mennonite women wear a black veil over their heads during worship.

The Mennonite Church holds firmly to Biblical nonresistance, believing that the calling of the Christian is to lead people to personal salvation, not to destroy men's lives. They therefore refuse to participate in any military activity, either as combatants or as members of a noncombatant unit, as well as in the manufacture of munitions of war. This position they base on the spirit and the letter of the New Testament (Matt. 5:38-48; Rom. 12:17-21; etc). Similarly they do not resort to litigation to realize their "rights" (I Cor. 6:1-8). And they refuse to unite with any organization which ever resorts to force for the accomplishment of its ends, labor unions, for example. Mennonites also refuse to swear oaths, giving only a solemn affirmation; they base this refusal on such Scriptures as Matthew 5:33-37; 23:16-22; and James 5:12. The oath is one of the factors which makes them oppose membership in secret orders which are oath-bound fraternities. In brief, Mennonites believe in separation from the "world," a life of full conformity to the will of God as revealed in the Scriptures, in reliance upon the sustaining grace of God.

Another cardinal point with members of the Mennonite Church is simplicity. This applies to the entire life of the Christian. Mennonites hold that the Christian ought to live a simple life, avoiding the luxuries and the selfish indulgence of the rich. Clothing has become more or less a symbol of the simple life for them. The men dress conservatively avoiding the styles and fashions of the day. In some cases they do not wear neckties, considering them "worldly." Some of the laity and all ordained men wear a coat without a lay-down collar, the so-called "plain" coat of Mennonite and Brethren circles. The women likewise wear plain headgear without brim or ornament, such as the bonnet or hood, avoiding fashionable hats; they also wear such dresses as they consider becoming to Christian women. In some areas a standard "plain" dress is worn which includes a cape over the shoulders. Mennonites take seriously the Scriptural prohibition against the wearing of gold and pearls (I Tim. 2:9, 10; I Peter 3:3, 4), applying this principle of simplicity and nonconformity to all jewelry including wedding rings.

Simplicity is also applied to worship. The Mennonite "meeting-house" is a plain structure without steeple, bell, organ, altar, or works of art. Emphasis falls not on aesthetic stimulation but on worshiping God in the heart. The minister who is addressed as "Brother" rather than "Reverend" is chosen from the congregation and in many cases has had no special training for his work. In former years, however, the ministers were often schoolteachers, and today many young men who feel that God is calling them to the work of the church are attending Bible school or seminary to prepare themselves. There are frequently two ministers in a congregation, both of whom earn their own livings by farming or some other occupation, although there is growing conviction in many congregations that ministers ought to receive support in order to devote their time more fully to ministerial duties (I Cor. 9:1-14; II Cor. 11:7-9; 12:13; Gal. 6:6; Phil. 4:10-17; I Tim. 5:17, 18). The ministers meet regularly in conference and make regulations which are binding upon the brotherhood. In some districts elected lay delegates also participate in the conference work. The worship service is simple and dignified, not demonstrative or emotional. The congregations sing four-part music, unaccompanied by any instruments; the worshipers kneel for prayer; the sermon is simple and earnest with a constant appeal to the Bible in support of the message.

Marriage is to be entered into only with those of "like precious faith," meaning those who believe in "nonconformity to the world" and nonresistance. Formal separation from one's life companion is recognized only for unfaithfulness on the part of the companion (Matt. 5:32; 19:9).

Mennonites emphasize separation of church and state. Office-holding which would infringe on the life of love and nonresistance is not permitted. Many Mennonites refuse even to vote, holding that it is not consistent for one whose citizenship is in heaven (Phil. 3:20).

In recent years considerable emphasis has been placed on the temperate life including total abstinence in reference to alcohol and tobacco. Members of the church are also expected to stay away from the theater and from moving picture shows inasmuch as they have a carnal emphasis rather than drawing men toward God.

Members of the Mennonite Church have a strong historical consciousness, being keenly aware that they are members of a martyr-church. This consciousness and their sense of mission are being nourished by scholars and writers who are producing books and articles for the strengthening of the brotherhood.

2. *The General Conference of the Mennonite Church of North America*

The chief figure in the formation of this body of Mennonites was an eastern Pennsylvania minister named John H. Oberholtzer, 1809-95, ordained in the Swamp district of the Franconia Conference in 1842. Oberholtzer was a schoolteacher and locksmith, and a man of progressive views. For refusing to wear a "plain" coat, for urging the keeping of conference minutes when the older ministers were opposed, and for writing a constitution and trying to get it adopted, he, along with fifteen other ministers and deacons including the conference moderator, was disfranchised by the Franconia Conference on October 7, 1847. Three weeks later most of Oberholtzer's party, consisting of one bishop, five ministers, and six deacons—there were present twelve in all—met in the Lower Skippack Mennonite Church and organized a new conference now the *Eastern District* of the General Conference of the Mennonite Church of North America. The new conference claimed six of the twenty-two meetinghouses of the Franconia Conference, built two new ones, and worshiped every two weeks in six others, alternating with the old congregations. It now (1945) has 3,700 members.

It is evident that the stated "issues" of 1847 were but symptoms of more fundamental differences. Oberholtzer himself stated: "Our [new] conference was not opposed to go to law in a just cause." This attitude was of course regarded by the Franconia Conference as the surrender of a New Testament principle (I Cor. 6:1-8). Other points of difference between the two groups concerned their respective attitudes toward other denominations, toward marrying non-Mennonites, toward open communion, etc., the Oberholtzer group in each case taking the more tolerant and lenient attitude. As early as 1850 the new conference seemed to weaken on the matter of barring lodge members from communion. In the course of time the worship veil was discarded, all "plain" clothing forms were abandoned, educated and salaried ministers began to serve the congregations, musical instruments and choirs were introduced into the church services, and various other changes from the "old order" were tolerated. Discipline was reduced to a minimum; the ministers taught Mennonite principles but allowed the members to make their own decisions with little danger of a loss of church fellowship. From the standpoint of the Franconia Conference perhaps the most serious departure from the historic faith and practice of the Mennonite brotherhood was the weak position taken in respect to secret orders and to nonresistance. The matter of lodge membership has been mentioned already. In reference to nonresistance the Oberholtzer Conference faced the question of what to do about those Mennonites who took up arms during the American Civil War (1861-65). Conference felt it was "best to refrain from action at this date"; the matter was left to the congregations involved.

The Oberholtzer Conference was active and alert. Men were ordained and new activities were inaugurated. Oberholtzer became a publisher, issuing conference minutes, catechisms, his constitution, and after 1852 a German periodical entitled *Religioeser Botschafter* (Religious Messenger). Indeed, it should be emphasized that his group pioneered in Sunday-school work, in publication and education, and in missions and charities—in all of which fields the Franconia Conference and its sister bodies later followed. What a tragedy that the division of 1847 had to occur. Each group needed the other.

About a decade after the division Oberholtzer began to urge the creation of an all-Mennonite general conference. In 1859 two progressive Mennonite ministers in Iowa, Daniel Krehbiel and Christian Showalter, held a joint meeting of their two congregations which proved to be a sort of preliminary meeting to the 1860 General Conference—if such it may be called. This first session, May 28, 1860, was attended by delegates from the West Point and Zion (Iowa) congregations—those of Krehbiel and Showalter—another Iowa minister, Oberholtzer and one other Pennsylvania delegate, Enos F. Loux. At this meeting was born the General Conference of the Mennonite Church of North America, a movement designed to unite all American Mennonites, not to create another branch. The following six resolutions were adopted May 29, 1860 as a platform on which all American Mennonites should stand as they worked together in the new conference:

1. That all branches of the Mennonite denomination in North America, regardless of minor differences, should extend to each other the hand of fellowship.

2. That fraternal relations shall be severed only when a person or church abandons the fundamental doctrines of the denomination;

namely these concerning baptism, the oath, etc., (wherein we follow Menno Simon) as indeed also all those principal doctrines of the faith which we with Menno base solely upon the Gospel as received from Jesus Christ and His apostles.

3. That no brother shall be found guilty of heresy unless his error can be established on unequivocal Scripture evidence.

4. That the General Conference shall consider no excommunication as Scripturally valid, unless a real transgression or neglect, conflicting with the demands of Scripture, exists.

5. That every church or district shall be entitled to continue, without molestation or hindrance and amenable only to their own conscience, any rules or regulations they may have adopted for their own government; provided they do not conflict with the tenets of our general confession.

6. That if a member of a church, because of existing customs or ordinances in his church, shall desire to sever his connection and unite with some other church of the General Conference such action shall not be interfered with (Krehbiel: *General Conference,* 56f).

The spirit of the General Conference has been set forth by the phrase, "In essentials unity, in nonessentials liberty." At the 1861 session another "essential" was added to the 1860 basis of union, namely, "That no one may be a member of the Mennonite denomination who is a member of a secret society." This made three or four great planks of distinctive Mennonite doctrine in the platform of the General Conference: believers' baptism, opposition to the oath, the stand against membership in secret orders, and nonresistance—assuredly taken for granted for it seems not to be mentioned.

The General Conference has enjoyed a healthy growth. At the 1861 session eight congregations with about 800 members were represented. Fifty years later (1911) one hundred ten congregations with about 15,000 members were united in the General Conference. Today (1946) there are about two hundred congregations with 44,000 members in the General Conference. Whence the great increase since 1861? The answer is: The Mennonites from Russia.

The congregations of the General Conference are now affiliated with six district conferences—counting the *Central Conference of Mennonites* (3,200 members) which merged with the General Conference in 1946—in the United States, besides the congregations in Canada, and the following mission congregations: India (31); China (24); North America (9). The General Conference group does work among the North American Indians of Arizona and Montana; in Africa; and in Colombia, South America. It has 3,000 members in India and 2,300 in China. But as noted above the bulk of the present membership of the General Conference consists of congregations of Mennonites who emigrated from Russia to North America. The *Northern District* Conference with 5,400 members has strong "Russian" congregations at Mountain Lake, Minnesota; at Henderson, Nebraska; and at Freeman, South Dakota. The *Western District* with 12,300 members has large congregations (Russian) in Kansas and Oklahoma—some a thousand members strong (Alexanderwohl, 1,049; Eden, 803; Newton, 678; Pretty Prairie, 609). The *Middle District* Conference, with 5,400 members is spread over Ohio, Indiana, Illinois, and Iowa and is made up of a variety of congregations; for example, the Swiss churches at Bluffton and Dalton, Ohio; and at Berne, Indiana (1,313 members); the former Amish congregations at Trenton, Ohio; Nappanee, Indiana; and Noble, Iowa; etc. The *Pacific District* is the smallest of them all, having only sixteen congregations scattered through Idaho, Oregon, Washington, and California with a total of 2,900 members. The *Canadian Mennonite Conference* is not affiliated with the General Conference, but works closely with it; some of these Canadian congregations (The Canadian Conference has over sixty "Russian" congregations with 13,800 members) belong to the General Conference. In fact that is always true of the General Conference—it is made up of *congregations* not of conferences, and these congregations may or may not be affiliated with a district conference.

The two causes to which the General Conference has given the most attention are missions and education. As early as 1858 the Oberholtzer Conference instructed their founder to write to the European Mennonites to learn more about their missionary work. Letters in reply were received from J. Mannhardt and B. C. Roosen but led to no definite missionary work immediately. The first major achievement of the General Conference was a church school which was operated at Wadsworth, Ohio, from 1868 to 1878. The first principal was Christian Showalter who was succeeded by C. J. Van der Smissen who was called from Friedrichstadt, Germany, to head the school. The school exerted much influence over a goodly number of men who were destined to become influential in the General Conference in coming years. Missionary work was begun among the American Indians in 1880 and in India in 1900.

C. Henry Smith writes of the conference of the General Conference of the Mennonite Church of North America:

> The conference meets every three years, and is composed of delegates elected by the participating congregations, which are given voting power according to the size of their individual membership. These sessions are devoted largely to the discussion of reports from the various standing boards—Missions, Education, Publication, and in recent years, Peace and Emergency Relief, and such committees as have been appointed for special purposes. Church government among the congregations is strictly congregational, each minister usually being an elder with full power to administer all the religious rites demanded of the church. There are no superior officers, and the title "bishop," common among the Mennonites and the Amish, is unknown.
>
> The General Conference has no printing establishment, but the Publication Board publishes the official organs of the church, the *Mennonite* and the *Christlicher Bundesbote,* an annual Year Book, Sunday-school supplies, and numerous other books and pamphlets of a religious and denominational character (*Mennonites in America,* 1942, 54f).

3. The Mennonite Brethren Church of North America

The Mennoniten Brüdergemeinde originated as a revivalist movement in the Molotschna Mennonite Colony in South Russia in 1860. Eighteen family heads signed a statement of withdrawal from the parent Mennonite body on January 6 of that year. On May 30, 1860, the Brethren elected two ministers whom they set apart for the work by the laying on of hands on June 5. One of the men who had aroused sentiment against the spiritual coldness of the old church was an earnest evangelist named Edward Wüst from a near-by colony of German Evangelicals. Two years later, in 1862, a similar congregation of "awakened" Brethren arose in the conservative Chortitza colony under the leadership of Abraham Unger. In this case the revival came about through the reading of the sermons of Ludwig Hofacker. From the first the Baptist influence was strong in Unger's group. Indeed it was a Baptist who ordained Unger as an elder. Yet it should be emphasized that the *Brüdergemeinde* was ever a truly Mennonite body. And although there were certain excesses in the early years of the movement, these were soon overcome. By 1872, when three Mennonite Brethren groups in South Russia united in a conference, the group consisted of about six hundred members; by 1885 it had arisen to 1,800. In 1926 the Ukraine contained a Mennonite Brethren population of 7,242, of which 3,112 were baptized members.

The first Mennonite Brethren members settled in North America in 1873, locating in the state of Kansas. Yearly conferences of the ministers were inaugurated in 1878, but it was not until 1889 that the organization, *Konferenz der Vereinigten Mennoniten-Brüder in Nord-Amerika* (Conference of the United Mennonite Brethren in North America), was created.

One of the leading ministers of the Mennonite Brethren, P. C. Hiebert, chairman of the Mennonite Central Committee, has summarized the distinctive views of his church as follows:

1. A definite religious experience followed by a changed life, as a prerequisite of admission to membership.
2. Baptism by immersion upon confession of faith as the only recognized form.
3. A negative reaction against all tendencies toward formalism as it hindered early church procedure, and toward systematic religious instruction of children.
4. Definite opposition to all participation in military training and service.
5. Limiting communion to baptized members in good standing in the local church.
6. Active evangelism characterized by a keen personal interest in the personal conversion and salvation of one's associates.
7. A thorough study of all the Scriptures, which is recognized as the word of God, and an urgent demand that every member live up to what God requires in the Bible of those who have accepted Christ as their personal Saviour (Smith: *Mennonites in America,* 1942, 46).

By 1887 the American membership of the Mennonite Brethren had reached 1,200. Through the years since that time the group has enjoyed a healthy growth. The Canadian portion of the church consists largely of the Mennonites from Russia who arrived some twenty years ago. The M.B. Church is now organized into a number of district conferences—Ontario, Northern, Central, Southern, and Pacific—and numbers about seventeen thousand communicants. They are strongly missionary-minded, having missionaries in Africa, India, and China, and among the Comanche Indians and the Mexicans on this continent.

4. *Old Order Amish Mennonites*

In an earlier chapter, the story of Jacob Ammann and his 1693 schism in Switzerland and Alsace was told in some detail. In the first half of the eighteenth century a number of Amish families settled in southeastern Pennsylvania: Yoders, Zooks, Lapps, Schlabachs, Hostetlers, Beilers, Koenigs (Kings), Hartzlers, etc. In the course of time some of the early settlements such as those in the Oley and Chester Valleys died out, but thriving colonies were established in Lancaster and Somerset counties and in the "Big Valley" (the Kishacoquillas, now in Mifflin County). In 1800 Joseph Schantz (Anglicized as Johns) founded a settlement called Johnstown, made famous by the disastrous flood of 1888. (Johns has a number of descendants who are now active ministers in the Mennonite church in Ohio and Indiana.) In the course of the nineteenth century the Pennsylvania Amish settlements expanded by establishing daughter colonies in Ohio, Indiana, and points farther west. And during the time from 1815 until the American Civil War many more European Amish came to this country, although these were less conservative than the eighteenth century immigrants. The attitudes of the latter are illustrated by the Amish disciplines of 1809, of 1837, and of 1865 which have been preserved and published (*The Mennonite Quarterly Review,* VIII, 2, 1934: 90-98). The brethren were much concerned not to adopt any modern methods of cutting the hair and trimming the beard. Dresses, trousers, and clothing in general were not to be "proud," that is, made in conformity with the current styles. All buildings, house furnishings, and vehicles were to be simple and plain. The vehicles were not to be painted two colors of paint. As new things were invented by the "world" an effort was made to exclude them from the church. The 1865 discipline prohibits the wearing of oilcloth and rubber raincoats. In brief the Amish wished to perpetuate the simple culture of their Swiss forebears, ignoring new inventions which might create new ethical problems in relation to "conformity to the world" (Romans 12:2), and resisting changes of any kind at least for a time.

About the year 1850, however, there began to be a breaking down of the absolutist position of making no changes at all. Certain parties in the Amish congregations began to make innovations which reduced the differences between them and the Mennonites. These Amish progressives began to build meetinghouses and to depart from some of the time-honored life patterns of their fathers. These "Amish Mennonites," known variously as "church Amish," "high Amish," etc., eventually merged with their Mennonite brethren. One of the most interesting of the Amish Mennonite innovations was administering baptism in streams. Some Amish Mennonite meetinghouses were built at or near streams, perhaps for convenience in baptizing. The mode of baptism remained pouring, but the bishop and the convert stood in the water, following the example of some New Testament baptisms (Matt. 3:16; Acts 8:38).

Not all the Amish adopted the new ways of their progressive brethren. They regarded their changes not as progress but as declension, a compromising with the world and its pride, a conformity to the spirit of the times. They held tenaciously to their older European culture and civilization, identifying this pattern of life with that which was demanded in the Scriptures. Only thus, they believed, could they resist the entrance of "worldliness"; only in this way could they remain in God's will and please Him. Consequently, to strangers, the Amish seem like people from another world. And in a sense they are. They seek to live as pilgrims in this world, knowing that eternity is before them. With them their distinctive life patterns are not sociological aids for the perpetuation of their way of life; they are believed to be the concrete applications of a Biblical separation from the world.

Amish life is simple and beautiful. Every two weeks worship services are held in their homes. They have no church buildings. In daily life the Amish use the Pennsylvania German dialect (Palatine German with an admixture of English words). In the worship services however the ministers use the German; a German Bible; a German prayer book; and a German hymnal, traditionally the *Ausbund* which they call the "thick songbook." Their preaching is done in a modified high German, or perhaps more accurately in a modified Pennsylvania German. They sing their German hymns to ancient tunes which have only recently been written and printed (J. W. Yoder: *Amische Lieder,* 1942). Following their service, which lasts for hours, a meal is eaten at the home of the family which entertained the worshipers. During the afternoon the several families hitch their horses to their plain buggies and slowly wend their way homeward. They thus present a most picturesque appearance. The men wear dark clothing of a plain style all their own, with large, black, broad-brimmed hats, and with long beards. The women wear large, plain bonnets; and long, full dresses of solid color, not flowered, checked, or figured. Their homes are as simple as their clothes, often without plumbing, and having no electric lights and no telephones. But this is no indication of a lack of energy or of concern for property. For the Amish are among the best farmers in the land, taking good care of the soil, keeping fine stock on their farms, and maintaining their premises in a first-class condition. Their wives are diligent homemakers, keeping their houses spic-and-span, and excelling as cooks. Their families are large and home life is strong. In short, the Amish are usually devout and earnest, and among the sturdiest citizens of the land. They have succeeded in maintaining the life patterns of their forefathers of two centuries or more ago, and on such essential Mennonite emphases as believers' baptism, opposition to the oath, and nonresistance they stand firmly. But they have been slow in awakening to the need of doing mission work, in adopting such agencies for Bible-teaching as the Sunday school, and in teaching against such unworthy practices as the use of alcohol and tobacco. They have been "slow" on these points, but they are moving in the right direction.

The Old Order Amish Mennonites, commonly called "The Amish," are strict congregationalists, having neither district conferences nor a general conference. In some areas however ministers' meetings are held to discuss church matters and to seek to maintain a more nearly uniform discipline. Their most numerous congregations are found in Pennsylvania, Ohio, and Indiana. They are one of the fastest growing Mennonite bodies, not because of mission work, but because of their large families; their present membership is about 13,600. Anyone wishing to get accurate information on the Amish can do so by reading the charming little book of J. W. Yoder, *Rosanna of the Amish,* 1940, Herald Press, Scottdale, Pa., a thoroughly reliable work.

5. The Mennonite Brethren in Christ

The origin of the M.B.C. Church was summarized in an earlier chapter. The group is most strongly represented in Ontario, Pennsylvania, Ohio, Indiana, and Michigan. In faith the M.B.C. Church is in line with the historic Mennonite confessions. With few exceptions their Confession of Faith is in substantial agreement with the Dordrecht Confession. The unique emphases of the group fall on a vigorous program of evangelism, on a somewhat emotional type of conversion and religious life, on a theory of instantaneous and complete sanctification often called "holiness," on immersion as the mode of baptism, and on the simple life, but without any required and uniform expressions of "nonconformity to the world." Feet washing is practiced as an ordinance. Membership in secret orders is not permitted. This group "has perhaps more non-Mennonite family names in its membership than any other wing of the denomination" (C. H. Smith). They actually win converts from non-Mennonite homes. In this respect the Mennonite Brthren in Christ have more nearly recaptured the Anabaptist vision of 1525-30 than any other branch of Mennonites. Their membership is now 12,800.

6. *Old Order Mennonites*

During the nineteenth century when various innovations in methods of church work were introduced into the Mennonite Church certain ministers and members found themselves unable to adopt the newer ways of doing things. The opposition centered largely in the Sunday school. The conservatives also frowned on English preaching, evening meetings, evangelistic meetings, and any other new thing. Mennonitism for them meant clinging to the ways of the fathers rather than adopting such new measures as modern Christendom had devised. But the issues were not confined to church work. New inventions were rejected as they issued from the factory —such items as telephones, automobiles, and the like. Eventually the group divided into two or more levels of strictness. The mildest group is today taking a fraternal attitude toward the "Mennonite Church" though it is still somewhat reticent about adopting all which the latter group permits and employs. The total membership of the Older Order bodies is 4,600.

Not in any way affiliated with the Old Order Mennonites but even more conservative than the strictest sects thereof are several settlements of Russian Mennonites in southern Manitoba in Canada. (1) The "Chortitz" congregations are named for the old Chortitza colony in South Russia and number today (1946) 1,400 members. (2) Most of the so-called "Old Colony" Mennonites in Manitoba, also from the Russian Chortitza in the Ukraine, migrated to Mexico to maintain the German language undisturbed by any government, but 500 of them are left in Manitoba. These people are as strict as the Old Order Amish in many respects. (3) The "Sommerfelders," named for the village of Sommerfeld, are also quite conservative, some of their members having followed the "Old Colonists" to Mexico. In Manitoba they number 4,000 members. (4) The "Rudnerweide" congregation, 1,500 members strong, is also independent of any conference connections and is located in southern Manitoba.

To the more progressive bodies of Mennonites it appears that the various "old order" bodies of Mennonites are more interested in preserving the *status quo* of a past culture and civilization than in carrying out the Great Commission. But the "old order" groups regard their way of life as that of "nonconformity to the world" (Romans 12:1).

7. Conservative Amish Mennonites

The Conservative A. M. Church is made up of individuals who have withdrawn from the Old Order Amish Mennonites, those who have "drifted" away from the Old Order. In practice they vary from a slight deviation from the attitudes of the parent body to an almost complete parallelism with the "Mennonite Church." In some communities the chief difference between the Conservative A. M. and the Old Order Amish Mennonites consists in their respective attitudes toward the ownership and use of automobiles. The Amish prefer the use of horse and buggy while the "Conservatives" permit the use of automobiles. In other communities the Conservatives are hardly distinguishable from members of the "Mennonite Church." The Conservative A. M. Church has about 4,000 members of whom over one fourth do not belong to their conference.

8. Church of God in Christ, Mennonite

Commonly known as "Holdemans" this is another of the strict Mennonite bodies. The founder of the group was a layman named John Holdeman, 1830-1900, of Medina County, Ohio. Holdeman believed that he was the recipient of special revelations and that he was called of God to preach. For twenty years he was not successful in winning many converts. But after the Russian Mennonites settled in Kansas in the years 1873-80 a goodly number of them united with Holdeman's group. Holdeman himself spent the latter part of his life in Jasper County, Missouri. Holdeman emphasized avoidance or shunning, and this is still a point of emphasis with his group. The men are required to wear beards, for this is considered a part of the moral law of God. They have but two types of ordained men: ministers or elders who preach, and deacons who are stewards of the alms monies. They are said to be "quite active in their church work, especially in their benevolences" (Smith). They have approximately 4,000 members, rather widely scattered in the United States and Canada.

9. *Evangelical Mennonite Brethren*

One of the active promoters of the emigration of the Mennonites from Russia to America was Isaac Peters, 1826-1911, a school teacher and minister in one of the villages of the Molotschna colony. Ordained as an elder in 1867 he was a strong advocate of emigration to America in 1874 and as such was ordered into exile by the Russian government. He lived at Henderson, Nebraska, and linked hands with Aaron Wall of Mountain Lake, Minnesota, in church work. Peters was a well-informed man and a popular speaker.

Aaron Wall, 1833-1905, was ordained as an elder at Mountain Lake, Minnesota, in 1876. Wall was a conservative leader and in 1888-89 he withdrew from the *altkirchlich* church and founded a congregation of like-minded followers. His group practiced feet washing, baptized in the water with pouring as the mode, and had a Sunday school. They opposed the use of tobacco. Their married women, like those of the other Mennonite groups at Mountain Lake, wore hoods, which were brought to them in a formal ceremony after their weddings. Wall's congregation was known as the *Bruderthaler-Gemeinde.* Though without formal training, Wall exhibited great skill as a physician. He was also a very spiritual man, a good leader, and an excellent pastor. With Wall's approval P. A. Friesen, later a missionary to India, started young people's Bible meetings about the year 1904.

As indicated above Peters and Wall worked together in church work. Indeed they were the leaders of a small conference called the Nebraska-Minnesota Conference with congregations at Mountain Lake, Minnesota; Henderson, Nebraska; Dalton and Marion Junction, South Dakota; and near Inman, Kansas. For some years they sent delegates to the General Conference of the "Mennonite Church," ceasing to do so about 1914. For a time they were known as the Conference of Defenseless Mennonites of North America and co-operated with the Illinois group known as Defenceless Mennonites. But later (1937) they adopted the present name, Evangelical Mennonite Brethren. Today the E. M. B. Church is much like their General Conference and Mennonite Brethren neighbors except that they have a somewhat stricter discipline, particularly on such matters as the use of alcohol and tobacco and attendance at theaters. C. Henry Smith writes:

> Many of the early distinctive demands of this church have since been modified, but they are still conservative in their practices. They are actively

evangelistic, however, and support a strong mission and relief program. They baptize either by pouring or by immersion, and observe footwashing at the communion service. Their membership numbers about two thousand including some in Canada *(Mennonites in America,* 1942, 49).

10. *Defenseless Mennonite Church of North America*

The *Church Manual* of this group contains a "Brief History of the Defenseless Mennonite Church" from which the following is reproduced (abbreviations were eliminated by the present author):

> The Defenceless Mennonite Church had its origin, through the direction of God and the instrumentality of the Holy Ghost, in the person of Henry Egly of Geneva, Indiana, an Elder of the now so-called "Old Order Amish Mennonites," who hitherto had not experienced a change of heart, was truly and happily converted, and at once introduced these means of grace into his church insisting on a personal experience of forgiveness of sins and a change of heart of all those who wished to partake of the Lord's Supper. He also required re-baptism of those (but only those) who had not made this experience, before uniting with the church, believing that baptism was but the answer of a good conscience towards God.
>
> Upon making his position known one-half of his congregation withdrew and refused to have anything more to do with him. Of the other half of the congregation about one-half of the members had made a personal experience of salvation, either before they were baptized in the old church, or after they had been baptized. The remaining half of the members requested prayer that they too might see the light and receive the experience of conversion and regeneration. This occurred in the years of 1864-1866.
>
> The movement spread to other places in Indiana, Ohio, and Illinois. There the cause was espoused by such church leaders as Joseph Rediger of Gridley, Illinois; Michael Mosiman and Nicholas Roth near Peoria, Illinois; Joseph Gerig of Leo, Indiana; Christian Zimmerman, Edna Mills [near Lafayette], Indiana; Jacob Rupp, Archbold, Ohio; and later by Abraham Steiner of Bluffton, Ohio.
>
> Later on there were also congregations and churches established by settlement of members and church extension in Hickory County, Missouri; Reno County, Kansas; Seward County, Nebraska; Centralia, Missouri; Zurich, Ontario; and Elkton, Michigan.
>
> A division took place in the Church in the year 1890, dividing nearly all of the then existing congregations, caused by some of the ministers and members adopting immersion as the only mode of baptism *(Manual,* 7, 8).

The total membership of the Defenseless Mennonite Conference of North America is 1,700. In many ways they resemble the General Conference Mennonites except that they place more emphasis on "experimental" Christianity and teach "The Baptism with the Holy Ghost" as an experience separate from regeneration. They also teach divine healing: "that God has made provision in the atonement for the healing of the body, Isa. 53:3, 4, R.V.; Matt. 8:16, 17; that it is to be administered by the elders, in the name of the

Lord, by anointing with oil, and laying on of hands and praying over any who are sick and desire it, Mark 16:18; 6:13; James 5:14, 15."

11. Krimmer Mennonite Brethren Church

The word *Krimmer* is the German word for "Crimean" and indicates that this wing of the Russian Mennonite family originated on the Crimean Peninsula which projects southward into the Black Sea. The founder was a revivalist minister named Jacob A. Wiebe, 1836-1921. The group, in number eighteen persons, withdrew from the *Kleine Gemeinde* (described below) and in 1869 organized their new church in the village of Annafeld. In 1874 the group migrated to Marion County, Kansas, and founded the village of Gnadenau near Hillsboro.

The *Krimmer* Mennonites today have 1,600 members located in Kansas, South Dakota, and a few other states and provinces including Alberta and Saskatchewan. In many respects they resemble the Mennonite Brethren, except that they immerse their converts forward while the M. B. Church immerses backward. Since 1899 they maintain mission work among the American negroes, having about a hundred members (1934) in North Carolina and Tennessee; since 1902 they have a foreign mission, Shantung, China; and since 1923 an additional station in Mongolia.

12. Kleine Gemeinde

This name is rather appropriate for it is in reality a "small church," having in 1945 but 1,560 members. The group withdrew from the Mennonites of the Molotschna Colony in South Russia in 1812. The leaders were Claas Reimer and Cornelius Janzen who favored a stricter church discipline and a firmer stand on nonresistance. Reimer was regarded by his fellow Mennonites in the Molotschna as being rather contentious, but it is evident that he was really a man of a sensitive conscience. For example he was much disturbed by the use of force on the part of Mennonites against their religious fellows. It hurt his conscience to see a Mennonite lead an offender to the whipping post or to jail. He also objected to the use of tobacco. A pamphlet which came from his group in 1838 pictures the members of the old church as sitting at weddings with pipes in one hand and songbooks in the other.

The *Kleine Gemeinde* has now lived in North America about seventy years and is found mainly in Manitoba and Kansas. They maintain no mission stations, resembling in this respect the Old Order Mennonites and the Old Order Amish. However they have adopted Sunday schools and young people's Bible meetings.

13. Reformed Mennonites

About a century and a half ago a layman of Lancaster County named Francis Herr, 1747-1810, found himself out of fellowship with the Mennonite Church and unable to agree on terms of reconciliation with the ministers of that day. Consequently he began to hold meetings in his dwelling, having singing and prayer, and exhorting those who came to hear him. He remained seated while speaking, even at funerals. After Herr's death a man named David Buckwalter was appointed as leader of the meetings, but soon John Herr, 1781-1850, son of Francis, took his father's place as the unordained exhorter. Indeed John had never been baptized. Finally, after much prayer and earnest discussion it was unanimously agreed to form a new organization. The solemn meeting took place May 30, 1812. Herr, a young man of thirty, was unanimously elected by the group as pastor and bishop, and Abraham Landis was selected to baptize him. Consequently, Landis baptized Herr, and he in turn baptized Landis as well as Abraham Groff. Groff served as the first deacon of the group. Soon Landis was chosen as minister and on October 10, 1812, his brother John Landis was chosen as an additional minister.

The group has never thrived. It is quite exclusive, not permitting its members to listen to the sermons of other religious bodies. The members dress very plainly. They practice avoidance or shunning. In fact they regard their group as being truly a reformation movement within Mennonitism; what they aim to do is return to the Biblical teaching of Menno Simons, 1496-1561. They cling to the ways of Mennonites before the introduction of Sunday schools, young people's Bible meetings, mission work, and evangelistic services. They have something like twelve hundred members in the United States and in Ontario. Further information about their beliefs may be obtained from the book, *Christianity Defined: A Manual of New Testament Teaching* . . . , published by Reformed Mennonite Church, Lancaster, Pa., 1940.

* * *

All Mennonite groups have similar doctrinal standards and agree with each other that the New Testament prohibits participation in warfare and in litigation; that the Christian shall not swear an oath but make only a solemn declaration of the truth; that the Church consists of those who have voluntarily turned from sin and accepted Jesus Christ as their Saviour; that the Christian life involves a separation from the sin of the world, and positively the living of the "simple life"; that Christians shall not unite with secret orders; that baptism shall be administered only to those who accept Christ, not to infants (who are saved without baptism); and that the Christian congregation shall maintain a Scriptural discipline, excluding from its membership impenitent sinners. The differences between the several conferences of Mennonites relate mostly to their differing attitudes toward such newer institutions of Christendom as the Sunday school, toward the adoption of new inventions in the realms of transportation and communication, and toward newer forms of clothing. While all this may seem amusing to some people, even to the more progressive Mennonite groups, it is nevertheless a testimony to the ethical earnestness and the tender consciences of the brotherhood.

READINGS

Bachman, C. G.: *The Old Order Amish of Lancaster County* (Proceedings of the Pennsylvania German Society. Volume XLIX, 1941, pp. 1-297), Norristown, Pa., 1942.

Bender, H. S.: *Two Centuries of American Mennonite Literature* . . ., Goshen, Indiana, 1929 (Contains the titles of books produced or published by the several Mennonite groups).

Church Manual of the Defenseless Mennonite Church . . . , Printed by Economy Printing Concern, Inc., Berne, Indiana, 1937.

Fretz, J. Winfield: *Mennonite Colonization in Mexico,* M.C.C., Akron, Pennsylvania, 1945.

Getz, Jane C.: "The economic Organization and Practices of the Old Order Amish of Lancaster County, Pennsylvania," *The Mennonite Quarterly Review,* Goshen, Indiana, I, January 1946; II, April 1946.

Hartzler, J. S. & Kauffman, Daniel: *Mennonite Church History,* Scottdale, Pa., 1905.

Huffman, J. A.: *History of the Mennonite Brethren in Christ Church,* New Carlisle, Ohio, 1920.

Kauffman, Daniel, Editor: *Mennonite Cyclopedic Dictionary* . . . , Mennonite Publishing House, Scottdale, Pa., 1937.

Kollmorgen, W. M.: *Culture of a Contemporary Rural Community: The Old Order Amish of Lancaster County, Pennsylvania,* Washington, D. C., 1942.

Krehbiel, H. P.: *History of the General Conference of the Mennonite Church of North America,* Volume I, Canton, Ohio, 1898; Volume II, Newton, Kansas, 1938.

Mennonite General Conference, Mennonite Publishing House, Scottdale, Pennsylvania, 1921.

Smith, C. Henry: *The Mennonites of America,* Goshen, Indiana, 1909.

Smith, C. H.: *The Mennonites,* Berne, Indiana, 1920.

Smith, C. H.: *The Story of the Mennonites,* Berne, Indiana, 1941.

Smith, C. H.: *Mennonites in America,* M.C.C., Akron, Pennsylvania, 1942.

Weaver, William B.: *History of the Central Conference Mennonite Church,* Danvers, Illinois, 1926.

Yoder, J. W.: *Rosanna of the Amish,* Huntingdon, Pa., 1940.

Consult also the yearbooks and the published conference reports of the several Mennonite Conferences.

CHAPTER XII

Literature and Hymnody

1. Literature

The Mennonite immigrants to America naturally brought along the same books which they and their fathers had read in Europe. At the head of the list of course is the German Bible. It is interesting to note the fact that the early Mennonites preferred the Froschauer (Zurich) Bible to Luther's. Another book carried along to the new world was the *Ausbund,* the old Swiss Brethren hymnal of 1564. One of the best-loved books was the *Foundation-Book* of Menno Simons, which appeared in the original Dutch in 1539 and in German translation as early as 1575. It was printed in America in five German and in four English editions between 1794 and 1869. The greatest book ever written by a Mennonite was T. J. van Braght's *Martyrs' Mirror,* 1660. One of the first things the Pennsylvania Mennonite pioneers did was to have this enormous tome published at Ephrata in 1749. Some of the pioneers also owned the *Enchiridion* or *Handbook* of Dirck Philips. The *Enchiridion* passed through five German editions in America, 1811-1917, and appeared in English in 1910. Then there were books of sermons by Jacob Denner, 1659-1746, and by John Deknatel, 1698-1759, two European Mennonite ministers. A popular yet queer book was J. P. Schabalje's *The Wandering Soul,* originally published in Dutch in 1635. Then there was also the catechism of Gerhard Roosen, *Conversation on Saving Faith,* published originally in the year 1702. The American pioneers also had a German book called *The Christian's Serious Duty* which was apparently the prayer book of the Palatine Mennonites. American Mennonites also made considerable use of some Lutheran books such as John Arndt's *True Christianity.* Arndt lived from 1555 to 1621.

The first American Mennonite writer was Bishop Henry Funk of Franconia. In 1744 he wrote a little book in German called *Mirror of Baptism.* And three years after his death, which occurred in 1760, Funk's children published another of their father's German treatises entitled, *Restitution, or How Christ Fulfilled the Law and the Prophets.* In 1770 Christopher Dock, "the pious Mennonite schoolmaster of the Skippack," finally allowed his German treatise of 1750 entitled, *School-Management,* to be published—the earliest American treatise on pedagogy. A Doylestown minister, Abraham Gottshall, published both in German and English a book on regeneration entitled, *A Description of the New Creature,* in 1838. In 1804 Bishop Christian Burkholder of the Lancaster Conference published a German book, *Anrede an die Jugend* (*Address to Youth*), a volume which has passed through eight German and five English editions.

In more recent times one of the successful authors of the church was A. D. Wenger of Virginia. After making a thirteen-month tour of the world Wenger published his *Six Months in Bible Lands,* 1902. This book is found in Mennonite homes all over the country. *Jacob's Ladder,* a little book of sermons by J. E. Hartzler, published in 1908, is also found in many Mennonite libraries. The first sizable book on the teachings of the Bible as understood by modern Mennonites, *Bible Doctrine,* appeared, with Daniel Kauffman as editor, in 1914. The only book to be written by an American Mennonite which achieved any considerable circulation outside the church is *Modern Religious Liberalism* (1920), by John Horsch, 1867-1941, of Scottdale, Pennsylvania.

If one wishes to study the literature published by American Mennonites, the book of Harold S. Bender, *Two Centuries of American Mennonite Literature, 1727-1928,* Goshen, Indiana, 1929, will be found indispensable. More recent works by Mennonites are listed in the catalogs of the several Mennonite bookstores.

2. Confessions of Faith

A few introductory remarks must be made in connection with Mennonite Confessions. At the outset it should be stated that a number of individuals in the Mennonite Church have prepared formal doctrinal statements. Such statements, therefore, oftentimes represent single individuals rather than the church. It is also apparent that only the more significant confessions can be mentioned here. Attention should also be called to the fact that Mennonites are not a creedal church, strictly speaking. In the final analysis Mennonites are bound only by the Word of God, not by any human interpretation of it, although confessions of faith as adopted by the church have great weight. (Compare the Editorial note on page 214.)

The earliest known Mennonite confession is called *The Seven Articles of Schleitheim.* Schleitheim, called "Schlaten" in the dialect of that region, is a village near Schaffhausen, Switzerland. The main author of the Seven Articles was Michael Sattler who was burned at the stake some three months later (May 21, 1527). The Seven Articles treat the following points: baptism, the ban (discipline), the Lord's Supper, separation from the world, pastors, nonresistance, and the oath. (See pages 206-213 of this book.)

One of the longer confessions is that of P. J. Twisck, 1565-1636, consisting of thirty-three articles. In the 1938 edition of *Martyrs' Mirror* this confession is printed, anonymously and without date, on pages 373-410.

Fifteen ministers produced the "Concept of Cologne" on May 1, 1591. Several decades later two Dutchmen, John de Ries and Lubbert Gerrits, published another confession (1610). And then followed three Dutch confessions in quick succession. The "Olive Branch," or "Scriptural Instruction" is dated September 27, 1627; it is printed in the 1938 edition of *Martyrs' Mirror* on pages 27-33. John Cents wrote another confession on October 7, 1630. It is found on pages 33-38 of *Martyrs' Mirror.* The well-known "Eighteen Articles of Dordrecht" were written in the first draft by an old bishop, Adrian Cornelis, and adopted at a conference of fifty-one Flemish and Friesian Mennonite ministers at Dordrecht, Holland, April 21, 1632. Cornelis died that same year. He had the great joy of seeing his confession unite two groups of Mennonites. The Alsatian Mennonites adopted the Dordrecht (or Dort) articles, February 4, 1660. It was probably due to the influence of the Dutch William Rittenhouse of Germantown that the Dordrecht articles became the standard confession of the "Mennonite Church." This confession has been used historically in the instruction of candidates for baptism. The Eighteen Articles are found on pages 38-44 of *Martyrs' Mirror.* The Dordrecht confession was formally adopted at a conference of Franconia and Lancaster ministers in the year 1725.

One of the longer confessions is the Thirty-three Articles of Cornelis Ris of Hoorn, Holland, 1766. This confession was translated from the Dutch to the German by C. J. van der Smissen in 1849. A. S. Shelly translated it from the German into the English about 1902. It is the standard confession of the General Conference of the Mennonite Church of North America.

The Hutterian confession was written by Peter Riedemann about 1543.

Courtesy of the James A. Bell Publishing Co., Elkhart, Indiana

John F. Funk, 1835-1930; Pioneer Mennonite Publisher
(A photograph taken on his ninetieth birthday anniversary)

John S. Coffman, 1848-99; Pioneer Mennonite Evangelist
(Taken from a family picture made about 1892)

Reproduced from the "Wenger Family History," opposite page 56

Samuel Coffman, 1822-94; a Nineteenth Century Bishop in the Virginia Mennonite Conference

The

Christian

CONFESSION

Of the Faith of the harmless *Christians*, in the *Netherlands*, known by the name of

MENNONISTS.

AMSTERDAM.
Printed, and Re-printed and Sold by *Andrew Bradford* in *Philadelphia*, in the Year, 1727.

Exact Facsimile of the Title Page of the First American Mennonite Imprint, Reproduced from the Copy in the Library of the Historical Society of Pennsylvania

3. Hymnody

Mennonites have always delighted in music. They themselves have produced many hymns, but of these compositions many were originally not intended for publication. The bulk of the hymns of the Hutterians, for example, was unpublished through the centuries. Finally 344 of their hymns appeared in print for the first time in the year 1914. This hymnal had 894 pages. Some really beautiful German hymns are included in this collection.

The earliest Swiss Brethren hymnal was called the *Ausbund,* a term which means "Selection of the Best." The first known edition of *Ausbund* is of the year 1564, and the copy at Goshen College is unique. The book passed through at least twelve European editions and has been printed at least seventeen times in America, 1742-1935. The *Ausbund* contains hymns of George Blaurock, Felix Manz, Michael Sattler, and many other early leaders of the Swiss Brethren. Some of the tunes indicated in the *Ausbund* suggest the use of the tunes of popular folk songs: "Toward Morn One Hears the Crowing Cocks" and "There Went a Maiden with a Jug." The *Ausbund* is still used by the Old Order Amish in their services—the "thick songbook."

The first American Mennonite hymnal, in German of course, was produced in Franconia in 1803, *Zions Harfe* (Zion's Harp). The last edition was published in 1904. The Lancaster hymnal, also in German, the *Unpartheyisches Gesangbuch,* (Impartial Songbook), passed through fifteen editions, 1804-1923. Of the American Mennonites, those in Virginia became the leaders in the music world. Their best book (English), *A Compilation of Genuine Church Music,* first appeared in 1832 and passed through twenty editions by the year 1942. From the fourth edition on, this book was called *Harmonia Sacra.* Strictly speaking, however, *Harmonia Sacra* was not a hymnal and was not used in regular worship. The Virginia Mennonite hymnal was an English book entitled, *A Collection of Psalms, Hymns and Spiritual Songs,* first published in 1847. This was followed in 1902 by the book which still is a favorite with the main body of American Mennonites, *Church and Sunday School Hymnal.* A *Supplement* was added to this hymnal in 1911. One of the best Mennonite hymnals is the *Church Hymnal, Mennonite,* published in 1927 and edited by John D. Brunk, 1872-1926, but it contains less than twenty hymns by Mennonite authors. Among these authors are Deacon Henry B. Brenneman, 1831-1887, of Ohio;

Deacon Menno M. Brubacher of Canada; Elsie Byler; Minister John S. Coffman, 1848-1899; Bishop S. F. Coffman, 1872- , of Canada; Minister Samuel Good, 1878-1905, of Illinois; Bishop Amos Herr, 1816-1897, of Lancaster; A. B. Kolb, 1862-1925, of Canada; Levi Mumaw, 1879-1935, of Scottdale, Pennsylvania; and Bishop J. S. Shoemaker, 1854-1936, of Illinois.

The General Conference hymn book is entitled *The Mennonite Hymnary.* It was edited by Walter H. Hohmann and Lester Hostetler and was first published in 1940. It is an excellent hymnal.

READINGS

Bender, H. S.: "The First Edition of the Ausbund," *The Mennonite Quarterly Review,* III, 2 (April 1929), 147-150.

Bender, H. S.: "A Brief Summary of American Mennonite Literature," *Christian Monitor,* Scottdale, Pennsylvania, February 1928, 50-52.

Bender, H. S.: "Literature and Hymnology of the Mennonites of Lancaster County, Pennsylvania," *The Mennonite Quarterly Review,* VI, 2 (July 1932), 156-168.

Bender, H. S.: *Two Centuries of American Mennonite Literature: A Bibliography of Mennonitica Americana, 1727-1928,* Goshen, Indiana, 1929.

Enss, Frieda E.: "Dielman Kolb and the Martyrs' Mirror," *The Youth's Christian Companion,* August 4, 1935, 662f.

Friedmann, Robert: "The Devotional Literature of the Mennonites in Danzig and East Prussia to 1800," *The Mennonite Quarterly Review,* Goshen, Indiana, XVIII, 3 (July 1944), 162-173.

Friedmann, Robert: "Dutch Mennonite Devotional Literature from Peter Peters to Joannes Deknatel, 1625-1753," *The Mennonite Quarterly Review,* Goshen, Indiana, XV, 3 (July 1941), 187-207.

Friedmann, Robert: "The Devotional Literature of the Swiss Brethren, 1600-1800," *The Mennonite Quarterly Review,* Goshen, Indiana, XVI, 4 (October 1942), 199-220.

Hohmann, Walter H.: "Development of Music in the Mennonite Church," *Proceedings of the third Annual Conference on Mennonite Cultural Problems.* Held at North Newton, Kansas, August 18 and 19, 1944, 11-22.

Horsch, John: "The Hymns of the Anabaptists and Early Mennonites," *Christian Monitor,* Scottdale, Pennsylvania, August 1916, 625.

Ramaker, A. J.: "Hymns and Hymn Writers Among the Anabaptists of the Sixteenth Century," *The Mennonite Quarterly Review,* Goshen, Indiana, III, 2 (April 1929), 93-131.

(Roosen, Gerhard, 1612-1711:) *Conversation on Saving Faith for the Young, in Questions and Answers,* Scottdale, Pennsylvania, 1941. (Contains the Longer Catechism of 148 questions, the Shorter Catechism of 35 questions, the Dordrecht Confession of Faith of 1632, etc.)

Umble, John: "The Old Order Amish, Their Hymns and Hymn Tunes," *The Journal of American Folk-Lore,* The American Folk-Lore Society, New York, Vol. 52, No. 203 (January-March 1939), 82-85.

Wenger, J. C.: "An Old Mennonite Hymn," *Gospel Herald,* Scottdale, Pennsylvania, March 16, 1939, 1074.

Wenger, J. C.: "The Schleitheim Confession of Faith," *The Mennonite Quarterly Review,* XIX, 4 (October 1945), 243-253 (Introduction and text).

Wenger, J. C.: "T. J. van Braght," *Gospel Herald,* December 29, 1938, 834.

CHAPTER XIII

The Theology of the Mennonites

A number of monographs on Anabaptism have been written and several books on Bible doctrine have been issued by Mennonite publishers, but the definitive Anabaptist-Mennonite theology is yet to appear. All that can be attempted here is a brief summary of the main outlines of the theology of the Anabaptists and Mennonites. One handicap to a historical survey is the paucity of theological treatises from the leaders of the brotherhood, for most of their writings treat of practical questions of Christian living, or matters of church discipline, or isolated doctrinal points. This is true even of Menno Simons' WORKS which will be quoted extensively in this discussion. This lack of theological treatises is not without its significance; it indicates the fundamental fact that Anabaptism and Mennonitism are more Biblical than theological.

One thing is certain: Anabaptism was essentially the logical outcome of the Protestant reformation. It was not an unbalanced, bizarre or fanatical movement. It was rather *a more earnest effort than the other Protestant groups made to break with religious and ecclesiastical tradition in order to render absolute obedience to the text of Scripture.* This point of view was regarded as revolutionary in the sixteenth century—as it is in modern Christendom. The Protestant reformers regarded Anabaptism as a dangerous acid that would eat away the very foundations of society. But the Brethren were determined to "live dangerously,"—if following the Scriptures is ever really dangerous. The Protestant "Revolution" itself involved definite hazards, but the rewards of facing those hazards far outweighed them. Since Anabaptism was simply a radical form of Protestantism, on the so-called fundamental doctrines the Anabaptists were in agreement with the Lutherans and the Reformed. This basic unity on the major doctrines of the Christian faith has often been overlooked by writers on the Anabaptists.

I MAJOR DOCTRINES

1. God

The Brethren held to the same doctrine of God as did the Protestant reformers. They believed in His personality and goodness. In 1550

Menno Simons, 1496-1561, wrote his *Confession of the Triune, Eternal, and True God, Father, Son, and Holy Ghost.* This little treatise begins thus:

> We believe and confess with the Holy Scriptures, that there is an only, eternal and true God, who is a Spirit. One God, who created heaven and earth, the sea, and all that is therein. Such a God whom heaven and the heaven of heavens cannot comprehend. Whose throne is heaven and earth His footstool; who measures "the waters in the hollow of his hand," who spanneth the heavens; who comprehendeth the dust of the earth in a measure, and weigheth the mountains in scales and the hills in a balance; who is as high as heaven, deeper than hell, lower than earth and broader than the sea; "Who only hath immortality, dwelling in the light which no man can approach unto; whom no man hath seen, nor can see;" who is an almighty, powerful and an over-ruling King, in the heavens above and in the earth beneath; whose strength, hand and power none can withstand. A "God of Gods, and a Lord of Lords;" there is none like unto Him, but He is a mighty, holy, terrible, praiseworthy, wonderful, and consuming fire; whose kingdom, power, dominion, majesty and glory is eternal, and shall endure forever, and besides this only, eternal, living, almighty over-ruling God and Lord we know no other; and since He is a Spirit so great, terrible, and invisible, He is also inexpressible, incomprehensible and indescribable. . . . (WORKS, II, 183).

2. Jesus Christ

The Anabaptists also held to the Deity and the true humanity of Jesus Christ. They believed all that the Scriptures teach on His virgin birth, on His supernatural miracles, His vicarious and substitutionary death, His bodily resurrection, and His glorious second coming. Menno, in the same book on the Trinity, 1550, wrote as follows on Christ's Person:

> And this same incomprehensible, inexpressible, spiritual, eternal, divine Being, which is begotten of the Father before every creature, divine and incomprehensible, we believe and confess to be Christ Jesus, the first and only begotten Son of God, "the first-born of every creature," the eternal Wisdom, the power of God, the everlasting Light, the eternal Truth, the everlasting Life, . . . , the eternal Word. . . (WORKS, II, 183).

On the incarnation of the Son Menno stated:

> . . . We believe and confess that this same eternal, wise, almighty, holy, true, living and incomprehensible Word, Christ Jesus, which in the beginning was with God and which was God, incomprehensible—born of the incomprehensible Father, before every creature, is in the fulness of time become, according to the unchangeable purpose and true promise of the Father, a true, visible, passive, hungry, thirsty and mortal man, in Mary the pure virgin, through the operation and overshadowing of the Holy Spirit, and is thus born of her. Yea, that He was like unto us in all things except sin; that He grew up as other men; and at the appointed time was baptized and entered

upon His ministerial office, the office of grace and love, which was enjoined upon Him from the Father, and which He obediently fulfilled. . . (WORKS, II, 184).

On the Deity of Christ Menno wrote clearly:

. . . We believe and confess Christ Jesus, with His heavenly Father, to be truly God; and that because of the plain testimony of the holy prophets, evangelists and apostles, as we may learn from the following Scriptures, and also from other texts. Isaiah says, "Unto us a child is born, unto us a son is given; and the government shall be upon his shoulder; and his name shall be called Wonderful, Counsellor, The mighty God, The everlasting Father, The Prince of Peace . . . Again, "Say unto the cities of Judah, Behold your God! . . ." (WORKS, II, 185).

While it is true that the Obbenites and early Mennonites held to a strange view of Mary's relation to Jesus before His birth, the Swiss Brethren did not share this notion and the Mennonites themselves soon dropped it. Note the statement given in the third paragraph of Article IV of the 1632 Dutch Mennonite Confession of Faith: "But how or in what manner this worthy body was prepared, or how the Word became flesh, and He himself man, we content ourselves with the declaration which the worthy evangelists have given . . ."

3. The Holy Spirit

The Anabaptists also believed in the personality and Deity of the Holy Spirit, regarding Him as the One who convicts men of their sin and leads them to saving faith in Christ the Lord. Menno wrote:

. . . We believe and confess the Holy Ghost to be a true, real, or personal Holy Ghost; and that in a divine way—even as the Father is a true Father, and the Son a true Son; which Holy Ghost is a mystery to all mankind, incomprehensible, inexpressible and indescribable. . . divine with His divine attributes, going forth from the Father through the Son, although He ever remains with God and in God, and is never separated from the being of the Father and the Son. And the reason that we confess Him to be such a true and real Holy Spirit, is because we are impelled to this by the Scriptures, for He descended upon Christ at His baptism in the bodily shape of a dove, and appeared unto the apostles as cloven tongues like as of fire; because we are baptized in His name as well as in the name of the Father and of the Son; because the prophets through Him prophesied, performed miracles and works, had dreams and saw visions; for He is a Distributor of the gifts of God, and that according to His will (WORKS, II, 186f).

It is therefore evident that the Anabaptists believed in God as existing in three Persons, Father, Son and Holy Spirit. They engaged in no speculation concerning the philosophical aspects of the Trinity for they were Biblicists rather than theologians. Yet, Menno did write a brief treatise on the Trinity which contains the following:

> . . . We believe and confess before God, before His angels, before all our brethren, and before all the world, that these three names, operations and powers, namely, the Father, Son and Holy Ghost (which the fathers called three persons, by which they meant the three, true, divine Beings) are one incomprehensible, indescribable, almighty, holy, only, eternal and sovereign God. . . And although they are three, yet in Godliness, will, power and operation they are one. . . All the Father does and has wrought from the beginning, He works through His Son, in the power of His holy and eternal Spirit. . . If we deny the divinity of Christ, or the true existence of the Holy Ghost, then we counterfeit and depict unto ourselves a God who is without wisdom, power, light, life, truth, word, and without the Holy Spirit (WORKS, II,187).

The interested reader should examine also "The Theology of Pilgram Marpeck," in *The Mennonite Quarterly Review,* XII, 205-256 (October, 1938), especially pages 214-217.

4. Sin

The Anabaptists believed in the sinfulness of human nature (original sin) and in man's total inability to deliver himself from sin. Menno commented thus on human depravity and sin:

> A carnal man cannot apprehend or comprehend divine things, for by nature he has not that discernment; but on the contrary his mind is depraved; God is not in his mind. A carnal man cannot understand spiritual things, for he is by nature a child of the devil, and is not spiritually minded, hence, he comprehends nothing spiritual; for by nature he is a stranger to God; has nothing of a divine nature dwelling in him, nor has communion with God, but is much rather at enmity with Him; he is unmerciful, unjust, unclean, not peaceable, impatient, disobedient, without understanding and unhappy. So are all men by nature according to their birth and origin after the flesh. This is the first or old Adam, and is comprised in the Scriptures in a single word, ungodly, that is, without God, a stranger and destitute of the divine nature (WORKS, I, 232; cf. II 312f).

5. Regeneration

On the subject of the new birth Menno's friend and colleague, Dirck Philips, 1504-68, wrote:

> Jesus testifies of this to Nicodemus and says: "Verily, verily, I say unto thee, Except a man be born again, he cannot see the kingdom of God. Verily, verily, I say unto thee, Except a man be born of water and of the Spirit, he cannot enter into the kingdom of God."
>
> Here the kingdom of God is absolutely denied to all who are not born again of God, and who are not created by Him anew after the inner man in His image. . .

This regeneration is not external, but in the mind, reason, and heart of man; in the reason or intelligence, and mind, in this that he learns to know the eternal, true and gracious God in Jesus Christ, who is the eternal image of the Father. . . , and the brightness and express image of the Person of God. In the heart, in this that man loves this same almighty and living God, fears, honors and believes in Him, trusts in His promises, which cannot be without the power of the Holy Spirit, who must inoculate into the heart, as it were, with divine power, giving faith, fear, love, hope and all the divine virtues (ENCHIRIDION, English Edition, 1910, 376f).

In his treatise on *The New Birth,* 1556, Menno wrote:

True repentance and the birth from above, must take place; we must believe Christ and His word, and we must abide by His Spirit, ordinance and example willingly, or eternal misery must be our portion. This is incontrovertible (WORKS, 1, 171).

Menno wrote further:

The new birth consists, verily, not in water nor in words, but it is the heavenly, living and quickening power of God in our hearts which comes from God, and which by the preaching of the divine Word, if we accept it by faith, quickens, renews, pierces, and converts our hearts, so that we are changed and converted from unbelief into faith, from unrighteousness into righteousness, from evil into good, from carnality into spirituality, from the earthly into the heavenly, [and] from the wicked nature of Adam into the good nature of Jesus Christ. . . (II, 215).

6. Holiness of Life

The Christian life is one of holiness, of following after Christ Jesus as Lord. Menno wrote:

. . . The chosen of God are the church of Christ, His saints and beloved, who washed their clothes in the blood of the Lamb, who are born of God, influenced by the Spirit of Christ; who are in Christ and He in them, who hear and believe His word, who follow Him in their weakness, in His commandments, walk in His footsteps with all patience and humility, hate the evil, and love the good, earnestly desiring to apprehend Christ as they are apprehended of Him, for all who are in Christ are new creatures, flesh of His flesh, bone of His bone, and members of His body (WORKS, I, 161f).

Behold, this is the word and will of the Lord, that all who hear and believe the word of God shall be baptized. . . , thereby to profess their faith, and declare that they will henceforth not live according to their own will but according to the will of God. That for the testimony of Jesus they are prepared to forsake their homes, chattels, lands and lives, and to suffer hunger, affliction, oppression, persecution, the cross and death; yea, they desire to bury the flesh with its lusts, and arise with Christ to newness of life, even as Paul says, "Know ye not, that so many of us as were baptized into Jesus Christ were baptized into his death? Therefore we are buried with him by baptism into death: that like as Christ was raised up from the dead by the glory of the Father, even so we also should walk in newness of life" (WORKS, 25f).

In 1582 John Wouters, a Mennonite of Dordrecht in Holland, was burned to death for his faith. While awaiting execution he wrote numerous letters to his friends. In a letter addressed to his only daughter, a child of about seven years, Wouters wrote:

> Thus, my dearest daughter, lay it to heart, despise it not, for it is of great importance to you; and diligently search (when you have received understanding from the Lord) the holy Scriptures, and you will find that we must follow Christ Jesus and obey Him unto the end; and you will also truly find the little flock who follow Christ. And this is the sign: they lead a penitent life; they avoid that which is evil, and delight in doing what is good; they hunger and thirst after righteousness: they are not conformed to the world; they crucify their sinful flesh more and more every day, to die unto sin which wars in their members; they strive and seek after that which is honest and of good report; they do evil to no one; they pray for their enemies; they do not resist their enemies; their words are yea that is yea, and nay that is nay; their word is their seal; they are sorry that they do not constantly live more holily, for which reason they often sigh and weep. Let not this, however, be the only sign by which you may know who follows Christ; but [they are] also these, namely, who bear the cross of Christ, for He says: "If any man will come after me, let him deny himself, and take up his cross daily, and follow me." . . . For He has said: "If they have persecuted me, they will also persecute you." . . . The apostle Paul declares to them and says that "all that will live godly in Christ Jesus shall suffer persecution" (MARTYRS MIRROR, 1938, 915).

7. Divine Grace

While the Anabaptists emphasized regeneration they also recognized that even those who have experienced the new birth continue to fall short of God's glory. But Christians enjoy the grace of God. Menno says expressly:

> . . . For Christ's sake we are in grace; for His sake we are heard; and for His sake our failings and transgressions, which are committed involuntarily, are remitted. For it is He who stands between His Father and His imperfect children, with His perfect righteousness, and with His innocent blood and death; and intercedes for all those who believe on Him and who strive by faith in the divine word, to turn from evil, follow that which is good and who sincerely desire, with Paul, that they may attain the perfection which is in Christ. . .
>
> Mark, beloved reader, that we do not believe nor teach that we are to be saved by our merits and works, as the envious accuse us of without truth; but that we are to be saved solely by grace, through Christ Jesus . . . (WORKS, II, 263).

To a troubled sister in the church Menno wrote:

> . . . We must all acknowledge, whosoever we are, that we are sinners in thoughts, words and works. . . . In and by yourself you are a poor sinner . . .

but in and through Christ you are justified and pleasing unto God, and accepted of Him in eternal grace as a daughter and child (WORKS, II, 402).

On the subject of God's grace Menno stated further:

> . . . All the truly regenerated and spiritual conform in all things to the word and ordinances of the Lord; not because they think to merit the propitiation of their sins and eternal life; by no means; in this matter they depend upon nothing except the true promise of the merciful Father, graciously given to all believers through the blood and merits of Christ, which blood is and ever will be the only eternal medium of our reconciliation, and not works, baptism or Lord's supper. . .
>
> For if our reconciliation depended upon works and ceremonies, then it would not be grace, and the merits and fruits of the blood of Christ would be void. O no! it is grace, and will be grace to all eternity; all the merciful Father is doing or has done for us grievous sinners through His beloved Son and Holy Spirit is grace . . . (I, 158).
>
> . . . I have read in some books which they have written [undoubtedly he has in mind Luther, or perhaps Zwingli] that there is but *one* good work which saves us namely, FAITH, and but *one* sin which will damn us, namely, UNBELIEF. This I will leave as it is, and not find fault with it; for where there is a sincere, true *faith,* there are also all manner of sincere, good fruits. On the other hand, where there is unbelief, there are also all manner of evil fruits; therefore, is salvation properly ascribed to *faith,* and damnation to *unbelief* (WORKS, I, 159).

Dirck Philips, Menno's fellow-elder (bishop), taught the same doctrine of grace. Indeed Menno himself stated unqualifiedly: "Dirck and we are of the same mind" (II, 96). Dirck wrote:

> It must therefore be recognized that every Christian has sin and must confess himself a sinner, that he may humble himself under the mighty hand of God and pray the Lord for His mercy. Thus the Scripture remains true and unbroken which puts all men under condemnation and reproves them as sinners; but sin is not imputed to Christians, but has been forgiven them through the innocent death of Jesus Christ, and is covered with His everlasting love, by which He offered Himself up for us for an everlasting atonement for our sins, taking upon Himself our burden, and paying our debt with His bitter suffering, and making us a free gift of all that He has, so that He is one with us and we with Him, whereby we are made acceptable unto God, yea, accounted as saints of God. Therefore David says: "Blessed is he whose transgression is forgiven, whose sin is covered. Blessed is the man unto whom the Lord imputeth not iniquity (ENCHIRIDION, English edition, 1910, 282).

Matthew Cervaes, c. 1536-1565, a Mennonite elder of the Lower Rhine who was beheaded June 30, 1565 at Cologne, wrote:

> . . . We may not seek righteousness or salvation from our works, from what we do or do not do; for by the works of the law shall no flesh be justified before the Lord, as Paul says. Nor shall we be able to pay what we owe; but we hope to be justified and saved only through the grace of God,

through the merits of our Lord Jesus Christ (MARTYRS MIRROR, 1938 edition, 694).

In 1568 a Mennonite schoolteacher named Valerius was arrested as an Anabaptist in Zeeland in the Netherlands and after a long imprisonment was put to death as a heretic. During his imprisonment he wrote two books, one of which, *The Proof of Faith,* contains the following statement of salvation by grace:

If then we are to be saved through God's mercy, we must repent, must be obedient children of God, born again of Him, and must follow Christ in the regeneration and the footsteps of faith, through the narrow way unto eternal life; nor are we then saved through the merit of good works, but by the grace which came through Christ . . . For though we lived holy, blameless, and perfect in all righteousness (as the Scriptures require), and suffered for the truth a death more bitter than that of Christ, which with us men is impossible, yet we could not be saved through our own good works, but only by God's mercy, and the grace of our Lord Jesus Christ, who alone has wrought out our salvation. And if we sought or placed our salvation in our good works or our sufferings we should commit idolatry, and we were our own idol, if we trusted in ourselves. But now our salvation depends only on the mercy of God, and not on our running and following after . . . though we should run and follow after ever so well (which is our bounden duty), so that we attained, and already had, the perfection (that for which we are apprehended of Christ), and had done all those things which are commanded us, and which it is our duty to do, we were yet only unprofitable servants . . . How much more unprofitable then are we now, with our many defects, though we willingly strive after and should gladly perform that which is good, and are sorry that we are not perfect (Quoted in MARTYRS MIRROR, 1938, 730f).

8. The Church

The quotations on the Christian life have already indicated in part the Anabaptist conception of the church; it is nothing more or less than the fellowship of the saved. Menno describes the church thus:

In the first place, it should be taken into consideration that the community of God, or the church of Christ, is an assembly of the pious and a community of the saints as is represented by the Nicene symbol; who, from the beginning have firmly trusted and believed in the promised Seed of the woman, which is the promised Prophet, Messiah, Shiloh, King, Prince, Emmanuel and Christ; who accepted His word in sincerity of heart, follow His example, are led by His Spirit, and who trust in His promise in the Scriptures. . . (WORKS, II, 77).

9. Eschatology

The Swiss Brethren and the Mennonites also agreed with the Lutherans and the Reformed on eschatology. They looked for the personal return of the Lord Jesus to raise the dead, judge the world, and usher in the eternal state. The only "golden age" to which they looked forward was in heaven, not on this earth. Nicholas Blesdijk, c. 1500-1556, a Davidian, stated: "The followers of Obbe Philips, who are today called Mennonites, taught that no other condition of Christ's kingdom is to be expected than that which exists today, namely persecution by the world." The *Vindication* of Pilgram Marpeck, c. 1495-1556, contains fifty references to the Return of Christ. Menno Simons, after quoting from Luke 19, comments:

> This Scripture clearly testifies that the Lord Christ must first come again before all His enemies are punished. And how Christ will come again He Himself testifies, saying, "For the Son of man shall come in the glory of His Father, with His angels; and then He shall reward every man according to his works." Again, "For as the lightning cometh out of the east and shineth even unto the west; so shall also the coming of the Son of man be." "And then shall appear the sign of the Son of man in heaven: and then shall all the tribes of the earth mourn, and they shall see the Son of man coming in the clouds of heaven, with power and great glory." The two angels also testified how Christ would come again, saying, "Ye men of Galilee, why stand ye gazing up into heaven? This same Jesus, which is taken up from you into heaven, shall so come in like manner as ye have seen Him go into heaven."
>
> Further, the evangelist says, that Christ will take account with His servants, which will not be until the day of judgment. . .
>
> . . . "The Lord Jesus shall be revealed from heaven with His mighty angels, in flaming fire, taking vengeance on them that know not God, and that obey not the gospel of our Lord Jesus Christ." These angels will be the reapers who, at the end of the world, that is, in the day of judgment, will root up all the tares and cast them into the lake of fire. Until that time the tares will be left among the good seed; let none think that we should root up the tares now, or that we should now separate the goats from the sheep. "When the Son of man shall come in His glory, and all the holy angels with Him, then shall He sit upon the throne of His glory: and before Him shall be gathered all nations; and He shall separate them one from another, as a shepherd divideth His sheep from the goats; and He shall set the sheep on His right hand, but the goats on the left."
>
> These words are as clear as the sun, yet some do not understand them. . . (WORKS, II, 438f).

10. *Inspiration of the Bible*

On the great doctrines of God, Christ, the Holy Spirit, the Trinity, depravity and sin, regeneration, holiness of life, grace, and eschatology, the Brethren held common views with the Protestant bodies. In some respects they agreed also on the doctrine of the church. And, in common with all branches of the Christian Church in the sixteenth century, the Brethren believed in the absolute authority of the Bible. Menno said it was "impossible" for the Word of God to prove untrue (II, 438). The Scriptures are "the true witness of the Holy Ghost and the plummet of our consciences" (I, 167).

> . . .The whole Scriptures, both of the Old and New Testaments, were written for our instruction, admonition and correction; and . . . they are the true scepter and rule by which the Lord's kingdom, house, church and congregation must be governed and adjusted . . . Everything contrary to Scripture, whether it be in doctrines, faith, sacraments, worship or conduct, should be measured by this infallible rule, and demolished by this just and divine scepter, without any respect to persons, and brought to nothing (Menno's WORKS, I, 53f).
>
> Brethren, I tell you the truth and lie not. I am no Enoch, no Elias; I have no visions, am no prophet who can teach and prophesy differently from what it is written in the Word of God; (and whoever tries to teach something else will soon miss the right way and be deceived in his learning). I trust that the merciful Father will keep me in His Word so that I shall write or speak nothing but that which I can prove by Moses, the prophets, the evangelists or by other apostolic Scriptures and doctrines, explained in their true sense, spirit and intent of Christ. Judge ye that are spiritually minded. Again, I have no visions nor angelic inspirations, neither do I desire such lest I be thereby deceived. The Word of Christ alone is sufficient for me (II, 248).

In view of the above discussion of the position of the Brethren on the major doctrines of the Christian faith—and on those doctrines the Swiss and Dutch Anabaptists largely agreed—it is not surprising to find Zwingli addressing the Brethren in these words: "If one looks into this matter closely it is seen that you contend only for unimportant outward things." At the Zofingen debates, 1532, the Swiss Reformed clergy stated: "We are of one mind in the leading articles of faith, and our controversy has to do only with external things which are not in accordance with the gospel. . . " Again, Zwingli stated: "But that no one may suppose that the dissension is in regard to doctrines which concern the inner man, let it be said that they make us difficulty only because of questions such as these: whether infants or adults should be baptized and whether a Christian may be a magistrate."

In controversy however this basic agreement was quite overlooked and the Reformers spoke of the Anabaptists in most abusive terms. Zwingli stated that the Brethren "seek nothing but disturbance and confusion of affairs, both human and divine." Calvin referred to "the nefarious herd of Anabaptists." Luther spoke of the Anabaptists as "the devil's emissaries" and "the birds who devour the seed sown by the wayside." In the heat of their polemic the Reformers hurled charges against the Brethren which came wide of the truth. Indeed, most sixteenth century writers, no groups excepted, were lacking in grace and courtesy when they engaged in "religious" controversy.

II. MENNONITE EMPHASES

The unique tenets and emphases of the Mennonites theologically can perhaps be subsumed under three heads, relating to (A) the Bible, (B) the Church, and (C) the Christian Life and Ethic.

A. THE BIBLE

1. Evangelism, Not Theology

The Anabaptists were above all else men of the Word. They accepted the Bible, both the Old and New Testaments, as inspired of the Holy Spirit, as the very oracles of God. This was not unique with them for the Lutherans and the Reformed, as well as the Catholics, also believed in divine inspiration. But the Anabaptists made their attitude toward the Bible operate in daily life to a degree which seemed fanatical to many sixteenth century Christians. Furthermore, Luther in his reaction to ecclesiastical tradition and authority relaxed somewhat in his attitude toward the Biblical canon. Menno Simons took offense at Luther's derogatory remark concerning the Epistle of James (WORKS, I, III). In brief, the Anabaptists used the Bible not so much to erect a human system of theology as to redeem men from sin. In this sense they had a "practical" attitude toward the Bible, making it function in the salvation and the sanctification of men, rather than placing much stress on systems of thought or entering into the speculative problems of theology. And there is something wholesome about this point of view. It is much easier to theorize about the order of the divine decrees than to win converts for the Lord Jesus. It is much easier to get an intellectual grasp of the doctrines of Scripture than to apply the Scriptures to the whole man, to all of life. A few quotations from Menno's works will help elucidate the redemptive and Bible-centered attitude of the Brethren:

> I have served you all with this small gift as I received it from my God. I gladly would that I could serve you longer with great and abundant grace, to the praise of the Lord. Therefore have I renounced praise, honor, ease, and

forsaken all, and willingly submitted to the pressing cross of my Lord Jesus Christ, which ofttimes weighs very heavily on my weak flesh. I seek neither gold nor silver (the Lord knows this), but am ready with faithful Moses to suffer affliction with the people of God rather than to enjoy the pleasures of sin for a season; and I esteem the reproach of Christ greater riches than the treasures in Egypt, for I know what the Scriptures have promised us. And this is my only joy and desire of my heart, that I may extend the borders of the kingdom of God, publish the truth, reprove sin, teach righteousness, feed the hungry with the word of the Lord, lead the stray sheep into the right path, and win many souls to the Lord through His Spirit, power and grace, and so act in my weakness, as He taught me who purchased me, a miserable sinner, with His crimson blood, and gave me this mind, by the gospel of His grace, namely Jesus Christ: to Him be praise and glory and the eternal kingdom, Amen (I, 75).

. . . The Word of God is eternal. Neither princes, nor power, nor the commands of men with all their imperial edicts are to constitute faith, neither can a soul be saved by them. Only the heavenly counsel we must hear and follow, that which Jesus Christ, God's first and only begotten Son Himself brought from heaven and taught from the mouth of His Father and confirmed by signs and wonders, and finally sealed it with His crimson blood. This counsel stands and can never be changed or prevailed against by the gates of hell. By this counsel we are, in common, taught that we must hear Christ, believe in Him, follow His footsteps, repent, be born from above, become as little children, not in understanding but in malice, be of the same mind with Christ, walk as He did, deny ourselves, take up His cross and follow Him. . . (I, 175).

. . . The surest and best fruits are to so preach the Word of God in power that many may be born of Him and be led to sincerely fear and love Him, to cordially serve their neighbors, to die unto flesh and blood, to believe on Jesus Christ with all the heart, and tremble at His Word, that they may do nothing contrary to it, may truly worship God and conform their whole life or walk according to His Spirit, Word and example. . . (II, 24).

It was because of their wholehearted obedience to the Word of God, their determination to recognize only the Scriptures in matters of faith, that the Anabaptists defied all efforts of the state and of organized Christendom to coerce them in matters of faith. They were determined at all costs to follow God as He revealed His will in the Scriptures. They therefore demanded for themselves the right to have freedom of conscience. They resented and repulsed all efforts to settle matters of Christian faith by an appeal to church authority or to ecclesiastical tradition. In his *Exhortation to All in Authority* Menno wrote:

O you high-renowned lords and princes, turn to the truth of God and receive reproof and wisdom, for through wisdom kings reign and princes decree justice. Observe how far your spirit, faith and lives differ from the Lord's Spirit, Word and life (WORKS, I, 77).

> Do not excuse yourselves, beloved sirs and judges, that you are the servants of the emperor; this will not acquit you in the day of vengeance. . . (I, 86).
>
> Do not interfere with the right and kingdom of Christ, for He alone is the Ruler of the conscience, and beside Him there is none other. . . (I, 86).

2. *Biblicism*

The genius of Mennonitism has been to reject completely the traditional distinction between those New Testament commandments on the one hand which are binding both in form and spirit upon Christians for all time, and those on the other hand which are to be observed only in spirit. Most Christians hold that to the former class belong such items as baptism, communion and ordination, and that to the latter class belong such commands as to greet one another with a holy kiss, to wash one another's feet, and to anoint the sick with oil. The Mennonites, however, in the course of time began to stress the parity of all New Testament commands; this is of course a parity in authority, not in significance. The Mennonite Church of today has numerous ordinances and restrictions.

(*a*) Ordinances

Dirck Philips comments thus on (1) baptism (2) communion, and (3) feet washing:

> . . . The penitent, believing and regenerated children of God must be baptized, and for them the Lord's Supper is ordained. . . . These two symbols Christ gave and left behind and subjoined to the gospel because of the unspeakable grace of God and His covenant, to remind us therof with visible symbols, to put it before our eyes and to confirm it; in the first place by baptism, to remind us that He Himself baptizes within and in mercy accepts sinners, forgives them all their sins, cleanses them with His blood. . . , bestows upon them all His righteousness and the fulfilling of the law, and sanctifies them with the Spirit. . . In the second place, by the Lord's Supper, which testifies to divine acceptance and redemption by Jesus Christ . . , namely that all believing hearts who are sorry for their sins hasten to the throne of grace, Jesus Christ, believing and confessing that the Son of God died for them and has shed His blood for us . . . , obtain forgiveness of sin, deliverance from the law, everlasting justification and salvation, by grace through Jesus Christ. . . .
>
> These two symbols are left us by the Lord that they might admonish us to a godly walk. . . , to a crucifixion of the flesh, the burial of sin, a resurrection into newness of life, to thanksgiving for the great benefits which we have received of the Lord, to a remembrance of the bitter suffering and death of Christ, to the renewing and confirming of brotherly love, unity and fellowship. . . . (ENCHIRIDION, 1910, 386f).

[3] The third ordinance is the washing of feet of the saints which Jesus Christ commanded His disciples to observe [John 13:1-17], and this for two reasons. First, He would have us know that He Himself must cleanse us after the inner man, and that we must allow Him to wash away the sins which beset us. . . (*Ibid.*, 388).

The second reason why Jesus instituted the ordinance of foot washing is that we shall humble ourselves among one another. . . , and that we hold our fellow believers in the highest respect for the reason that they are the saints of God and members of the body of Jesus Christ, and that the Holy Ghost dwells in them. . . (*Ibid.*, 389).

(4) There seems to be no extended discussion of the holy kiss by the early Anabaptists. But Thomas of Imbroich, 1533-58, beheaded for Anabaptism at Cologne, wrote to his wife, "Greet all the saints with the kiss of love, and all who love the Lord Jesus, and tell them to be kind . . . (MARTYRS' MIRROR, 1938, 581). The *Martyrs' Mirror* contains a number of cases of Brethren greeting one another with a kiss (471, 474, 591). In 1565 Matthew Cervaes several times encouraged his fellow believers to practice this "holy kiss of love" (*M. M.*, 697, 700, 702). Menno Simons says that "the greeting or kiss of peace signifies the communion" [that is, Christian love in Christ's fellowship, the church]; he states that if an apostate should come "we should not greet him as a brother lest we have communion with him" (WORKS, II, 278). The Brethren were of course correct in regarding the "holy kiss" of the New Testament (Rom. 16:16; I Cor. 16:20; II Cor. 13:12; I Thess. 5:26; I Pet. 5:14) as a symbol of fervent Christian love. How often the Anabaptists practiced this greeting or on what occasions we do not know.

(5) There seems to be no mention in Anabaptist writings of anointing with oil. Modern Mennonites, when ill, sometimes send for the elders of the church and ask to be anointed with oil for the healing of the body (James 5:14, 15). How long this has been observed is not known. In 1527 Michael Sattler stated that the Roman Catholic sacrament of extreme unction is not identical with the oil mentioned in James 5. In the same year an Anabaptist martyr, a woman named Weynken was asked, "What do you hold concerning the holy oil?" With facetious "misunderstanding" she replied, "Oil is good for salad, or to oil your shoes with" (*M. M.*, 423; cf. 778). But the woman had in mind extreme unction, not the modern Mennonite practice of anointing with oil for God to heal the body.

(6) Because of Paul's teaching (I Corinthians 11:2-16) that women should be veiled when participating in the worship of God the baptized girls and women of a number of Mennonite conferences now wear, while worshipping, a special "covering" or veil on their heads to symbolize the headship of man. This point received no literary treatment by Mennonites in previous centuries, perhaps because in other Christian groups the women used to worship with their heads covered. Mennonite women have long worn a prayer veiling similar to that of the "Mennonite Church" of today. For example, in the beautiful painting by Rembrandt of "The Mennonite Preacher C. C. Anslo and a Widow," now in the National Gallery of Berlin, Germany, if not destroyed during the second World War, the woman is wearing a covering on her head much like that of the modern Mennonite church. (Claesz Anslo, 1592-1646, was a Waterlander Mennonite Minister, ordained in 1617. Rembrandt's painting was made in 1641, more than three centuries ago.)

Each of the above practices has a valuable symbolical significance; none has any value apart from faith and obedience. Baptism symbolizes the convert's faith in the power of Christ to cleanse from the guilt of sin. The Lord's Supper symbolizes faith in Christ as the One who has given His life for the redemption of the race. Feetwashing is a symbol of Christian brotherhood within the church. The holy kiss is a symbol of fervent Christian love in the fellowship of the saints. Anointing with oil symbolizes the power of God to heal the body. The prayer veiling is a symbol of the preeminence of man in administration and function (not in importance or in personal gifts).

(7) About the close of the nineteenth century certain ministers in the "Mennonite Church" began to teach that the Bible prescribes *seven* ordinances. In this sense an ordinance is a practice commanded in the Word of God; it is binding upon the Church; and it symbolizes a Christian virtue or truth. We have just listed six ordinances, but what is the seventh? The modern formulation is that it is marriage. Marriage is indeed a God-ordained relationship, and it therefore does seem appropriate for the wedding ceremony to be performed before the Christian congregation by a minister of the church. The *Martyrs' Mirror* indicates that some sixteenth-century Mennonite weddings did take place before the assembly (pages 515, 516, 675, 925, 927, 929, 936, 1004).

(8) One other rite has been committed to the church, namely the laying-on of hands in ordination (I Timothy 4:14; Titus 1:5; Hebrews 6:2; Acts 14:23). For four centuries the Mennonite Church has had three types of ordained men: (1) the elders or bishops, each of whom is the chief pastor of one or more congregations; (2) the ministers who serve as teachers of God's Word and as assistant pastors of the congregations; (3) the deacons who assist the elders in administering such ordinances as baptism and communion, and who have charge of administering the alms of the church.

As noted above Mennonites reject the traditional distinction between ordinances which are binding upon the church for all time and those which are to be kept only in spirit. They hold that all New Testament commandments are to be kept literally by all believers everywhere as long as the world stands. There is no exegetical consideration against the observance of feetwashing, for example, which would not also bear against the observance of baptism.

(*b*) Restrictions

There are other portions of Scripture which are taken in an absolute sense by Mennonites but which are not so understood by most Protestant bodies. This accounts for some of the distinctive positions held by Mennonites in the field of Christian ethics.

(1) A number of New Testament verses teach unqualified love for and nonresistance to evil men as the divine ethic for Christian believers. Among these passages are Matthew 5:38-48; Luke 6:27-36; John 18:36; Romans 12:17-21; I Thessalonians 5:15; II Timothy 2:24; Hebrews 12:14; I Peter 2:20-23; 3:8, 9, 13, 17. These verses require no "interpretation"; they are entirely clear. Consider the following, for example, from Romans 12:

> Dearly beloved, avenge not yourselves, but rather give place unto [God's] wrath: for it is written, Vengeance is mine; I will repay, saith the Lord. Therefore if thine enemy hunger, feed him; if he thirst, give him drink: for in so doing thou shalt heap coals of fire on his head. Be not overcome of evil, but overcome evil with good.

In a simple acceptance of this as the Christian ethic Mennonites oppose the use of force in private life and also reject military service in every form. They hold this position humbly, aware of the fact that there are many believers who cannot understand them.

They base their ethic of nonresistance on both the letter and spirit of the New Testament, believing that the Christian's calling is to "make disciples of all nations" (Matt. 28:19). The question is not so much "how far to take" the verses on nonresistance; it is rather this: If one seeks to obey these verses at all, can one participate in warfare? Can there be a more complete violation of the law of love than the waging of modern warfare?

It is because of these verses on nonresistance that Mennonites also refuse to do police service, or to be a magistrate. They frown even on jury service. *The calling of the Christian is evangelism, not the dispensing of justice in the state.* It does not follow, however, that Mennonites condemn the state. On the contrary the state is ordained of God to administer law and justice *in a society of evil-doers.* In that sphere the state is absolutely necessary. Evil men must frequently be restrained by force. But that task is not assigned by God to the saints. Christians are obligated, however, to obey the government in all matters (Rom. 13:1-7; Titus 3:1; I Pet. 2:13, 14) save where the demands of a ruler may conflict with the law of God (Acts 4:19; 5:29). All taxes are to be paid (Matt. 22:15-21; Rom. 13:7). The Schleitheim Confession of Faith, 1527, asserts that the state is ordained of God *outside the perfection of Christ.* This is based on the belief that the Christian ethic is for Christians, not for the state. The only means which the church has to cope with transgressors is admonition, and finally excommunication in case of impenitence.

Critics of the nonresistant Anabaptists sometimes try to point out certain logical difficulties in connection with their position. But the critics have some difficult exegetical considerations to deal with themselves, as well as the problem of just how to divide a man into two persons: the Christian who seeks the welfare and salvation of all men, and the policeman or soldier who must take human life in the pursuit of his work.

From its very inception in 1525 the Mennonite Church has held the principle of nonresistance. Conrad Grebel, the founder of the Swiss Brethren Church, wrote in September 1524: "True, believing Christians are as sheep in the midst of wolves. . . . They use neither the worldly sword nor engage in war, since among them taking human life has ceased entirely, for we are no longer under the Old Covenant." Felix Manz, a colleague of Grebel, said, "No Christian smites with the sword nor resists evil." Pilgram Marpeck said of the Christians, "All bodily, worldly, carnal earthly fighting, conflicts and wars are annulled and abolished among them through such law." The Dutch Mennonites took the same stand as the Swiss Brethren. Dirck Philips testified that "The people of the Lord arm themselves not with carnal weapons . . . but with the armor of God, with the weapons of righteousness . . . and with Christian patience, with which to possess their souls and overcome all their enemies." Menno Simons wrote, "The regenerated do not go to war, nor engage in strife. They are the children of peace . . . and know of no war. They render unto Caesar the things that are Caesar's and unto God the things that are God's. Their sword is the sword of the Spirit which they wield with a good conscience through the Holy Ghost."

The Mennonites of Europe have largely given up the Anabaptist position on war. The first country in which the Mennonites weakened on the doctrine of nonresistance was Holland. After the Napoleonic period the Dutch Mennonites took a progressively weaker stand, and by the middle of the last century nonresistance among them was about dead. Mention has already been made of the determined group of Mennonites who emigrated from Balk, Holland, to New Paris, Indiana, in 1853, to maintain the doctrine of nonresistance. Very few Dutch Mennonites took a stand for the historic faith of the church during the first World War. However, the new "Gemeentedag" Movement has nonresistance as one of its emphases.

About the middle of the past century the Prussian Mennonites were also weakening in their stand for nonresistance. King Wilhelm I issued a cabinet order in 1868 which permitted the Mennonites to do noncombatant service, but in the Franco-Prussian war of 1870-71 many German Mennonites voluntarily accepted combatant service. German militarism led many nonresistant Mennonites to emigrate to the western part of the United States, especially Kansas, in the nineteenth century. In World War I almost all the Mennonite soldiers of North Germany voluntarily bore arms. The doctrine itself was formally given up in 1934.

The story in South Germany is similar to that of Prussia, a gradual giving up of the doctrine of nonresistance. A large emigration of nonresistant Mennonites took place to America between the years 1817 and 1860 because of a fear of military service. Today there is not even sympathy for the nonresistant position on the part of many German Mennonites.

It was in France that compulsory military service began. Beginning in 1688 certain men were conscripted by lot. Since the time of Napoleon there has been no place in France for conscientious objectors to military duties. Everyone simply takes military training or faces the consequences, which means imprisonment at the least, or possible death in time of war. The French Mennonites of today are therefore not nonresistant. Many Alsatian Amish emigrated to America after 1815 to escape the rigid militarism of the French.

Switzerland is the only country where Mennonites suffered any hardships because of nonresistance prior to the time of Napoleon. Not only did the Swiss hire out their young men as mercenary soldiers to other countries, Berne also made a law making it obligatory for all her citizens to be armed. The Mennonites of course refused to carry any weapons and were constantly harassed on this account, even as late as the early part of the nineteenth century. They won the right to pay a fine in lieu of military service in 1815, but lost this right in 1874 when they were at last given the full privilege of citizenship. In 1937 when Bishop Johann Kipfer of Langnau, the oldest Mennonite congregation in existence, wrote a little confession of faith, he did not even mention nonresistance, though this was displeasing to some of his brethren. Most of the Swiss Mennonites today stop short of bearing arms, although all accept the military uniform. They are taking a stronger stand for nonresistance than any other European Mennonites.

When the Prussian Mennonites settled in South Russia in the last decades of the eighteenth century, they were promised military exemption forever. About 1870 it began to appear that the "forever" had already expired and the Russian Mennonites began to look for a new national home. A key man at this time of crisis was John F. Funk of Elkhart, Indiana. On June 11, 1895, Peter Jansen, 1852-1923, wrote to Funk as follows: "I would call your attention to the fact that the correspondence of Father with yourself was really the first step towards the Mennonite Immigration to the U. S. I recently found some of your letters written to Father in Russia in 1871 & 72." The father of Peter Jansen was Cornelius Jansen who led the Russian emigration of 1873 to North America.

In the end, however, the Mennonites who remained in Russia were not required to bear arms. A system of nonmilitary forestry service was devised, a system which was fairly satisfactory to the church. The Russian Mennonites remained nonresistant until the crises of the first World War bore down upon them. When bands of ruthless bandits plundered in the Mennonite colonies of the Ukraine, some young men, unable to remain passive, disregarded the protests of the majority and took up arms, forming a self-defense corps. Even from a practical point of view, this was a mistake, for when the little Mennonite army was overpowered the abuse became more horrible than before. Since that time cold-blooded execution and Siberian exile have broken the organized church life of the Russian Mennonites. Nonresistance is probably one of their lesser worries, for even faith in Christ is probably dying in the younger generation.

Prior to 1940 nonresistance was not put to a test in the United States except in time of war. There is no guarantee in the constitution of the United States that pacifists shall enjoy military exemption. The Supreme Court of the United States in 1946 granted citizenship to a pacifist of some sort. The United States has, moreover, shown consideration to those whose conscience forbids participation in warfare. During the American Civil War, 1861-65, Mennonites secured military exemption by the payment of a fee of $300, or by hiring a substitute. Farm furloughs and release for relief work were provided for Mennonites, Friends, and Brethren during the first World War, 1914-18. The matter was handled quite admirably during the second World War, 1939-45, by creating Civilian Public Service camps and units. In "C.P.S.," as it was familiarly known to hosts of Mennonites, conscientious objectors to warfare did work of national importance, such as forestry service and soil conservation work, under civilian direction. Many objectors also served as attendants in mental hospitals where they rendered a splendid service. The cost of the C.P.S. program to the Mennonite Central Committee for the fiscal year ending November 30, 1945 was about $825,000. Congressional action prevented large numbers of inducted Mennonites from serving as relief workers in Europe and Asia during the war. Nevertheless the Mennonite Central Committee was able to launch a relief program, which by November 30, 1945, amounted to $285,000 per year. C.P.S. and relief for 1945 did not mean a retrenchment in missionary receipts. The Mennonite Board of Missions and Charities, which handles only a part of the contributions of one group, the "Mennonite Church," received over $390,000 for missions during the fiscal year which ended April 1, 1946.

Both Brazil and Argentina have compulsory military training. This creates a problem both for the Russian Mennonite colonists of Brazil and for the North American missionaries of the Mennonite Church who are working in Argentina.

Of the countries where Mennonites live only two guarantee them military exemption: Canada and Paraguay.

Nonresistance and believer's baptism were the two most distinguishing tenets of the Swiss Brethren and the Dutch Mennonites. On the subject of nonresistance those interested may consult further Guy F. Hershberger's monograph, *War, Peace, and Nonresistance,* and John Horsch's treatise, *The Principle of Nonresistance as Held by the Mennonite Church;* also the writings of Conrad Grebel, Pilgram Marpeck, Menno Simons and Dirck Philips; and the several Mennonite confessions of faith.

Some of the writings of the early Dutch Mennonites seem to grant eternal salvation to good Christian rulers; note especially the last four paragraphs of page 87 of Part I of Menno's WORKS, and the last sentence of Article XIII of the Dordrecht Confession. It is extremely doubtful that these statements would have been acceptable to the Swiss Brethren. Modern Mennonites follow the Swiss in those points where they differed from the Brethren in the Netherlands.

(2) The Bible also forbids Christians to sue at law. The New Testament advises that it is better for Christians to suffer injustice than to achieve their "rights" by resorting to litigation. This position is a particular application of the broad principle of love and nonresistance. The New Testament says expressly:

> Dare any of you, having a matter against another, go to law before the unjust, and not before the saints? . . . Now therefore there is utterly a fault among you, because ye go to law one with another. Why do ye not rather take wrong? Why do ye not rather suffer yourselves to be defrauded? Nay, ye do wrong, and defraud, and that your brethren (Cf. I Cor. 6:1-7).

(3) Another point where Mennonites and other Protestant bodies differ is on the swearing of oaths. Jesus stated emphatically that although the Old Testament condemned only false oaths His followers should never swear at all. Rather they should let their every word be strictly truthful. The pertinent New Testament Scriptures are Matthew 5:33-37; 23:16-22; and James 5:12. Mennonites therefore merely make an affirmation when asked to take an oath.

Menno wrote in his *Clear Confession,* 1552:

> We are aware that the magistracy claim and say, *We are allowed to swear when justice is on our side.* This we simply answer with the word of the Lord. To swear truly was allowed to the Jews under the law; but the gospel forbids this to Christians. . . (WORKS, II, 273).

In his *Epistle to Martin Micron,* Menno added:

> The oath is required for no other purpose but that we shall truthfully testify. Can the truth not be told without being sworn? Do all testify to the truth, even, when under oath? To the first question you must answer in the affirmative, and to the last in the negative. . . (II, 410).

> . . . Christ's foundation and doctrine is that Moses had commanded not to forswear thyself, but that under the New Testament one should not swear at all. James says that we should not swear "neither by heaven, neither by the earth, neither by any other oath. . ." (Mark, he says neither by *any other oath*) and you gloze it . . . that it is not so but that we may swear to the truth. . . (WORKS, II, 410).

> I will let you teach and counsel . . . to fight and retaliate as did Moses and the patriarchs. . . ; teach them to punish, scatter, imprison and destroy their enemies; to adjudge the criminals no matter whether they repent or not, as you write. Teach them also to swear and be sworn after the manner that Moses commanded the Israelites. But I shall and will by the grace of God faithfully teach and counsel all truly regenerated children of God and followers of Christ, both rulers and subjects, according to the sure word of the holy gospel, to use no other sword than the one Christ Jesus and His holy apostles used; to be merciful unto the penitent sinners as Christ is merciful unto us; mercifully to punish the impenitent and to admonish them in love as Christ admonished us; and scrupulously to stand by their yea and nay as the true Teacher and Executor of the New Testament, the ever blessed Christ Jesus Himself, has distinctly commanded and taught us with His guiltless mouth; no matter what the consequences to my person may be . . . (II, 412).

(4) The awful oaths which bind the members of secret orders make it unthinkable for a non-swearing Christian to unite with such societies. But it is not only the oath which keeps Mennonites out of secret societies. The very principle of organized secrecy is unchristian. Jesus protested to the Jewish authorities that He had no secrets; His doctrine and teaching were open to all men (John 18:19, 20). It is the church which is to be *the* brotherhood of Christians. For a Christian to unite with a fraternal society, especially when some members are not even professing Christians, and share with this mixed body certain secret information which he may not divulge to his fellow believers in Christ's church, is utterly out of the question (II Corinthians 6:14—7:1). Furthermore, in the minds

of many people secret societies are a substitute for church membership. Being a lodge "brother" is often regarded as practically equivalent to being a member of Christ's body, the church. All Mennonite conferences therefore oppose membership in secret societies.

(5) Mennonites also teach the permanence of marriage, permitting a second union only when a life companion dies, and allowing formal separation only for adultery. This position they base on the following Scriptures: Matthew 5:31, 32; 19:3-9; Mark 10:2-12; Luke 16:18; Romans 7:1-3; I Corinthians 7:1-16, 39. In his *Foundation* Menno wrote:

> We acknowledge, teach, and approve of no other matrimony than that one which Christ and His apostles publicly and plainly taught in the New Testament, namely one man and one woman [Matt. 19:4], and that they may not be divorced except in case of adultery [Matt. 5:32], for the two are one flesh; but if the unbelieving depart, a sister or brother is not under bondage in that case [I Cor. 7:15]—WORKS, I, 83. (Cf. article "Ehe," in *Menn. Lexikon.*)

In speaking of Christ's kingdom Menno states:

> . . . Under this kingdom and under this King no other wedlock must be tolerated except between *one* man and *one* woman as God had in the beginning established in the union of Adam and Eve; and Christ has further said that these two are one flesh, and that they shall not separate, save for the cause of fornication [Matt. 5:32]—WORKS, I, 95f; cf. II, 277.

(6) Mennonites have for centuries placed much stress on simplicity of life. Considerable emphasis fell on the external appearance of the Christian; the wearing of jewelry, for example, is proscribed. Here are a number of quotations from the *Complete Works* of Menno Simons:

> And even as all things are pure to the pure, and are for the good of the pious, so also to the impure all things are impure, and to the evil all things are evil; because they are impure they use all the creatures of God impurely. They eat and drink to excess; they dress gorgeously; and engage in lewdness; they raise their children to idleness; they avariciously hoard gold, silver, houses and lands, and there is nothing they use purely according to the will of God; for they are impure, sensual, disobedient to the Word, and are earthly-minded, as the Scriptures say (I, 71).

> Beloved reader, take notice that all the proud, haughty, avaricious, carnal and adulterous who call themselves Christians, but who are by no means such, testify by their disposition, heart, mind and walk that they hate and are inimical to Christ. . . .
>
> They say that they believe, and yet there are no limits nor bounds to their accursed wantonness, foolish pomp, show of silks, velvet, costly clothes,

gold rings, chains, silver belts, pins, buttons, curiously adorned shirts, handkerchiefs, collars, veils, aprons, velvet shoes, slippers and such like foolish finery; never regarding that the enlightened apostles, Peter and Paul [I Pet. 3:3, 4; I Tim. 2:9, 10] have in plain and express words forbidden this to all Christian women. If this is forbidden to woman how much more then should men abstain from it, who are the leaders and heads of their women, notwithstanding all this they still want to be called the Christian church (I, 144).

This is not a kingdom in which a display is made of gold, silver, pearls, silk, velvet and costly finery, as is done by the proud, wicked world, and which also your leaders teach and give you liberty to do under this deception, viz., that it is harmless if you do not desire and serve them from your heart . . . (I, 96).

(7) In recent years the Mennonite Church has had to resist the unnatural and unscriptural practice of women cutting their hair. Paul stated that it was "a shame for a woman to be shorn or shaven" (I Cor. 11:6). On the same point he asks, "Does not even nature itself teach you that if a man have long hair it is a shame unto him? But if a woman have long hair it is a glory to her . . . ." Then he adds these significant words, "for her hair is given her for a covering." The verb for *given* is in the Greek perfect tense which, as Professor G. G. Findlay states, "connotes a *permanent* boon." It was none other than God who gave woman long hair in the first place. It is God who intends that woman should wear her hair long. And it is God who regards woman's hair as a natural covering to accompany the prayer veiling. The prayer veiling in turn, as indicated above, symbolizes the authority of man.

(8) In recent decades Mennonites have also found it necessary to warn their young people against worldly recreation in general and the moving picture theater in particular. It is well known that the moving picture industry, with its sensuous stars divorcing and remarrying continually, caters to those human desires which are not spiritual. Commercial moving pictures, by gratifying the carnal mind deaden spiritual life and draw the human heart away from God and His Word. Moving pictures create in young people false standards of life in general. Particularly do they portray impossible economic standards and an utterly unchristian view of courtship and of home life. On the subject of the moving picture theater the warning of the Apostle John is apropos: "Love not the world, neither the things that are in the world. If any man love the world, the love of the Father is not in him. For all that is in the world, the

lust of the flesh, and the lust of the eyes, and the pride of life, is not of the Father, but is of the world" (I John 2:15, 16), and Paul warns, "Therefore, brethren, we are debtors, not to the flesh, to live after the flesh. For if ye live after the flesh, ye shall die: but if ye through the Spirit do mortify the deeds of the body, ye shall live" (Romans 8:12, 13).

(9) From the very beginning of the church, Mennonites have emphasized the fact that the New Testament teaches church discipline. The Christian congregation, the entire brotherhood, is responsible to warn and restore those who may fall into sin (Gal. 6:1). In case the transgressor remains impenitent it becomes necessary to make known to the entire brotherhood that he is no longer a member of the church. This is what Paul meant when he told the Corinthian Church to "put away from among yourselves that wicked person" (I Cor. 5:13). This is not a matter of a minister's self-will and selfish love of power or of lording it over the congregation, all of which is condemned in the New Testament (Matt. 20:25-27; Mark 10:42-45; Luke 22:25-27; I Pet. 5:3). It is rather a solemn act with a threefold purpose: (1) It makes known to the obdurate sinner his true state before God—for Scriptural excommunication is attended by divine sanction (Matt. 16:18; 18:18). (2) It indicates to the brotherhood the awfulness of unrenounced sin and warns believers against such social fellowship with the sinner as might lead them into sin (I Cor. 5:9-11; Rom. 16:17; II Thess. 3:14; Tit. 3:10, 11). (3) It protects the good name of the church, the members of whom are to glorify God by their life. Menno Simons sets forth his views on church discipline in his books, *Excommunication, Ban, Exclusion . . .* , WORKS, I, 239-268, revised by him in the latter years of his life; and *Scriptural Explanation of Excommunication,* II, 121-137.

(10) It is amazing to observe how severely the Anabaptists were maligned by the state churchmen four centuries ago for seeking to maintain Scriptural standards of life and faith in their congregations. It is because of the same desire to uphold Biblical standards in the congregations of today that the Mennonite Church continues to practice close communion. It is not intended to suggest that there are no children of God in other denominations; both Menno Simons and Pilgram Marpeck acknowledged that there were saved people in other religious groups. Nor is close communion an anathema pub-

lished against all other Christians. Close communion is practiced because of a desire to maintain faithfully the Biblical ethic, for some professing believers are not Scripturally qualified to come to the Lord's table. Since it would be impossible and odd to try to exercise a Scriptural discipline over those who are not affiliated with one's particular group, the only position open to those who believe that the brotherhood is obligated to maintain Scriptural standards of faith and life is to offer the communion emblems only to those who share those standards and are faithful members of that Christian group.

In the liberalism of the present era this Mennonite "Biblicism" with its ordinances and restrictions may seem like a neo-legalism. It is not so intended. The obedience of love is never legalism; it is loveless conformity to a code which is legalism. A joyful awareness of the centrality and foundation of Christ's redemption and of God's grace will prevent this simple and earnest obedience to Christ's Word from degenerating into a formalistic legalism. Furthermore, the "danger" of taking the Bible too seriously is far less grave than the peril of secularism and worldliness.

3. *New Testament Finality*

All the ordinances and restrictions of the Mennonites, as shown above, are based on a literal obedience to the text of Scripture. Some of them, it should be noted, are also grounded on the distinction between the covenants of Moses and of Christ, a distinction which will here be examined briefly.

Mennonites regard the entire Bible as God's holy Word, "inspired and profitable." But they hold that Jesus Christ and His redemption stand at the center of time. All of God's dealings with man before Christ were in preparation for His redemption. The Old Covenant stood until the death of the One who instituted the New Covenant, until "the death of the Testator" (Heb. 9:16). The Old Covenant was not perfect in the sense that its blessings were inferior to those of the New (Heb. 8:6ff). The Old Testament prophets looked forward to the glory of the New Covenant with its deeper blessings, the New Covenant being less nationalistic and external and more personal and spiritual in character (Jer. 31:31-34; Heb. 8:7-13). Jesus Christ established this predicted New Covenant (Heb. 8:6; 9:13-17). The Old Testament *as a religious system* is therefore done away. It is displaced by the New Covenant with its better promises (Heb. 8:6), this New Covenant being in force since the death of Jesus (Heb. 9:15, 16). The New Covenant brought with it complete forgiveness for sin forever, with no need of further sacrifices for sin (Heb. 10:14-18).

Jesus Christ who established the New Covenant during His earthly life served as God's Prophet making known the will of God for man. All that Christ taught was by command of the Father. Christ's words were therefore the Word of God (John 12:49, 50). The four Gospels contain almost all that we know of the words of Jesus. In the fifth chapter of Matthew the Lord Jesus discussed His attitude toward the Old Testament, "the law and the prophets." He indicated first of all the durability and permanence of the Old Testament Scriptures; they will not fail (5:18). But they are fulfilled in Jesus and His teaching (5:17, 18). Then Jesus proceeded to give five illustrations of how He "fulfilled" the Old Testament. These relate to murder (5:21), adultery (5:27), divorce (5:31), oaths (5:33), and retaliation (5:38). In every case Jesus built upon the essential moral principles of the Old Testament and made those principles more penetrating and extensive than they had been in the Law. Not only is murder wrong, but he who hates is equally guilty of a lack of love (cf. I John 3:15). Not only is adultery wrong, but the lustful gaze indicates the same corrupt heart (cf. Mark 7:21). Not only shall divorce be strictly legalized, it shall be restricted to but one ground, infidelity (cf. Matt. 19:9). Not only are all false oaths prohibited, but all oaths whatsoever are to be done away (cf. James 5:12). Not only is illegal retaliation wrong, but all retaliation shall be desisted from (cf. Romans 12:17-21). In every respect the disciple of the Lord shall take an attitude of perfect love toward his enemies and wrongdoers; he shall imitate the Father in heaven who is beneficent toward both the evil and the good, toward those who defy Him and those who obey Him. He shall be perfect in love, even as God is perfect (5:48).

With this general interpretation the leading reformers of the sixteenth century were in basic agreement. They too believed that there was a difference between the Old Covenant and the New; indeed John Calvin wrote an excellent discussion of the matter (INSTITUTES, II, 11). The reformers also believed that Jesus had established the New Covenant. They believed further that Jesus gave His disciples an authoritative interpretation of God's moral law. But at that point the agreement ceases. The reformers ultimately limited that which Christ displaced to the Mosaic tabernacle, sacrificial system, priesthood, holy days and festivals, and ceremonially unclean foods. They refused to concede that what was permitted in the Old Testament could now be forbidden. They were of course not totally consistent in this point of view; for example, it was only in an awkward situation that Luther joined in permitting Elector Frederick to have two wives. But the reformers did not believe in granting religious liberty to the "heretical" Anabaptists—and in the Old Testament they found abundant authorization to suppress deviation from the faith of the covenant people. Furthermore, since wars and oaths were freely engaged in by Israel of old, even with divine sanction, the reformers refused to believe that Christ and His apostles meant in an absolute sense what they said about being nonresistant and not swearing at all. In addition to this the Anabaptist stress fell on the *fulfillment* of the Old Covenant by the New, while the reformers emphasized the essential *unity* of the two covenants. Consequently it was natural for the reformers to think in terms of a national church with all children of the citizen-members being baptized as infants quite as Israelitish children were circumcised from Abraham to Jesus.

Little wonder then that the Anabaptists were regarded as heretics when *they stated that the Old Testament was done away and when they demanded New Testament backing for every church ordinance and for the entire ethic of the Christian.* Pilgram Marpeck compiled an entire volume consisting of contrasting citations from the two testaments on every conceivable point of doctrine. Dirck Philips wrote as follows on the unity in spirit of the two covenants:

> So then the gospel and the law are divided so far as the figures, shadows and the letter of the law are concerned, which are all done away by the gospel. But it is essential that we take heed to the spirit of the law (for the law is spiritual, as Paul says. . .). We will then find that the signification, purport and real meaning of the law accords and agrees in every way with the gospel, yea, that it is one and the same truth. For as there is but one God so there is but one truth, for God Himself is the truth; but the letter (in which the truth is hidden) comes to an end. Thus the literal command of the Lord regarding circumcision of the flesh has come to an end, but the command regarding the spiritual circumcision of the heart remains [Rom. 2:25-29; Phil. 3:3; Col. 2:11] Thus all symbols of the law (which are too numerous to speak of here) have come to an end so far as the letter is concerned, nevertheless the true and essential signification of these same figures remains and accords with the gospel . . . . Thus the apostles and even the Lord Jesus Christ Himself many

times proved and confirmed the truth of the gospel with sayings and testimonies of the law and the prophets, thereby showing us that the truth of the gospel is embodied in the law and the prophets (ENCHIRIDION, 260, 261).

But in the preface to his book, *Of Spiritual Restitution,* Dirck stated that he had written

> . . . to the end that simple minds may be thereby instructed and that they may not be deceived by the false prophets who embellish and disguise their deceptive doctrine with the old leaven of the letter as shadows and figures; for whatever of the New Testament they cannot defend they try to prove with the Old Testament and with the letter of the prophecies. From this fallacy many sects have come, many false forms of worship have been established . . . (ENCHIRIDION, 323).

Menno Simons made numerous remarks regarding the necessity of having New Testament support for one's ethic and practice. Here are a few of them:

> . . . Even though an Elias himself were to come, he dare not teach anything against the foundation and doctrine of Christ and the apostles, but he must, if he would preach aright, teach and preach conformably to the same, for by the spirit, word, actions and example of Christ all must be judged and receive the last sentence; otherwise the whole Scriptures are false (I, 97).

In the course of a discussion on baptism he wrote:

> It is our determination in this matter as in all other matters of conscience . . . that we will not be influenced by lords and princes, nor by doctors and teachers of schools, nor by the influence of the fathers, and long established customs; for in this matter neither emperors nor kings nor doctors nor licentiates nor councils nor proscriptions against the Word of God will avail. We dare not be bound to any person, power, wisdom or times, but we must be governed alone by the expressed and positive commands of Christ, and pure doctrines and practices of His holy apostles. . . (I, 31).

After condemning "infant baptism, masses, matins, vespers, caps (of cardinals, etc.) palms, crosses, chapels, altars, bells, etc.," Menno adds:

> The true evangelical faith looks upon and has respect to the doctrine, ceremonies, commands, prohibitions and unblamable examples of Christ alone, and strives to conform thereto with all its powers. . . (I, 118).

> . . . We acknowledge the ever blessed Jesus alone for our Redeemer, Mediator, Intercessor, spiritual King, Example, Shepherd, infallible Teacher and Master; . . . we judge and prove all spirits, doctrines, councils, ordinances, statues and ceremonies as far as regards spirit and faith with the spirit, doctrine, ordinances, commands and ceremonies of Christ, and thus esteem the commands and ceremonies of men which are contrary to the commands and ceremonies of God not only as vain and useless but also as accursed and idolatrous according to the Scriptures. . . (I, 185).

The Anabaptists were above all else *men of the Word,* believers who insisted on striving to achieve absolute obedience to Christ and His New Testament.

B. THE CHURCH

1. Those Espousing Discipleship

Luther and Zwingli both decided to continue with the state system, to have a *Staats- und Volks-Kirche.* In this arrangement the common people had no choice but to accept the official religion of their land or emigrate. But large numbers of them did not take the matter of religion very seriously, as the reformers themselves lamented. In the early years of Luther's reform work his colleague, Philip Melanchthon, 1497-1560, stated that "Many believe themselves very pious and holy when they upbraid priests and monks or eat meat on Friday." This agrees with Menno's severe charge against the Lutherans:

> If anyone can simply say with them, Ah! what dishonest knaves and villains these desperate priests and monks are; . . . The ungodly pope with his shorn crew, say they, have deceived us long enough with purgatory, confession, and fasting; we now eat as we have hunger, fish or flesh, as we desire; for every creature of God is good, says Paul, and is not to be rejected. But what follows they do not want to understand or know; namely to [live as] the believing who know the truth and enjoy it with thanksgiving. They further say, How shamefully they have deceived us poor people; they have robbed us of the blood of the Lord and directed us to their mummery and to their enchanting works. God be praised, we now know that all our works avail nothing, for the blood and death of Christ alone must blot out and pay for our sins. They begin to sing a *psalm: Der Strick ist entzwei und wir sind frei,* etc, i.e., *The cord [of restraint] is cut asunder and we are free,* while the smell of beer and wine issues from their drunken mouths and noses. Anyone if he can but read this *distich,* if he live ever so carnally, is a good evangelical man and a fine brother. And should someone come who would in true and sincere love admonish or reprove them and direct them to Jesus Christ, to His doctrine, sacraments and unblamable example, and show that it does not become a Christian to carouse and drink, and to revile and curse, etc., he must from that hour hear that he is a legalist *(Werkheiliger),* a heaven-stormer or a factionist, a fanatic or hypocrite, a defamer of the sacrament or an Anabaptist (I, 112).

Menno listed six earmarks by which the true church of Christ may be known:

> 1. By an unadulterated, pure doctrine . . . 2. By a scriptural use of the sacramental signs . . . 3. By obedience to the Word . . . 4. By unfeigned brotherly love . . . 5. [By] an unreserved confession of God and Christ . . . 6. By oppression and tribulation for the sake of the Lord's Word. . . (II, 83).

Again Menno wrote to his "true brethren and sisters in Jesus Christ":

> . . . You must be conformed unto Christ in mind, spirit, courage and will, both in doctrine and life, as Christ Jesus is conformed unto the nature and image of His blessed heavenly Father, to which He was so conformed that He did nothing but what His Father did, Jn. 5; that He taught nothing but the word of His Father, Jn. 7. In the same manner with those who are begotten of the living, saving Word of our beloved Lord Jesus Christ; they are by virtue of their new birth so conformed unto Christ, so like unto Him, so really implanted into Him, so converted into His heavenly nature, that they do not teach nor believe any doctrine but that which conforms unto the doctrine of Christ; do not make use of any religious ceremonies but Christ's ceremonies which He has taught and commanded in Holy gospel. . . .
>
> . . . Such regenerated and godly minded live unblamably, even according to the measure of the rule of the holy gospel of Jesus Christ and His apostles. Therefore He kisses them as His beloved chosen ones with the mouth of His peace, Cant. 1, and calls them His church, His bride, flesh of His flesh, and bone of His bone. . . (II, 443).

In other words, for the Anabaptists it was impossible to accept the idea of a provincial church which embraced the entire population of the land, reckoning them all as Christians because they were *christened* as babes. The only people the Anabaptists could consider members of the church were *those who had made a personal commitment to Christ*. Let the indifferent and the carnal know where they are; let them be outside the church, lost and in need of evangelization. It was because of this conception of church membership as a commitment to an earnest Christian life that the Brethren insisted on believers' baptism. No infant could make a personal commitment to Christ nor assume the obligations of church membership. It does not follow however that the Anabaptists regarded infants as lost. Menno protested thus:

> . . . If it should be said that we rob the children of the promise and of the grace of God you will observe that they contradict us out of hatred and envy and do not tell the truth. Say, who has the strongest ground and hope of the salvation of their children? Is it he who places his hopes upon an outward sign [infant baptism]? Or is it he who bases his hopes upon the promise of grace given and promised of Christ Jesus? (II, 226).

Menno believed in the salvation of children because of,

> . . . The word of the Lord that the kingdom is promised them by grace, by the election of God our heavenly Father through the merits of Jesus Christ, as He says, "Suffer little children and forbid them not, to come unto me; for of such is the kingdom of heaven" . . . not the baptism of antichrist [infant baptism] but the promise of Jesus Christ assures us of the salvation of our little children if they die and depart from here. But if the good Father

suffer them to grow up and grant them His grace, then we would educate them in the instruction and fear of the Lord as much as we are able. When they can understand God's Word and believe it the Scripture directs them to be baptized [Matt. 28:19; Mark 16:16]—II, 318.

. . . For Jesus' sake sin is not imputed to infants that are innocent and incapable of understanding. [Eternal] life is promised not through any one ceremony but out of pure grace through the blood of the Lord. . . (I, 33).

On the subject of adult baptism Menno pleaded:

True Christians believe and obey. Are you a sincere Christian, born of God? Then why do you dread baptism which is among the least that God commanded you? . . .

He then made an extensive list of the demands which God makes upon His children to conform to Him in heart and life, and added:

We think that these and the like commands are more painful and difficult to perverse flesh, which is naturally so prone to follow its own way, than to have a handful of water applied; and a sincere Christian must be ready to do all this; if he is not, he is not born of God, for the regenerated are of one mind with Christ Jesus (I, 38).

2. *Kept Pure By Discipline*

The necessity of church discipline is the negative counterpart of the high calling of the church. If the church is composed of born-again, obedient disciples of the Lord Jesus, then any who grow cold and revert to a life of sin must be regarded as in need of restoration. The church must put forth every effort to win the backslider to a renewal of his Christian life. But if in spite of earnest entreaty and prayer the offender insists on continuing in his sin it becomes obligatory for the church to make known to him that he has placed himself outside the pale of the church. This is well set forth in Article XVI of the Dordrecht Confession of Faith, which should be consulted at this point. (Page 224 of this book.)

The reformers ridiculed the Anabaptists for exercising church discipline, claiming that it was practiced in violation of the teaching not to uproot the tares until the harvest (Matt. 13:24-30, 37-43). They also accused the Brethren of considering themselves an assembly of absolutely perfect Christians—an odd charge to bring against a group which insisted on dealing with its transgressors!

Menno Simons made it abundantly clear that church discipline did not apply to every kind of transgressions; only open transgressions are to be dealt with by the church.

> . . . Should it ever happen that anyone should sin against God in private, from which may His power preserve us all, and should the Spirit of grace which works repentance again operate upon his heart and cause genuine repentance, of this we have not to judge, for it is a matter between him and God. For since it is evident that we do not seek our righteousness and salvation, the remission of our sins, satisfaction, reconciliation and eternal life in or through excommunication but alone in the righteousness, intercession, merits, death and blood of Christ. There are but two objects and ends why the ban [excommunication] is commanded in the Scriptures, which can have no reference to such an one. Because in the first place his sins are private, hence no offense can follow. And secondly because he is in deep contrition and is penitent in life; therefore he has no need then of being brought to repentance. Nor are we anywhere commanded of Christ to put him to open shame before the church. Reflect on these things (I, 254; repeated, I, 283).

> Not the weak but the corrupt members are cut off lest they corrupt the others. . . . I desire that excommunication be practiced in a sincere, paternal spirit, in faithful love, according to the doctrine of Christ and His apostles. . . (I, 284).

> . . . None is cut off by us or ejected from the communion of the brethren . . . but those who have already ejected themselves either by false doctrine or by a blamable life from Christ and His communion. For we do not wish to eject any but to accept them; not to cut them off but to restore them; not to reject but to win them back; not to afflict but to console them; not to condemn but to save them. . . .
>
> But those whom we cannot raise up and admonish unto repentance by tears, threatening, reproving, or by any other Christian service and divine means, we should reluctantly separate from us, sincerely deploring the fall and damnation of such erring brethren. . . (II, 446).

3. The High Calling of the Church

The Anabaptist concept of the church composed of individual souls who were saved by accepting the Lord Jesus Christ as their Saviour, and who were glorifying God by a holy walk and a life of Christian witnessing, was only one aspect of their view of the church. *They also thought of the church as a corporate body achieving the will of God for society.* This doctrine distinguished them more sharply than any other from the large Protestant groups. They held that the state had to live its life on a sub-Christian level, restraining unregenerate men by the employment of police force and the magistracy. But when a person became a Christian and accepted baptism he was lifted up into the society of the redeemed, a body of people who loved one another and were mutually concerned for the welfare of their fellow believers and for the corporate witness of the brotherhood, a society in which there was no need of force and coercion. Church discipline aided in keeping this society holy. Here Jesus

Christ was sovereign, directing His people by His Word, in the power of the Holy Spirit. His servants, the ministers or teachers in the congregations, were confident that the Holy Spirit would so bless their teaching of the Word that the members of Christ's body, being regenerated believers, would seek to conform themselves to Christ and His Word.

Needless to say, this vision, if the state churchmen had it at all, was an empty dream for a people's (provincial) church. Such a body did not achieve a high ethical level in Christ. In the state churches one could think of the vertical relation only, the individual soul reaching up to God. It was the Anabaptists who sought earnestly to build Christ's *kingdom* here and now. And that kingdom was not a theoretical concept for them, but a glorious reality, composed, as it was, of their fellow believers, the members of their congregations. The Lutherans thought of individual believers forsaking a sinful society and finding forgiveness and grace; (Pietism is Lutheranism at its highest level of devotion). The Reformed dreamed of Christianizing the social order: Christian mayors, Christian magistrates, Christian Policemen, Christian soldiers; but they had to be dual personalities, faithfully bearing the sword of the Spirit as believers and (in violation of the Christian ethic) bearing the sword of steel as citizens of this world. The Anabaptists with their conception of separation of church and state agreed with the Lutherans that the social order could not be Christianized, and they agreed with the Reformed in desiring to create a Christian society—*but they sought to do this only in the church.* This involved a certain "withdrawal" from one sector of the life of society, not a physical withdrawal into monasteries, but a certain "abandonment" of non-Christian society to its own management and a concentration on the evangelization of individuals from that non-Christian society. The church of Christ was therefore the society in which Christ exercised His glorious reign. The highest achievement of this life was to participate in extending that kingdom of glory. The statements of the Anabaptists on the subject of the kingdom will therefore help us to see their vision of the nature, place and function of the church. Here are some extracts from Menno Simons' writings:

> . . . Spiritually we acknowledge no king, neither in heaven above nor upon earth beneath, [other] than the only, eternal and true King, spiritual David, Christ Jesus who is Lord of lords and King of kings. . .

But according to the flesh we teach and exhort to be obedient to the emperor, kings, lords and princes, yea, to all in authority in all their transactions and civil regulations so far as they are not contrary to the Word of God. . . .

We teach and confess that we know of no sword nor commotion in the kingdom or church of Christ other than the sharp sword of the Spirit, God's Word . . . , which is sharper and more piercing than any two-edged sword. . . . But the sword of worldly policy we leave with those to whom it is committed. . .

We acknowledge, teach and seek no other kingdom than that of Christ which shall endure for ever, in which there is no pomp, splendor, gold, silver, meat and drink, but righteousness, peace and joy in the Holy Ghost; we confess with Christ that our kingdom is not of this world. . . (I, 82, 83, cf. I, 95).

. . . We know that all the promises to the fathers, the waiting of the patriarchs, the whole figurative law, and all the predictions of the prophets, are fulfilled *in* Christ, *with* Christ, and *through* Christ; that Christ is our King, Prince, Lord, Messiah, the promised David. . . (I, 116).

. . . All those who are born of God with Christ, who thus conform their weak life to the gospel, are thus converted and follow the example of Christ, hear and believe His holy Word, follow His commands which He in plain words commanded us in the holy Scriptures, form the holy, Christian church which has the promise; the true children of God, brothers and sisters of Christ, for they are born with Him of one Father and of the new Eve, the pure, chaste bride. They are flesh of Christ's flesh, and bone of His bone, the spiritual house of Israel, the spiritual city, Jerusalem, temple and Mount Zion. . . .

These regenerated have a spiritual King over them who rules them by the unbroken scepter of His mouth, namely with His Holy Spirit and Word. He clothes them with the garment of righteousness, of pure white silk; He refreshes them with the living water of His Holy Spirit, and feeds them with the bread of life. His name is Christ Jesus. . . (I, 170).

. . . Now the bright light of the holy Gospel of Christ shines again in refulgent splendor in these vexatious times of all anti-Christian abominations; God's own and first-begotten Son, Christ Jesus, is gloriously revealed; His good will and pleasure and holy Word concerning faith, regeneration, repentance, baptism, the Lord's Supper, and the whole saving doctrine, life and ordinance, have again come to light through much seeking, prayer, reading, teaching and writing; . . . now all things—God be praised for His grace—proceed according to the true, apostolic rule in the church, whereby the kingdom of Christ rises in honor, and the kingdom of antichrist is sinking. . . (I, 242).

. . . We do not teach and practice the doctrine of having goods in common. But we teach and maintain by the Word of the Lord that all truly believing Christians are members of one body and are baptized by one Spirit into one body. . . , that they are partakers of one bread. . . , that they have one Lord and one God. . . .

. . . All those who are born of God, who are gifted with the Spirit of the Lord, and who according to the Scriptures are called into one body of love in Christ Jesus, are prepared by . . . love to serve their neighbors, not only with money and goods but also after the example of their Lord and Head, Jesus Christ, in an evangelical manner with life and blood. They show mercy and love as much as they can; suffer no beggars among them; take to heart the need of the saints; receive the miserable; take the stranger into their houses; console the afflicted; assist the needy; clothe the naked; feed the hungry; do not turn their face from the poor; and do not despise their own flesh . . . (II, 309).

. . . I beseech you as my sincerely beloved brethren by the grace of God, nay I command you with holy Paul, by the Lord Jesus Christ who at His coming will judge the living and the dead, diligently to observe each other unto salvation in all becoming ways, teaching, instructing, admonishing, reproving, threatening and consoling each other as occasion requires, not otherwise than in accordance with the Word of God, and in unfeigned love, that we may all grow up in God and become united in faith and in the knowledge of the Son of God into one perfect man, and according to the measure of the gift of Jesus Christ. . . .

Therefore take heed. If you see your brother sin, then pass not by him as one that does not prize his soul; but if his fall be curable, from that moment endeavor to raise him up by gentle admonition and brotherly instruction before you eat, drink, sleep or do anything else, as one who ardently desires his salvation, lest your poor, erring brother harden and corrupt in his fall, and perish in his sin (II, 444, 445).

In view of the emphasis of the Brethren on need for the grace of God and on the necessity of fraternal helpfulness in spiritual matters it is clear that the Anabaptists did not claim to be morally perfect, a church without spot or wrinkle,—though indeed that was their goal, and toward it they pressed earnestly.

Menno held that there are four kinds of sin: (1) The corrupt nature or inherent sin, which "for Christ's sake . . . is not accounted as sin." (2) Acts of sin, such as "adultery, fornication, avarice, debauchery, hatred, envy, lying, theft, murder and idolatry;" for which there is no forgiveness apart from repentance. "If this inherent sin is to lose its effect and actual sin be forgiven, then we must believe the word of the Lord, be regenerated by faith, and thus by virtue of the new birth, by true repentance resist the inherent sin, die unto actual sin and be pious." (3) "The third kind are human frailties, errors and stumblings which are yet daily found among the saints and regenerated, such as untempered thoughts, careless words and rashness in our actions . . . . The unbelieving . . . commit sin unrestrainedly and fearlessly . . . .

"But those who are born from above are fearful of all sin; they know by the law that all which is contrary to the first righteousness is sin, be it inwardly or outwardly, important or trifling; and therefore they daily fight in spirit and faith with their weak flesh; sigh and lament about their errors . . . they daily approach the throne of grace with contrite hearts and pray: Holy Father, forgive us our trespasses as we forgive those that trespass against us. And thus they are not rejected by the Lord on account of such transgressions which are not committed willfully and intentionally, but contrary to their will out of mere thoughtlessness and frailty.

(4) The fourth type of sin is connected with becoming an apostate (WORKS, II, 312-314).

It is evident that the moral earnestness of the Brethren and their vision of the high calling of the church were both derived from the New Testament; they were sorely needed in the world four centuries ago; and even the Christian world of today could profitably follow the Brethren as they sought to follow Christ.

C. THE CHRISTIAN LIFE

1. The Essence of Christianity

It was pointed out above that the Anabaptists were simple Biblicists, little concerned with systems of theology. Neither were the Anabaptists sacramentarians. They did not teach that baptism effected regeneration, nor did they base their hope of salvation on baptism. It was Luther who fell back on his baptism when his faith wavered; but never did an Anabaptist make such a statement. Both Pilgram Marpeck and Menno Simons lamented the fact that professing Christians, however careless in their life, claimed to be Christians because of having been baptized as infants. For the Brethren there was no divine efficacy in the ceremony of baptism; rather, baptism was the external seal of having espoused discipleship; it was the sign of the covenant between the new disciple and God (cf. I Peter 3:21 in the German Bible). In commenting on Peter's statement that baptism was "the covenant of a good conscience with God" Menno writes:

> Here Peter teaches us how the inward baptism saves us, by which the inner man is washed, and not the outward baptism by which the flesh is washed; for only this inward baptism . . . is of value in the sight of God, while outward baptism follows only as an evidence of [the] obedience which is of faith. For could outward baptism save without the inward washing, the whole Scriptures which speak of the new man would be spoken to no purpose, the kingdom of heaven would be bound to elementary water, the blood of Christ would be shed in vain, and no one that is baptized could be lost. No, no! Outward baptism avails nothing so long as we are not inwardly renewed, regenerated, and baptized of God with the heavenly fire and the Holy Ghost. But when we receive this baptism from above we will be constrained through

the Spirit and Word of God by a good conscience . . .to believe sincerely in the merits of the death of the Lord, and in the power and benefits of His resurrection. And henceforth . . . we submissively covenant with the Lord through the outward sign of baptism, which is enjoined on all the believers in Christ . . . that we will no longer live according to the evil, unclean lusts of the flesh but walk according to the witness of a good conscience before Him.

. . .Baptism is a sign of obedience, commanded of Christ, by which we testify when we receive it that we believe the Word of the Lord, that we are sorry for and repent of our former life and conduct, that we desire to rise with Christ unto a new life, and that we believe in the forgiveness of sin through Jesus Christ. Not, my beloved, that we believe in the remission of sins through baptism; by no means. Because by baptism we cannot obtain faith and repentance; neither do we receive the forgiveness of sins, nor peace, nor liberty of conscience. But we testify thereby that we have repented, received pardon and faith in Christ. . . . In short, had we forgiveness of sins and peace of conscience through outward ceremonies and elements then the REALITY would be superseded and His merits made of no effect. (WORKS, I, 28).

Baptism was for the Brethren merely an outward testimony to their inner experience of salvation and to their intention to live the Christian life. It is therefore wholly wrong to state that the Anabaptists placed much stress on baptism. Indeed they placed little stress on any external ordinances. Everywhere they baptized believers, observed the Lord's Supper, and exercised church discipline—and in some communities they practiced feet washing as an ordinance—but that was the extent of their church ceremonies (cf. Menno's WORKS, II, 242-244). Menno Simons wrote a vigorous reply to the charge that the Brethren were "new monks" (WORKS, II, 316ff).

Not only did the Brethren refuse to rely on the observance of ordinances for their salvation; they did not consider regeneration or even faith, as the final essence of Christianity. They believed in and stressed both the new birth and saving faith, to be sure, but they were only the indispensable foundation of the Christian life, not ends in themselves. *The essence of Christianity was thought of as discipleship,* as a faithful "following-after" (*Nachfolge*) of Christ, a resolute obedience to the ethical demands of the New Testament. The Brethren were sharply critical of hearing people boast of baptism, of theology and faith while they lived in the lusts of the flesh. Baptism has its place, of course, but not to confer supernatural grace. Doctrine has its place, but not as a substitute for life. It is faith that saves, and faith alone, *but where there is no discipleship there is no saving faith.* Menno's outburst is typical of the attitude of the Brethren four centuries ago:

> . . . The reckless people are chained to and consoled in their unbelief and licentious, carnal life by their light minded doctrine, sacraments and easy life, for they preach and teach you, "There are none that can truly believe; we are all sinners—therefore none can rightly keep the commandments of God. In your baptism (they say) you became a regenerated Christian and received the Holy Ghost. Although you could not understand the Word, although you have no faith in Christ Jesus nor knowledge of good or evil, nor any change or renewing of heart, because you were an unconscious child,"—and similar false consolations. You hear their absolutions and receive their bread, as if that were sufficient, and never mind that you are yet an impenitent, avaricious, proud, drunken, unclean, envious and idolatrous man. . . (II, 265)).

In another treatise Menno says succinctly:

> Verily they are not the true church of Christ who merely boast of His name. But those are the true church of Christ who were converted, who are born from above of God, who are of a regenerated mind, and by the operation of the Holy Spirit from the hearing of the divine Word have become children of God; who obey Him and live unblamably in His holy commandments and according to His holy will all their days, or after their calling (II, 241).

There is abundant evidence, even from the pens of the most bitter opponents of the Anabaptists, that *the Brethren did succeed in reaching a distinctly higher level of Christian living than the state church groups of the sixteenth century.* This was the result of their insistence that the essence of Christianity was the realization of God's will in the lives of Christian disciples, that redemption must inevitably bear rich fruit in daily life. Without holiness of life and effective witnessing there is no real Christianity. The new life must be *in evidence* for the glory of God and the salvation of the lost.

2. Taking Up the Cross

The Anabaptists emphasized separation from the "world," meaning the mass of unregenerate men together with all their sinful ways and life. And they expected a certain amount of opposition and persecution from the world. They spoke much of bearing "the cross," of being faithful unto death, of being willing to shed their blood for their testimony to the truth. Menno described true Christians as "prepared to take upon themselves the cross of Christ, and to forsake father, mother, husband, wife, children, possessions and self, for the sake of the testimony of His holy Word when the honor and praise of God require it" (II, 110). This did not indicate an unhealthy desire for martyrdom. But when they lay in prison with no hope of release they naturally turned their minds toward their eternal Home. Yet even then they did not forget their families and congregations. In 1567 Christian Langedul, a Dutch Mennonite imprisoned for his faith, wrote the following in one of his letters to his wife:

> I must stop since my paper is used up. Greet all the friends much in the Lord whenever you have a proper opportunity, as also all friends according to the flesh; especially greet grandmother and comfort her as best you can since I have great anxiety for her sake, and for you and my children. I often think of my sweet P., but I am glad when he is out of my thoughts. Do the best in everything. I greet you with a holy kiss of peace. I hope the Lord will shorten my days, because He loves me. To L. E. I hope to write yet when I get time; greet her much in my name. Herewith I commend you to the Lord. . . .
>
> By me your very weak husband, Christian Langedul, from prison in which I am for the testimony of the Lord.

After being sentenced to death he wrote the following to his wife:

> Grace and peace from our heavenly Father through Christ Jesus, this I wish you my dear and chosen wife and sister in the Lord. And may the comforter, the Holy Ghost, comfort you in your tribulation as He will do according to His promise. . . . I expect to inherit salvation through the grace of the Lord and am of good cheer herein. I will therefore thank the Lord forever for His love. O my love, the winepress must now be trodden and I am quite ready for it: the Lord be praised. Truly He is a God of all comfort. . . . Oh, that I could fully thank the Lord for all the comfort and strength He grants to me, unworthy one. . . .
>
> Herewith I commend you to the Lord and to the Word of His grace. Greet all the friends most cordially with the peace of the Lord. Greet warmly R. Langedul, also your sister and all the friends whenever it is convenient, and bid them all adieu. Adieu my dear lamb, adieu. Written on the twelfth of September, 1567, by me, Christian Langedul, your husband and weak brother in the Lord, imprisoned and sentenced to death for the testimony of Christ and for our conscience. . . .

In 1573 a young man and his wife, John and Janneken van Munstdorp, were seized in a meeting of Dutch Mennonites and imprisoned at Antwerp in the first year of their marriage. Here are some extracts from his letter to his wife, written in prison:

> An affectionate greeting to you my beloved wife whom I love from the heart and greatly cherish above every other creature, and must now forsake for the truth for the sake of which we must count all things loss and love Him above all. I hope though men separate us here that the Lord will again join us together in His eternal kingdom where no one will be able to part us and we shall reign forever in the heavenly abode. . . .

. . . adieu and farewell, my lamb, my love; adieu and farewell to all that fear God; adieu and farewell until the marriage of the Lamb in the New Jerusalem. Be valiant and of good cheer; cast the troubles that assail you upon the Lord and He will not forsake you; cleave to Him and you will not fall. Love God above all; have love and truth; love your salvation and keep your promises to the Lord (MARTYRS MIRROR, 984).

John was executed first, by burning. Soon after his martyrdom Janneken bore a little daughter to whom she gave her own name. Before her death at the stake Janneken wrote a long letter to her month-old child, which letter was preserved and incorporated in the *Martyrs' Mirror.* Parts of the letter set forth the sixteenth century Mennonite belief in the cross of the Christian. After reporting to the child how her parents had died, and entreating her not to be ashamed of her executed parents, she continued:

Hence, my young lamb for whose sake I still have and have had great sorrow, seek when you have attained your understanding this narrow way though there is sometimes much danger in it according to the flesh as we may see and read if we diligently examine and read the Scriptures, that much is said concerning the cross of Christ. And there are many in this world who are enemies of the cross, who seek to be free from it among the world and to escape it. But, my dear child if we would with Christ seek and inherit salvation we must also help bear His cross. And this is the cross which He would have us bear: to follow His footsteps and to help bear His reproach, for Christ Himself says: "ye shall be persecuted, killed, and dispersed for my name's sake." Yea, He Himself went before us in this way of reproach and left us an example that we should follow His steps, for His sake all must be forsaken, father, mother, sister, brother, husband, child, yea, one's own life. . . .

. . . And, my dear child, this is my request of you since you are still very little and young—I wrote this when you were but one month old—, as I am soon now to offer up my sacrifice by the help of the Lord I leave you this: "That you fulfill my request, always uniting with them that fear God; and do not regard the pomp and boasting of the world, nor the great multitude whose ways lead to the abyss of hell, but look at the little flock of Israelites who have no freedom anywhere and must always flee from one land to the other as Abraham did, that you may hereafter obtain your fatherland. For if you seek your salvation it is easy to perceive which is the way that leads to life, or the way that leads into hell. . . ."

. . . I leave you here; Oh, that it had pleased the Lord that I might have brought you up. I should so gladly have done my best with respect to it; but it seems that it is not the Lord's will. And though it had not come thus, and I had remained with you for a time, the Lord could still take me from you; and then too you should have to be without me,—even as it has now gone with your father and myself: that we could live together but so short a time when we were so well joined; since the Lord had so well mated us that we would not have forsaken each other for the whole world. And yet we had to leave each other for the Lord's sake. So I must also leave you here, my dearest lamb; the Lord that created and made you now takes me from you: it is His holy will. I must now pass through this narrow way which the prophets and martyrs of Christ passed through and many thousands who put off the mortal clothing, who died here for Christ, and now they wait under the altar till their number shall be fulfilled, of which number your dear father is one. And I am now on the point of following him. . . .

. . . I herewith commend you to the Lord and to the comforting Word of His grace, and bid you adieu once more. I hope to wait for you; follow me, my dearest child.

Once more adieu, my dearest upon earth; adieu and nothing more; adieu, follow me; adieu and farewell. . . (984-987).

The Brethren read in the Scriptures the words of Christ that "Ye shall be hated of all nations for my name's sake (Matt. 24:9); "If they have persecuted me, they will also persecute you" (John 15:20); and Paul's testimony that "all that will live godly in Christ Jesus shall suffer persecution" (II Tim. 3:12). Consequently *the only way to glory is the way of the cross.* Menno wrote:

Yea, this is and remains the only narrow and straight way and door through which we must all enter, neither can we ever desire in any other way to enter with the saints into eternal life, rest and peace. . . . Yes, my brethren, would you be the people and disciples of the Lord you must also bear the cross of Christ. . . (I, 192).

The world pressed the heavy cross on the shoulders of the Christians because it could not bear their testimony of the truth and their protest against its sin. Because of the separation of the Brethren from the world the wicked were convicted of their sin and persecuted them. Therefore the bearing of the cross became the earmark of the true children of God. *Only those who were truly saints excited the opposition of the world.* And only those who were born of the Spirit were willing to bear the cross. Menno expressed it thus:

. . . Forasmuch as we thus separate ourselves from them and testify by word and deed even unto death that their works are evil, therefore they are filled with the most inhuman rancor and indignation. . . .

. . . Our actual confession, that is to say, our separation from them is the sole reason why the blind, blood-thirsty world, frantic with rage, tyrannizes over us with so much cruelty, and why we must suffer and bear so much. . . .

. . . Our separation has no other foundation nor design than this, that we desired in our weakness to observe with all our heart the Word of God and keep His commandments, and that we might in real charity and in fact show to the whole world that they lie in wickedness and are strangers to God and His Word,—to the end that they may in due time awake and turn from iniquity. . . (II, 202f).

But the cross which the witness of Christ brings is no mere human arrangement; God has ordained it for the good of His saints. The cross plays a significant role in the sanctification of Christians. In his treatise on *The Cross* Menno sets forth the place of the Christian's cross in the crucifixion of the believer's affection for the things of time and sense. "The gracious God and Father," says Menno,

> has prepared and left in His house an excellent remedy therefor, namely the oppressive cross of Christ, so that we who in unbounded mercy are received through Christ Jesus to the glory of the Father, believing in pureness of heart on Christ Jesus, and [who] love Him in our weakness may through the aforesaid cross, that is, through much affliction, oppression, anxiety, apprehension, bonds, robbery, etc., forsake all the transitory delights and enjoyments of earth, die unto the world and the flesh, love God alone, [and] set our affections on things above, where Christ sitteth on the right hand of God. . . (II, 205f).
>
> Forasmuch as eternal Wisdom recognizes an extreme weakness, and since earthly ease, peace and prosperity have so great a tendency to ruin and undo us before our God and to render us careless, refractory, lukewarm, and drowsy, He has appointed His cross as an awakening rod for the use of all His followers. . . (II, 206).

Menno believed that the number of the true saints would always remain comparatively small, for the world does not relish the heavy cross and the narrow way (I, 100; II, 75, 307). But he was not certain whether persecution unto martyrdom would always be the lot of the saints. Indeed he would have accepted gratefully a cessation of bloodshed in matters of faith, and for such cessation he pleaded eloquently (WORKS, 84-87).

The Anabaptists may never rate as outstanding and erudite theologians, but they did have sound principles of interpretation, as well as the determination to make the Bible alone the norm of their faith and practice. They held to Biblical doctrines of God, man, sin and salvation. They had a high view of the place and calling of the church, a view which has even today not been realized by Christendom as a whole. Their ethic of love and nonresistance is sorely needed in a world of wars and rumors of war. Upon the Mennonite Church of today rests the responsibility of holding aloft the Anabaptist torch of truth, a lamp which burns with the light of divine revelation, and a beacon which can give guidance to thousands of souls as they grope for the light of life.

READINGS

Bender, H. S.: "The Anabaptist Vision," *The Mennonite Quarterly Review,* Goshen, Indiana, XVIII, 2 (April 1944), 67-88.

Bender, H. S.: "The Mennonite Conception of the Church and Its Relation to Present Day Needs," *The Mennonite Quarterly Review,* Goshen, Indiana, XIX, 2 (April 1945), 90-100.

Bender, H. S., and Horsch, John: *Menno Simons' Life and Writings,* Scottdale, Pennsylvania, 1936.

Bender, H. S.: *Mennonite Origins in Europe,* M.C.C., Akron, Pennsylvania, 1942, 34-41

Blanke, Fritz: "Beobachtungen zum ältesten Täuferbekenntnis," *Archiv Für Reformationsgeschichte,* Jahrgang 38, Heft 2/3, Leipzig, 242-249.

Burckhardt, Paul: *Die Basler Täufer. Ein Beitrag zur Schweizerischen Reformationsgeschichte,* Basel, 1898, 103-125.

Burkhart, I. E.: "Menno Simons on the Incarnation," *The Mennonite Quarterly Review,* IV, 2 (April 1930), 113-139; IV, 3 (July 1930), 178-207; 2 (April 1932), 122, 123.

Complete Works of Menno Simons [1496-1561], The, Elkhart, Indiana, 1871.

Correll, Ernst H.: *Das schweizerische Täufermennonitentum. Ein soziologischer Bericht,* Mohr, Tübingen, 1925, 24-54.

Fretz, J. Winfield: "Mutual Aid Among Mennonites," *The Mennonite Quarterly Review,* Goshen, Indiana, I, XIII, 1 (January 1939), 28-58; II, XIII, 3 (July 1939), 187-209.

Friedmann, Robert: "The Anabaptist Genius and Its Influence on Mennonites Today," *Proceedings of the first Conference on Mennonite Cultural Problems,* Held at Winona Lake, Indiana, August 7 and 8, 1942, 20-25

Friedmann, Robert: "Anabaptism and Pietism," *The Mennonite Quarterly Review,* Goshen, Indiana, I, XIV, 2 (April 1940), 90-128; II, XIV, 3 (July 1940), 149-169.

Friedmann, Robert: "Spiritual Changes in European Mennonitism, 1650-1750," *The Mennonite Quarterly Review,* XV, 1 (January 1941), 33-45.

Friesen, J. J.: *An Outline of Mennonite History,* Newton, Kansas, 1944, 32-37.

Funk, Henry: *Restitution or An Explanation of Several Principal Points of the Law* . . . Originally Published in Philadelphia, A.D. 1763 . . . , (Elkhart, Indiana, 1915).

Händiges, Emil: *Die Lehre der Mennoniten in Geschichte und Gegenwart Nach den Quellen dargestellt* . . . , Eppstein und Ludwigshafen am Rhein, (c. 1921,) 5-78.

Hege, Christian and Neff, Christian: *Mennonitisches Lexikon,* Weierhof (Pfalz) und Frankfurt am Main, Bd. I. 1913-24; Bd. II, 1937. Note especially the following articles: *Bann, Bergpredigt, Bibel, Chiliasmus, Exegese, Eid, Gemeinde, Gemeindeverfassung, Gemeindezucht, Inspiration, Krieg, etc.*

Hershberger, Guy F.: *War, Peace, and Nonresistance,* Scottdale, Pennsylvania, 1944.

Horsch, John: "The Early Mennonite View on Christian Stewardship," *Christian Monitor,* Scottdale, Pennsylvania, May 1931, 145.

Horsch, John: "The Faith of the Swiss Brethren," *The Mennonite Quarterly Review,* I, IV,4 (October 1930), 242-266; II, V,1 (January 1931), 7-27; III, V,2 (April 1931), 128-147; IV, V,4 (October 1931), 245-259.

Horsch, John: *Infant Baptism, Its Origin Among Protestants and The Arguments Advanced For and Against It,* Scottdale, Pennsylvania, 1917.

Horsch, John: *Menno Simons, His Life, Labors, and Teachings,* Scottdale, Pennsylvania, 1916, 223-299.

Horsch, John: *Mennonites in Europe,* Scottdale, Pennsylvania, 1942, 293-380.

Horsch, John: *The Principle of Nonresistance as Held By the Mennonite Church. . . ,* [First Edition,] 1927; Second Edition, Revised and Enlarged, Scottdale, Pennsylvania, 1939.

Horsch, John: *Die biblische Lehre von der Wehrlosigkeit,* Scottdale, Pennsylvanien, 1920.

Horsch, John: "The Relation of the Old Testament Scriptures to the New Testament," *Christian Monitor,* Scottdale, Pennsylvania, November 1938, 329.

Horsch, John: "The Teaching of the Early Mennonite Fathers on Predestination," *Christian Monitor,* Scottdale, Pennsylvania, July 1938, 198f.

Horsch, John: "Washing the Saints' Feet," *Gospel Herald,* Scottdale, Pennsylvania, April 27, 1939, 83.

Kauffman, Daniel, Editor: *Bible Doctrine . . . ,* Scottdale, Pennsylvania, 1914.

Kauffman, Daniel, Editor: *Doctrines of the Bible . . . ,* Scottdale, Pennsylvania, 1928

Krahn, Cornelius: *Menno Simons (1496-1561), Ein Beitrag zur Geschichte und Theologie der Taufgesinnten,* Heinrich Schneider, Karlstrasse 28, Karlsruhe i. B., 1936, 103-179.

Mennonite Central Committee, Handbook of Information on the, M.C.C., Akron, Pennsylvania, July 1943, "Our Heritage of Faith," 23f.

Philip, Dietrich [1504-68]: *Enchiridion or Hand Book of the Christian Doctrine and Religion . . . ,* Elkhart, Indiana, 1910.

Rideman, Peter: *Rechenschaft unserer Religion, Lehr und glaubens, von den Brüdern, so man die Hutterischen nennt, ausgangen 1565.* Aufs Neue herausgegeben und gedruckt im Verlag der Hutterischen Brüder in U.S.A., Canada und England. Cotswold-Bruderhof, Ashton Keynes, Wilts., England, 1938.

Smucker, Donovan E.: "The Theological Triumph of the Early Anabaptist Mennonites," *The Mennonite Quarterly Review,* Goshen, Indiana, XIX, 1 (January 1945), 5-26.

Stauffer, Ethelbert: "The Anabaptist Theology of Martyrdom," *The Mennonite Quarterly Review,* Goshen, Indiana, XIX, 3 (July 1945), 179-214.

Twisk, Peter J. [1565-1636]: *The Peaceful Kingdom of Christ or An Exposition of the 20th Chapter of the Book of Revelations,* Elkhart, Indiana, 1913.

von Muralt, Leonhard: *Glaube und Lehre der Schweizerischen Wiedertaüfer in der Reformationszeit,* Zürich, 1938, 27-47.

Wenger, J. C.: "The Relation of the Christian to the Old Testament Scriptures," *Christian Monitor,* Scottdale, Pennsylvania, September 1939, 266f.

Wenger, J. C.: "The Theology of Pilgram Marpeck," *The Mennonite Quarterly Review,* Goshen, Indiana, XII, 4 (October 1938), 205-256.

Wenger, J. C.: "Pilgram Marpeck, Tyrolese Engineer and Anabaptist Elder," *Church History,* IX, 1 (March 1940), 24-36, especially 33-35.

Wenger, J. C.: "The Schleitheim Confession of Faith," *The Mennonite Quarterly Review,* XIX, 4 (October 1945), 243-253.

Wenger, J. C.: "Concerning the Satisfaction of Christ. An Anabaptist Tract on True Christianity," *The Mennonite Quarterly Review,* XX, 4 (October 1946), 243-254.

Wenger, J. C.: "Two Kinds of Obedience. A Swiss Brethren Tract on Christian Freedom." *The Mennonite Quarterly Review,* XXI, 1, (January 1947).

Wenger, J. C.: "Concerning Divorce. A Swiss Brethren Tract . . . ," *The Mennonite Quarterly Review,* XXI, 2 (April 1947).

Wenger, J. C.: "Martin Weninger's Vindication of Anabaptism," *The Mennonite Quarterly Review,* XXII, 3 (July, 1948), 180-187.

Wenger, J. C.: "Three Swiss Brethren Tracts," *The Mennonite Quarterly Review,* XXI, 4 (October, 1947), 275-284.

Wenger, J. C.: "Two Early Anabaptist Tracts," *The Mennonite Quarterly Review,* XXII, 1 (January, 1948), 34-42.

Yoder, Edward: *Our Mennonite Heritage,* M.C.C., Akron, Pennsylvania, 1942.

Yoder, Edward: "What Is Mennonitism?" *Proceedings of the second Annual Conference on Mennonite Cultural Problems,* Held at Goshen, Indiana, July 22 and 23, 1943, 106-112.

Mennonite Home Mission, 1907 South Union Avenue, Chicago, Illinois; Founded in 1893

Goshen College, Founded in 1903

Dirk Willems, a Dutch Mennonite, Saves His Captor's Life, 1569.
Willems was later burned at the stake.

Mennonite Publishing House, Established in 1908 with the New Annex Erected in 1949

CHAPTER XIV

Recapturing the Anabaptist Vision

1. The First Years of Anabaptism

One may learn the doctrine and program of the early Anabaptists by reading Harold S. Bender's Monograph, "The Anabaptist Vision," published in *Church History, XIII,* 3-24 (March, 1944) and in *The Mennonite Quarterly Review, XVIII,* 67-88 (April 1944). Certain it is that the Anabaptists were pre-eminently a missionary-minded group. This fact has been well demonstrated by Franklin H. Littell of the University of Michigan, in his doctoral dissertation (Yale) on the Anabaptist conception of the church (unpublished at this writing). And Professor Kenneth Scott Latourette of Yale University in his *History of the Expansion of Christianity,* Harpers, seven volumes, 1937-45, makes a number of illuminating references to and characterizations of the Anabaptists. The Mennonite writer, John Horsch, in his splendid work, *Mennonites in Europe,* 1942, states:

> The Mennonite Church at the beginning was pre-eminently a missionary church. This was one of the reasons for its rapid spread. In that period there were no special mission organizations, yet the church was engaged in aggressive evangelistic work. In the earliest years of its history its congregations, like the primitive Christian congregations, consisted of men and women who were noted for their zeal for propagating the gospel. . .
>
> In the first period of the history of the Mennonite brotherhood their principal fields of labor were Switzerland, South Germany, and Austria. The work of spreading the gospel was carried on under indescribable difficulties. They were in constant danger of apprehension and death. Their willingness to endure persecution was evidence, however, of their firm conviction that their message was the gospel truth. They endeavored to reach the common people, and their word of testimony, being spoken from sincere conviction, made a deep impression on their hearers. Sometimes their efforts resulted in the organization of a congregation within a few days after the arrival of a messenger of the gospel at a given place (314f).

The Swiss Brethren, the Hutterian Brethren, and the Obbenites believed that they alone were living in full obedience to the Word of God; only they baptized on confession of faith; only they taught Biblical nonresistance; only they rejected state churchism and sought earnestly to create anew Christian congregations patterned after those of the apostles in the first century. Because of their burning desire to win others to "the obedience of faith" they went about, as busy as bees, preaching a message which was regarded as dangerously revolutionary by the statesmen and theologians of that day, a faith which was almost from the first punishable by death. Yet the Brethren were able to win thousands of converts; people counted eternal salvation of more worth than temporal life. Conrad Grebel spent a few weeks in St. Gall, Switzerland, in the year 1525. In three weeks of evangelism, he won a host of converts; the Brethren congregation there numbered five hundred by the Easter season of 1525. Like Grebel, Felix Manz was an indefatigable evangelist, and for his successful effort to help establish a free church he was drowned in January 1527. Blaurock, who evangelized in various parts of Switzerland and in the Tirol until he was burned at the stake in 1529, has been credited with winning an estimated one thousand converts. Menno Simons, who had a fruitful ministry, twenty-five years in length, wrote:

> We would teach, proclaim, and imprint on the hearts of all mankind to the best of our ability this manifold grace of His great love toward us that they may enjoy with us the same joy and renewal of spirit and know and taste with all saints how sweet, good, and kind the Lord is to whom we have turned.
>
> We preach therefore as much as is in our power, both day and night, in houses and in the open air, in forests and in wilderness, hither and thither, in this and in foreign lands, in prisons and in dungeons, in water and in fire, on the scaffold and on the wheel, before lords and princes, orally and by writings, at the risk of possessions and blood, life and death. . .
>
> We would save all mankind from the jaws of hell, deliver them from the chains of their sins, and by the gracious help of God win them to Christ by the gospel of His peace. . .
>
> It is true that we sometimes have to serve the Lord and preach His Word at night, in the dead of the night. . . (WORKS, II, 10).

On the subject of the Great Commission (Matt. 28:18-20) Menno declared:

> We desire with ardent hearts even at the cost of life and blood that the holy gospel of Jesus Christ and His apostles, which alone is the true doctrine, and will remain so until Jesus Christ will reappear in the clouds, may be taught and preached through all the world as the Lord Jesus Christ commanded His disciples at the last moments while He was on earth (WORKS, II, 243).

It is not known how many converts Menno won. T. J. van Braght, 1625-1664, the Dutch Mennonite author, states modestly that "Menno Simons drew, turned, and won to God a great number of men from dark and erring popery, yea from the dumb idols to the living God" (MARTYRS' MIRROR, 455). It is known that Leonard Bouwens,

Menno's staunch colleague, baptized during a thirty-year ministry well over ten thousand souls. Bouwens himself kept the list of names of those whom he baptized.

On August 20, 1527, a group of Anabaptists met at Augsburg in Bavarian Swabia. Over sixty were in attendance, coming from Austria, South Germany, and Switzerland. At this meeting it was decided to send out missionaries to Basle and Zurich, to the Palatinate, to Upper Austria, to Franconia, to Salzburg, and to Bavaria. In a short time many of the participants at the 1527 conference became martyrs: Eukarius Binder and Joachim März at Salzburg, Leonard Spörle in a nearby Austrian village, Leonard Dorfbrunner at Passau, Leonard Schiemer at Rattenburg in the Tirol, Hans Schlaffer at Schwaz in the Tirol, Eitelhans Langenmantel near Ulm, Thomas Waldhausen in Moravia, John Leupold at Augsburg, John Mittermaier at Linz a. D., and Jacob Wiedemann at Vienna. Because of these executions the 1527 meeting has been called the martyr synod.

The Hutterian Brethren, the Moravian Anabaptists, had a remarkable missionary zeal. A description of their brotherhood is included in their oldest chronicle among the entries of 1569. Among other things their chronicler wrote:

> They carry out the Christian mission *(Sendung)* which the Lord commands and says, "As my Father hath sent me, even so send I you;" "I have chosen you, and ordained you, that ye should go and bring forth fruit." Therefore they sent out annually into the countries, since they had reason to do so, ministers of the gospel and their assistants. They sought out those who wished to amend their lives and who were zealous for the truth and asked about it. They led these out [of those countries into Moravia] by day and by night according to their request in spite of catchpoles and executioners and [notwithstanding the fact] that many had to lose their necks and give up body and life. They therefore gathered the Lord's people as is proper for the good shepherds (Zieglschmid edition, 1943, 433, translated from the German).

2. The Fire Burns Low

The missionary zeal of the Anabaptists was effectively dampened, if not extinguished altogether, during the dreadful persecution of the sixteenth century. The able leaders of the first years, some of them former priests and scholars, were in most cases succeeded by men of less ability. The authorities in both church and state continued their relentless persecution unto the death. In his book, *Against Sneaks and Hedgepreachers,* 1532, Luther condemned Anabaptist preachers and missionaries who labored in any territory without the permission of the civil authorities. As early as 1527 the duke of Bavaria ordered the imprisoned Anabaptists to be burned at the stake if they remained steadfast, and to be beheaded if they recanted. In 1529 the Diet of Spires, the national legislative assembly of the German Empire, issued an edict demanding that "every Anabaptist and re-baptized person of either sex shall be put to death by fire, sword, or in some other way."

It is an old adage, going back to Tertullian, c.155-c.225, that the blood of the martyrs is the seed of the church. Yet it is true that severe persecution can also succeed in its purpose, and the sixteenth century persecution was largely successful in the annihilation of the Anabaptists. Weak remnants managed to survive in Switzerland (the Swiss Brethren), in Moravia (the Hutterian Brethren) and in the Netherlands (the Mennonites). But by the time limited toleration came, the original Anabaptist vision of bringing the gospel to all men and gathering the believers into God's kingdom, the church, was lost. Society had made clear to the Brethren that it would have none of their "heresy." And slowly the Brethren unconsciously reached the point where they were content to be *die Stillen im Lande* (the quiet people of the country). They would henceforth seek only to perpetuate their faith in their families. The Brethren had had to maintain a more or less secret ecclesiastical life during the *Blutzeit* (bloody era) and when toleration at last was granted to them they had lost the vision of making disciples of all the nations. The Bernese Anabaptists went to the Palatinate by the hundreds after 1664, glad only for the limited toleration promised them, and little worried that "proselyting" was forbidden. The migration of the Dutch Mennonites from Prussia to Russia after 1789 was with similar restrictions. The fires of evangelism and missions had burned out.

3. *The American Mennonite Pioneers*

Several centuries rolled by before an interest in evangelism began to revive among the Mennonites. It was during the latter nineteenth century that an awakening took place among the Mennonites in Russia and in North America. Perhaps the story of this awakening in the American "Mennonite Church" is typical of some other American Mennonite bodies as well. Even in America the awakening did not come until a century and a half after the Mennonites first settled in Penn's Woods. Conditions in the days of the pioneers partly explain this seeming lethargy.

The pioneers who came to Pennsylvania during the eighteenth century first of all had to undergo a long and tedious sea voyage running into many weeks and under most unpleasant conditions due to vermin, poor food, small sailing vessels, etc. After arrival in the new world the settlers were faced with the task of clearing the forests, building homes, and manufacturing for themselves almost all their tools, clothing, and limited farm machinery. In those days there were no public schools, hospitals, trained physicians, dentists, or any other professional people or institutions available. Each rural community was largely self-sufficient with the people producing their own food and clothing and caring for their own needs. One of the first things done in each Mennonite settlement was to build a simple log building to serve as meetinghouse and school building. Later on separate buildings were erected but even today in southeastern Pennsylvania a schoolhouse often stands near the Mennonite meetinghouse, a silent witness to the dual-purpose building first erected in the early eighteenth century.

In daily life and even in the worship services the pioneers spoke the German dialect of the Palatinate. Those not familiar with this patois can get a good knowledge of it from the *Simple Grammar of Pennsylvania Dutch* by J. William Frey, Ph. D., 1942.

Ordinarily the church services were held every second Sunday in the forenoon. The men with their knee breeches and frock coats, and the women with their long, full dresses and hooded cloaks, together with the children, walked to the service or rode horseback. There they joined in singing the German one-part hymns and in the prayers, and listened to the reading of the Scripture, to the long sermon, and to the "testimonies" following the sermon. The meetinghouse was equipped with backless benches, with hatracks (boards with long pegs) above the men's seats, and with a table or pulpit for the use of the ministers.

Some special services were also held. Baptismal services were held for those who had "joined the class" and received catechetical instruction from Roosen's *Conversation on Saving Faith.* Once or twice a year, depending on the customs of the conference district involved, communion services were held. Counsel meetings were held a week or two before the observance of the Lord's Supper. Preparatory services were held the day before the communion service. In most congregations feet washing was observed as an ordinance (John 13) after the communion service. Harvest-Home services were held in the autumn in appreciation of God's bountiful gifts of the field. The pioneers were sturdy characters, self-reliant, pious, and a bit formal. But it never occurred to them to send out missionaries or make any innovations in their religious life. Many of them had no conscience against the moderate use of alcohol and tobacco, nor did their Lutheran and Reformed neighbors. The fire was still unkindled.

4. The Great Awakening

The American colonists of the eighteenth century were generally cold spiritually, rationalistic, and unfavorable toward the church. The Revolutionary War, 1775-83, made a bad situation worse. Consequently there was a great need for revival in the early nineteenth century. The great bulk of Americans were not even professing Christians. To meet this challenge to the Christian Church earnest believers created a host of Christian organizations during the first quarter of the nineteenth century: foreign mission societies, Bible societies, tract societies, temperance societies, and many others. By the end of the first third of the century the idea was becoming widespread that all children ought to be in Sunday school, but it was not until 1844 that any American denomination officially and fully recognized the Sunday school as an agency of their group.

The Great Awakening in the "Mennonite Church" which reached somewhat of a climax toward the close of the century was not the result of studying original Anabaptism. It was rather borne on the wings of the Sunday school, an institution which gained general acceptance in the Mennonite Church in the years from 1865-95. Perhaps the first Sunday school in the church was at the Wanner and Bechtel (Hagey) congregations, Waterloo County, Ontario, in 1840. In 1841 the Berlin (Kitchener) Mennonites established a school in "Benjamin Eby's schoolhouse." In 1842 Nicholas Johnson, 1787-1873, bishop of the Masontown congregation in southwestern Pennsylvania, organized a Sunday school in his congregation. In 1848 the Moyer congregation near Vineland, Ontario, established a school. But none of these early schools were permanent; not one survived. It was not until about 1860 that permanent schools were established. Quite a number came into existence between 1865 and 1875. By 1890 they were well established all over the Mennonite Church except in a number of eastern Pennsylvania congregations. Those who wish to read more on the history of the Sunday school may consult *Mennonite Sunday School Centennial,*

1840-1940, by Harold S. Bender, Scottdale, Pennsylvania, 1940. In that booklet the author lists a number of major contributions of the Sunday school to the Mennonite Church: (1) It stopped the exodus of young people from Mennonite homes into other denominations. (2) It greatly increased Bible study and Bible knowledge in the modern Mennonite Church. (3) It raised the level of spiritual life. (4) It improved the moral level of the Mennonites, making a particular contribution to the "clean life," that of total abstinence in reference to alcohol and tobacco. (5) It provided religious activity for the entire membership for the first time in centuries. (6) It created and developed lay leadership. (7) It made a direct contribution to the rise of mission interest in the church.

The two men who did the most to bring new vision to the modern Mennonite Church were John F. Funk, 1835-1930, and John S. Coffman, 1848-99. Funk was born in Bucks county in eastern Pennsylvania, attended Freeland Seminary (later Ursinus College), went to Chicago and entered the lumber business, was converted in a Presbyterian Church, united with the Mennonite Church at Line Lexington, Pennsylvania, founded the *Herald of Truth* in 1864, was ordained to the ministry in 1865, and located at Elkhart, Indiana, in 1867. As editor of the *Herald of Truth* Funk came to wield a powerful influence on the brotherhood. He was the chief figure in promoting and establishing Sunday schools. He called Mennonite young men of talent to Elkhart and made it the religious center of the denomination. He was ordained as bishop in 1892 in which office he was active for ten years. He was almost ninety-five years of age when he died in 1930, a man who undoubtedly did more for his church than anyone of his generation.

John S. Coffman, 1848-99, was born in the Shenandoah Valley, Virginia. As a youth he fled North to Pennsylvania to escape being drafted for military service during the Civil War, 1861-65, returning to Virginia after the war was over. As a young man he taught "singing schools," attended Bridgewater Normal School, taught school, farmed, was ordained to the ministry in 1875, and at Funk's invitation located at Elkhart, Indiana, in 1879 where he served as assistant editor of the *Herald of Truth.* Although John F. Funk had helped conduct the first series of evangelistic meetings at Masontown, Pennsylvania, in 1872, it was John S. Coffman who was destined of God to establish such meetings throughout the Mennonite Church. By 1880 Coffman was earnestly meditating on the need of missions and evangelism and was fasting as he prayed about his concern. Indeed he was fasting every few weeks in 1881, for "The mind is clear and the soul is less fettered with sensuality." In June 1881 he held his first series of meetings at Bowne, Michigan. Nine souls accepted Christ. Six months later he held meetings at Masontown, Pennsylvania, and there were twelve converts. At Cullom, Illinois, in February, 1882, there were fifteen applicants for church membership. At the Weaver Congregation in Virginia forty-five persons accepted Christ. And so the good work went on. Coffman was a man of much prayer, and his ministry as an evangelist was highly effective. In six weeks of evangelism in Canada he won one hundred forty converts. Among those whom he led to Christ were such leaders as Daniel Kauffman, 1865-1944; George R. Brunk, 1871-1938; Tillman M. Erb, 1865-1929; J. M. R. Weaver, 1858-1929; N. O. Blosser, 1859-1936; M. S. Steiner, 1866-1911; J. B. Smith, 1870- ; E. S. Hallman, 1866- ; and S. F. Coffman, 1872- . Today a large number of Mennonite ministers are doing "the work of an evangelist," a calling which God used John S. Coffman to restore to the Mennonite Church. Coffman was also a strong leader in establishing Elkhart Institute, now Goshen College, in 1895.

Another result of the Great Awakening was the rise of mission interest. In 1882 the Indiana-Michigan Mennonite Conference appointed an evangelizing committee. The members of the new committee were John F. Funk, Henry B. Brenneman, and Martin D. Wenger. A direct outgrowth of the work was the organization of the Mennonite Evangelizing Board of America (1892). Mennonite Benevolent Board, organized in 1890, later merged with the Evangelizing Board to form the Mennonite Evangelizing and Benevolent Board of America. The first city mission to be established by the main branch of the Mennonite Church, the Chicago Home Mission, was founded in 1893. Mennonite Board of Charitable Homes and Missions was established in 1897. The present Mennonite Board of Missions and Charities was organized in 1906 as a merger of the two existing boards and is still functioning. The India Mennonite Mission was founded in 1899 and the mission in Argentina, South America, in 1917. The mission board of Lancaster Mennonite Conference opened work in Tanganyika Territory, Africa, in 1934.

The first educational institution of the main branch of the Mennonite Church was Elkhart Institute, established as a private school in

Elkhart, Indiana, in 1894. In 1895 the Elkhart Institute Association was formed. In 1903 Elkhart Institute was moved to Goshen and renamed as Goshen College. The present Mennonite Board of Education was organized in 1906. Hesston College and Bible School was organized in 1909. Eastern Mennonite School was founded at Harrisonburg, Virginia, in 1917. Lancaster Mennonite School was established in 1942. Several more regional academies have been established since that time, also a number of church primary schools.

Mention has already been made of the pioneer work of John F. Funk in the field of publication. It was in 1864 that he founded *The Herald of Truth. The Gospel Witness* was established at Scottdale, Pennsylvania, in 1905. In 1908 *The Herald of Truth* was merged with *The Gospel Witness* to form the *Gospel Herald.* The *Words of Cheer* was founded in 1876. *Mennonite Year Book and Directory* began to appear in 1905. In 1909 the publication of the *Christian Monitor* was begun. *The Way* began to appear in 1912. From 1894 to 1906 the *Young People's Paper* was published; the place of this periodical has been filled since 1920 by *The Youth's Christian Companion.* Goshen College began to publish a historical journal entitled *The Mennonite Quarterly Review* in 1927. In 1908 the Mennonite Publication Board was organized as a church publishing agency. It has carried on its work through Mennonite Publishing House, Scottdale, Pennsylvania, the HERALD PRESS.

The Great Awakening was therefore the cause of many new methods of church work including Sunday schools, evangelism, missions, Bible conferences, young people's Bible meetings, education, and publication. It also occasioned the establishment of numerous charitable institutions. The first of these was an orphans' home at West Liberty, Ohio, founded in 1896. Two years later the Welsh Mountain Mission and Good Samaritan Home was founded at New Holland, Pennsylvania. A home for the aged was established at Marshallville, Ohio (the address is now Rittman), in 1901. The building was destroyed by fire in 1919 and was rebuilt in 1939. The first Mennonite home for the aged in the East was established near Lancaster in 1903. The Mennonite Hospital and Sanitarium at La Junta, Colorado, was founded in 1907. The Mennonite Publishing House, Scottdale, Pennsylvania, was established in 1908. Millersville Children's Home in Pennsylvania dates from the year 1911. In 1916 the Franconia Mennonites established the Eastern Mennonite Home at Souderton, Pennsylvania. The next year a children's home was founded in Kansas City, Kansas. Homes for the aged were established at Eureka, Illinois, in 1922, and at Maugansville, Maryland, in 1923.

Among the other modern developments in the "Mennonite Church" should be listed relief work, such new agencies for Christian education as summer Bible schools and winter Bible schools, and a renewed emphasis on nonresistance.

The first cause which prompted heavy giving in the church was the immigration of the Russian Mennonites in the years, 1873-80. The second occasion of this type was the India famine in the last decade of the nineteenth century. This latter situation occasioned the organization of the Home and Foreign Relief Committee in 1896. Postwar famine and poverty in Europe led to the organization of the Mennonite Relief Committee, in 1917. The all-Mennonite relief organization, the M.C.C. (Mennonite Central Committee), was set up in 1920 and is continuing relief work wherever needed. The M.C.C. cares for the Russian Mennonite colonists of South America; and it carried on an extensive program of relief during and after the second world war, 1939-45.

The Mennonite Church established the Commission for Christian Education and Young People's Work in 1937. The purpose of the Commission is to co-ordinate such various agencies of the church as young people's Bible meetings, Sunday schools, summer Bible schools, teacher training classes, and mission study classes. The Commission thus cares for the work previously in charge of three committees. These three committees, which were dissolved in 1937, were the Young People's [Bible Meeting] Topic Committee (established in 1909); the General Sunday School Committee (1915); and the Young People's Problems Committee (1923).

The "Mennonite Church" has done more in the last century toward recapturing the evangelistic and missionary vision of the early Anabaptists than had been done for the previous three centuries. Along with this external growth in agencies and institutions has come also a greater sense of historical consciousness, an awareness of linking hands across the centuries with the martyr evangelists of the sixteenth century as they walked in the ways of the apostles of Christ. Yet it must be admitted that in recent decades the rate of growth of the Mennonite Church has declined. Still more humbling is the recognition that the church has never entirely recovered the spiritual vigor of the Anabaptists. Missionary progress has been painfully slow. Evangelistic campaigns have generally reached but few people outside of Mennonite families. May God help the church of today to witness more effectively of His salvation and of His will for our lives to those who so sorely need that light in a world of awful sin and spiritual darkness. The light has been rekindled but it needs to be fanned into a brighter flame by the Spirit of God.

READINGS

Bender, H. S.: "The Anabaptist Vision," *The Mennonite Quarterly Review,* Goshen, Indiana, XVIII, 2 (April 1944), 67-88.

Bender, H. S.: *Mennonite Sunday School Centennial,* 1840-1940: *An Appreciation of Our Sunday Schools,* Scottdale, Pennsylvania, 1940.

Fiftieth Anniversary, Goshen College, 1895-1945, Goshen, Indiana, [1945].

Fiftieth Anniversary Addresses, April 29-May 1, 1945, Goshen, 1895-1945.

Hertzler, Silas: "Early Mennonite Sunday Schools," *The Mennonite Quarterly Review,* II, 2 (April 1928), 123f; II, 3 (July 1928), 205f.

Horsch, John: *Mennonites in Europe,* Scottdale, Pennsylvania, 1942, 314-318.

Horst, John L.: "The Rise of the Young People's Meeting," *Gospel Herald,* Scottdale, Pennsylvania, February 8, 1940, 970f.

Lehman, M. C.: *The History and Principles of Mennonite Relief Work—An Introduction. Students' Edition with Syllabus and Annotated Bibliography,* M.C.C., Akron, Pennsylvania, 1945.

Loucks, Aaron: "John F. Funk, Pioneer Publisher of Mennonite Literature," *Christian Monitor,* Scottdale, Pennsylvania, March 1930, 82f.

Umble, John: "Early Conditions Leading to General Conference," *The Mennonite Quarterly Review,* III, (January 1929), 13-25.

NOTE: In April 1946 Goshen College Biblical Seminary sponsored a conference on evangelism. The addresses given at that conference will probably be published in book form. They will be significant for the theme of this chapter.

CHAPTER XV

The Outlook for the Future

The discussion of the future of the Mennonite Church will be confined to the largest body of the Mennonite family, the "Mennonite Church," sometimes written (*Old*) *Mennonites* for identification. This small group of Christians can face the future with courage because it has a number of points of strength.

1. Assets

(1) Mennonites as a general rule are Christians with high moral standards and great moral earnestness. They have a conscience against both social evil and personal sin which is keen and discerning. They believe strongly that there is a personal devil who is trying to deceive and mislead the saints. They also have an instinctive distrust of "the world"—unregenerate society—being wary of any sort of "unequal yoke" which would make them unwilling participants in a program which they might ultimately find unscriptural. They reckon seriously with the non-Christian standards of society and hold themselves more or less aloof as they seek to keep "unspotted from the world." They do not expect to be fully understood since they are not of this world, but are strangers and pilgrims with their citizenship in heaven.

(2) Mennonites are usually Christians of a deep inner piety. They pray faithfully, regularly, and earnestly. In former years they made much use of prayer books. Today they emphasize free, spontaneous prayers. They do not look to professional pastors to do their praying and witnessing for them. Each believer feels that he must study the Bible for himself, mastering its doctrines, being ready always to give Scriptural support for the distinctive doctrines of his church, and memorizing choice portions of the Word.

(3) The homes of Mennonites are exceptionally strong. Mennonite women are serious-minded and courageous, eager to realize the highest possible level of achievement as homemakers. They are devout and earnest in their Christian lives, praying for their families and teaching their children the things of God. Being a homemaker is for them the highest calling on earth, a sacred trust from the Lord.

The typical home has perhaps four to eight children. The husband takes a serious view of his calling as the head of the home, conducting family worship, keeping a watchful eye on the religious development of the children, and seeking to provide a good income for his growing family. Little money is spent on recreation since Mennonites believe in living a "simple life." Cases of infidelity or separation are rare. Rather, the whole family learns to work for the common welfare, and learning to work is a major emphasis in Mennonite families. Mennonite homes are strong; family life is attractive; the ties of the parental home are never severed.

(4) Mennonites are staunch supporters of their church. The typical laymember knows the principles of his church and believes in them. Church attendance is good. In the services the entire brotherhood participates. Even today the Franconia Conference practice is to have the first prayer a silent one, each Christian being free to make his own prayer to God. The individual members enter wholeheartedly into the entire program of the church—praying, giving, singing, following the Scripture lesson in their own Bibles, and listening attentively to the sermon. The laity operate vigorous Sunday schools and young people's Bible meetings. In short, "the church" does not mean the ministry or the conference, it means the brotherhood as a whole. And the spirit of brotherhood is strong. This is evident in the warm spirit of fellowship which the members enjoy after the close of the Sunday service. The members do not file quietly out of the building after the bendiction is pronounced. Rather there is much handshaking and visiting, for each congregation feels itself as one large family, each member concerned for the welfare of the whole group.

(5) Mennonites have a growing consciousness of being stewards of all they possess. They are learning to be good givers to the Lord's work. Being an industrious and frugal people they have money to give to missions and charities. The general mission board of the "Mennonite Church" is beginning to approach an annual income of a million dollars, and this does not include the money received and expended by the district mission boards of the several conferences of the church. An increasing number of Mennonites are tithing their incomes.

(6) Mennonites excel as farmers and tradesmen. They are particularly concerned to keep their fields productive and in a high state of cultivation. Their buildings are kept in good repair. They

have large barns, particularly in the eastern part of the country, and substantial houses. They find deep satisfaction in their well-kept and productive estates. In recent years an increasing number of Mennonites are entering the professions, particularly teaching and medicine, and are enjoying good success.

2. Liabilities

(1) In the chapter, "Recapturing the Anabaptist Vision," it was pointed out that the Mennonite Church has never entirely recovered the original evangelistic zeal of Anabaptism. *There has been a tendency to substitute a quiet inner piety for an aggressive spirit which personally assumes the obligations of Christian discipleship in the face of a hostile world.* This has been the most serious liability of modern Mennonitism and it is still not entirely overcome. It manifests itself in an unwillingness to pay the price of following resolutely the New Testament ethic—for example, in nonresistance—as well as in catering to modern movements which are entirely foreign to the genius of Anabaptism. Such a modern movement is "Fundamentalism" which more or less rejects nonresistance, nonconformity to the world, some of the ordinances, and which minimizes the value and significance of church membership. If the Mennonite Church wishes to regain its power it must recapture the Anabaptist vision of the cross of the Christian and of making disciples of all the nations.

(2) Another challenge confronting the Mennonite Church is to preserve faithfully essential Mennonitism in a changing culture and in the face of the breakdown of those sociological barriers which formerly served as effective aids in the maintenance of the Mennonite faith and way of life.

Past generations of American Mennonites were a strongly rural people, and that in a day when five miles was a considerable distance, due to slow means of transportation. Mennonite young people went to country school for a few months each winter until they were in their late teens and quit school with no thought of high school or university. In their daily life the Mennonites used to speak the Pennsylvania German dialect exclusively; even today many Mennonites who are but fifty years of age report that they could not speak English until they went to school. Mennonites were also characterized by a certain plainness of attire. Morgan Edwards in his *Materials Toward a History of the American Baptists,* written in 1770, tells how scrupulous the Mennonites then were in avoiding even such things as fancy buckles. This care to avoid conforming to the ways of the world was no mere external peculiarity; it was the product of a sense of estrangement from the "world." Mennonites avoided being swallowed up in the broad stream of American life. There was also little marriage with non-Mennonites. In general it can be said that in past generations little pressure was exerted on the Mennonites to make them conform to the general standards of Americanism; the sector of their life which touched the stream of Americanism was small. Further it should be added that the pioneers had a hard struggle financially; they had no money to waste on luxuries. We of today cannot imagine the simplicity of life which obtained when people did not have money to waste on the fads and fineries of the rich.

Mennonites of today own speedy automobiles; they have telephones in their homes; and many of them also have radios. The distance factor in isolation has been practically eliminated. No longer does the young man or woman attend rural school only. Oftentimes the young children are taken by bus to a centralized school, right from the first grade of school on through high school. The average young Mennonite attends at least several years of high school, and an increasing number are securing a college education. Not only has the rural isolation disappeared, and with it the limited education of the past, but another barrier has also disappeared, the use of German. In the days when young people did not speak the national language with ease and beauty there was much less temptation to lose their religious identity. Today a terrific pressure is exerted on Mennonite youth to conform fully to the patterns of life which obtain in the world at large. This pressure is exerted through the schools, the press, and the radio. And the pressure is at least in part successful. In certain sections of the church the conscience against theater attendance, for example, is weakening. Some members of the church have even tried to make money in ways which are not consistent for nonresistant Christians. Some Mennonites also seem to have little hesitancy to let go of all that has been distinctive in the Mennonite way of life. The church is having some difficulty in maintaining the doctrine of nonconformity, and this in spite of the fact that today there is an increase in the wearing of "plain clothing" in some parts of the church. This situation presents a challenge to consecrated Mennonite youth to live as

Jesus would have them live. The problem of worldliness has always bothered the church and it always will, but only those who walk close to God can help in the solution. Evidently the difficulty with worldliness is part of a more fundamental lack of spirituality. This lack of spirituality is becoming evident in some sections in a decline not only in church attendance, but also in missionary interest and in support of the general program of the church.

What is the outlook for the future of the Mennonite Church? If the church remembers its assets, it will be able to do much good in the future. It can expect a numerical growth, which it is indeed already experiencing. Its many missions can look forward to a great harvest of souls as a result of the good seed which is now being sown. The church can anticipate expansion in educational work and in publication, as well as in missions. But the church will also have to guard against the loss of nonresistance, of nonconformity, and of brotherly love,—for there is grave danger of further trouble within the church on the problem of nonconformity, particularly as it applies to attire.

May the Mennonite Church face the future with hope, and with confidence in the great Head of the church, Jesus Christ. Only He knows how to direct its course. And He is able to guide it, no matter how difficult the times may be. If the church is faithful, He will certainly do His part by caring for His bride until that great day when He shall appear to take her unto Himself. "And every man that hath this hope in him purifieth himself, even as he is pure."

APPENDIXES

I

A Letter of Conrad Grebel to Vadian

Dr. Joachim von Watt (popularly known as Vadian) was married to Conrad Grebel's sister Martha, and was long a good friend of Grebel. More than fifty letters of Grebel to Vadian have been preserved. Vadian was a leading citizen later burgomaster (mayor), of St. Gall, a Swiss city near Zurich. The original of this letter is printed in Latin in the *Vadianische Briefsammlung,* edited by Emil Arbenz, St. Gall, Switzerland, Vol. III, 1897, 116-118. The translation was made by Edward Yoder, the late scholar of Scottdale, Pennsylvania, and was published, together with an introduction by Ernst H. Correll, in the *Christian Monitor,* XVII, 1 (January, 1925), 788, 789. The date of the original letter was May 30, 1525, four months after Grebel established Swiss Anabaptism.

Great earnestness is evident in this, the last letter of Grebel to Vadian which has been preserved. He hoped to persuade Vadian not to join the Zwinglian forces of persecution. He longed even for Vadian's conversion to the Swiss Brethren "obedience of faith." He hoped for his separation from worldly entanglements and from a compromising state church. But Vadian did not break with the world; rather, he carried information against Grebel to the city council of St. Gall, who in turn sent a delegation to warn the Zurich city council of Grebel and his revolutionary ideas.

The latter part of the fourth paragraph of Grebel's letter would undoubtedly be more clear if we had at hand all the correspondence of Grebel and Vadian. Ulrich Zwingli believed and taught a rigid view of divine predestination and election. Vadian was in general a follower of Zwingli. Grebel seems to be refuting, partly through irony, the arguments based on divine election which Vadian had communicated to him. For after rebuking Vadian for his position he adds, "See, how you catch yourself. . . ."

The last paragraph of Grebel's letter includes a defense of the right of the Swiss Brethren to baptize converts. The occasion for this vigorous emphasis on carrying out the Lord's commandments was undoubtedly the request of the city council of St. Gall (April 26, 1525) that the Swiss Brethren "stand still in regard to the observances of baptism and the Lord's supper until the questions at issue were further elucidated."

But Grebel's letter of appeal was written in vain. On June 16, 1525, Hans Kern, a minister of the Swiss Brethren in St. Gall, was taken from prison and banished. The St. Gall council had decided upon persecution as their method of checking the spread of Anabaptism. Vadian had refused to give heed to Grebel. And Grebel, oft imprisoned, a fugitive from "justice" died about fifteen months later.

For a more detailed account of developments in St. Gall, see John Horsch: *Mennonites in Europe,* Mennonite Publishing House, Scottdale, Pennsylvania, 1942, chapter 9, "The Swiss Brethren in St. Gall."

Greeting be to you and peace in the Lord, not in the world, so that it can be in the Lord. For the favors you have done me I thank you very much, and I wish and long that you may be exceedingly rewarded by the Lord our God, the God of good gifts. Still I think of it, when I call to mind your conflict with those who are my true Christian brethren, I speak freely, frankly, and like a Christian. I could not wish for more indulgent treatment for anyone than what you have done so generously for me, so that I might be free to tell you what it is my duty to say. For although you know this yourself, still you have not been led to lend a more willing ear to the doctrine of the spirit than to that of the flesh. Although you are annoyed by me, although you know it yourself, still you do not take heed. Although, I say, you do know, still I tell it: it is entirely or at least very largely your fault if anything will be decided against them [the Swiss Brethren] by means of prison, money fine, confiscation, or death.

Pray to keep yourself from innocent blood; innocent it verily is, both if you know it and if you do not; whether you wish it or not, it is innocent. Their suffering and the end of their lives and the great day of the Lord will prove it. You were born for your destruction at this point of sacred history, as you were into this city for this position of dignity, unless you beware and come to your senses. I call heaven and earth as witnesses; I beg you to bear with me as I say this, which through Christ our Lord and true Savior is the truth. The Lord willing, I shall even unto death bear witness to the truth, in which those men truly are and you could be too. I know what is urging you: their property is urging you, I think, or your own carnal wisdom or the unjust faction of Zwingli, who is an enemy of the truth in this matter. Do not destroy yourself, I beg you. If you deceive men here, you will not be hidden in the presence of the Lord God, the Searcher of hearts and the just Judge. Rather draw away from the enjoyment of wealth; trust in God, humble yourself, be content with a little, draw away from the bloody faction of Zwingli, flee from your own wisdom to the side of divine wisdom, so that you may become foolish in the world, and wise in the Lord; become a child, otherwise you cannot enter the kingdom of God. Why do you trust Zwingli even for your safety, who according to clear Scripture, Ps. 14, Ezek. 18, has publicly declared that money leads to condemnation? And Gregory, the ninth Pope of this name, excluded from the Lord's supper anyone who took from a debtor anything more than the principal.

If you do not wish to defend the brethren, at least do not resist them, so that you may be more excusable, and do not give an example of persecution to the other cities. Through my faith in Christ, through heaven and earth and whatever in them is, I tell you sincerely and without guile that it is out of my love to you that I have admonished you in this way. Therefore I implore you through Christ, do not despise my speaking and warning from Christ; and give careful thought that it may have been spoken to you for bringing you to your senses, not for a testimony against you. If you yield, I will lay down my life for you; If you do not yield, I will lay it down for these our brethren in the face of all men who are going to fight against this truth. For I will bear testimony to the truth with the spoiling of my goods, yea, of my home, which is all I have; I will testify to the truth with imprisonments, with confiscations, with death, and with my pen, unless God forbids. But if I had not written this reply all others will not sleep.

You accept the doctrine, Zwingli rejects it; why do you wait, when you know it beforehand? Do you expect that you may have a cover for rejecting the doctrine and even persecuting it. My dear Vadian! Why do you not bear testimony as we do, why do you exercise only the power and arm of the flesh, using the Scriptures against us instead of free-will? Do you believe that we are insane or full of hell itself, not only of demons, we who are ready to testify even to death, to that death however which Zwingli and others prepare, while they keep back the truth in falsehood? If the doctrine is sound, as it is, as you admit with partial consent and take away election from those, why do you not elect yourself or another or why are you not elected or why does not the council use force and baptize? Why does it not elect? Why do not the priests who strive against the doctrine and are not elected?

See, how you catch yourself and show in your own words that you have something else in mind than what the words indicate; for if those do not baptize, no one of you should baptize to whom you ascribe this duty and who you say are the elect. In this way you show that you want to have baptism held up in derision and contempt before the doctrine that you accept and so too the commandment of baptism. For the doctrine of the Lord and the commandments have been given for the purpose of being carried out and put into practice. I say again, if you deceive the council, who does not notice this, will you not deceive the Lord? Pray to the Lord for me, so that his just will alone may be willed in us, and I in turn will also pray in a brotherly manner and unceasingly. Bear with me in a patient Christian spirit and guard yourself. Farewell in the Lord Jesus Christ. Greet for me my sister and the family with thanks. *At Zurich, on the day of Mars before Pentecost, 1525.*

To Joachim Vadianus, my brother-in-law and brother in the Lord.

II

A Letter of Menno Simons to a Troubled Christian

Chosen beloved sister in Christ Jesus, Mercy, grace and peace be to thee! Most beloved sister whom I sincerely love in Christ. From your beloved husband's letter I understand that during all the winter you have been a sick and afflicted child, which I very much regret to hear. But we pray daily, "Father, Thy will be done." By which we commit ourselves to the Father to treat with us as is pleasing in his blessed sight. . . .

Secondly, I understand that your conscience is troubled because you have not and do not now walk in such perfection as the Scriptures direct us; on which account I write the following to my faithful sister as a fraternal consolation from the true word and eternal truth of the Lord: "The Scripture," says Paul, "hath concluded all under sin." "There is no man on earth," says Solomon, "who does righteously and sinneth not." Eccl. 7. At another place, "A just man falleth seven times, and riseth up again," Prov. 24:16. . . . "We are all as an unclean thing, and all our righteousnesses are as filthy rags;" Christ also says, "There is none good but one, that is, God;" "The evil which I would not, that I do;" "In many things we all offend;" "If we say that we have no sin, we deceive ourselves, and the truth is not in us," [Ps. 143:2; I Kin. 8:46; Isa. 64:6; Matt. 19:17; Mark 10:18; Rom. 7:19; I John 1:8].

As it is plain from all these Scriptures that we must all acknowledge ourselves to be sinners as we also are in fact; and as no one has perfectly fulfilled the righteousness required of God but Christ Jesus alone; therefore none can approach God, obtain grace and be saved except by the perfect righteousness, reconciliation and advocacy of Jesus Christ; however godly, righteous, holy and unblamable he is. We must all acknowledge, whosoever we are, that we are sinners in thoughts, words and works. Yea, if we had not before us the righteous Christ Jesus, no prophet nor apostle could be saved. Therefore be of good cheer and be consoled in the Lord. You can expect no greater righteousness in yourself than all the chosen of God had in them from the beginning. In and by yourself you are a poor sinner, and by the eternal righteousness banished, accursed and adjudged to eternal death; but in and through Christ you are justified and pleasing unto God, and accepted of Him in eternal grace as a daughter and child. In this all saints have consoled themselves, trusted in Christ, esteemed their own righteousness as unclean, weak and imperfect, with contrite hearts approached the throne of grace in the name of Christ and with firm faith prayed the Father, "O, Father forgive us our trespasses as we forgive those that trespass against us." Matt. 6; Luke 11. . . .

I herewith pray you and desire that you will wholly commend all your doings outward and inward unto Christ Jesus and His merits, believing and confessing that His precious blood alone is your cleansing, His righteousness your piety, His death your life, and His resurrection your justification; for He is the forgiveness of all your sins; His bloody wounds are your reconciliation; and His invincible strength the staff and consolation of your weakness. . . . So long as you find and feel such a spirit in yourself which is desirous of following that which is good and abhorring that which is evil notwithstanding the remnant of sin is not entirely dead in you, as also all the saints complained of from the beginning, so long you may rest assured that you are a child of God and that you will inherit the kingdom of grace in eternal joy with all the saints. . . . In the city of God, in the new Jerusalem, there we will wait on each other before the throne of God and of the Lamb, there sing hallelujah, and praise His name in perfect joy. Your husband and children I commend to Him who has given them to you, and He will do with them justly. The saving power of the most holy blood of Christ be with my most beloved child and sister, now and forever, Amen.

Your brother, who sincerely loves you in Christ,

MENNO SIMONS

III

The Schleitheim Confession of Faith

Adopted by a Swiss Brethren Conference, February 24, 1527

Editorial Note: The Seven Articles of Schleitheim were written with Michael Sattler of Stauffen, Germany, as the chief author, it is belived. Sattler was originally an officer in a Roman Catholic monastery. He early embraced the faith of the Swiss Brethren and served until his early martyrdom (May 1527) as an outstanding leader. Van Braght lists the nine charges on which Sattler was sentenced to death, together with Sattler's reply. He also gives a brief account of his trial and a copy of a letter from "Brother Michael Sattler of Staufen" to "the Church of God at Horb" (1938 *Martyrs' Mirror,* 416-420). In his farewell pastoral letter Sattler wrote, "Remember our assembly, and strictly follow that which was resolved on therein," an undoubted reference to the Seven Articles and a hint as to his own leadership in the meeting.

The Schleitheim Confession was widely circulated. Ulrich Zwingli translated it into Latin and attempted to refute it already in 1527. It was in print in its original German form as early as 1533. John Calvin used a now-lost French translation of the Seven Articles in his refutation of Anabaptism published in 1544. By 1560 there was also a Dutch translation of the confession. The English translation in W. J. McGlothlin's *Baptist Confessions of Faith,* Philadelphia, 1911, 3-9, was made from Zwingli's Latin translation. For an excellent survey of known manuscript copies and printed editions of the Schleitheim Confession, see Robert Friedmann's article in *The Mennonite Quarterly Review,* XVI, 2 (April, 1942), 82-87.

The Seven Articles are not at all a full statement of Christian doctrine. They were written in days of fierce persecution when there was little interest in or possibility of erecting a grand system of Christian theology. Sattler wished only to set up certain pillars of truth against the unsound teachings of that period. He seems in particular to be setting up a defense against the doctrines of some "false brethren" with antinomian tendencies.

Along with the writings of Conrad Grebel (very limited in extent) and Pilgram Marpeck (extensive, but not of the quality of the Dutch Menno Simons) the Schleitheim Confession is of great significance for the determination of the teaching of the first Swiss Brethren.

The following is my translation of the full text of the pastoral letter, apparently from "Brother Michael Sattler," and which includes the Seven Articles of faith. For the German text used, see Walther Köhler: *Brüderlich Vereinigung etzlicher Kinder Gottes sieben Artikel betreffend . . . (Flugschriften aus der ersten Jahren der*

Reformation, 2. Band, 3. Heft), Leipzig, 1908, 305-316, also Heinrich Böhmer: *Urkunden zur Geschichte des Bauernkrieges und der Wiedertäufer,* Bonn, 1910; second edition, 1921; reprint, Berlin, 1933, 27-35. The translation is somewhat free in places, particularly in the citation of Bible verses where the King James Version was followed unless the German text deviated too markedly. Here is the translation, reprinted from *The Mennonite Quarterly Review,* XIX, 4 (October, 1945), 247-253:

BROTHERLY UNION OF A NUMBER OF CHILDREN OF GOD CONCERNING SEVEN ARTICLES

May joy, peace and mercy from our Father through the atonement of the blood of Christ Jesus, together with the gifts of the Spirit—Who is sent from the Father to all believers for their strength and comfort and for their perseverance in all tribulation until the end, Amen—be to all those who love God, who are the children of light, and who are scattered everywhere as it has been ordained of God our Father, where they are with one mind assembled together in one God and Father of us all: Grace and peace of heart be with you all, Amen.

Beloved brethren and sisters in the Lord: First and supremely we are always concerned for your consolation and the assurance of your conscience (which was previously misled)* so that you may not always remain foreigners to us and by right almost completely excluded, but that you may turn again to the true implanted members of Christ, who have been armed through patience and knowledge of themselves, and have therefore again been united with us in the strength of a godly Christian spirit and zeal for God.

It is also apparent with what cunning the devil has turned us aside, so that he might destroy and bring to an end the work of God which in mercy and grace has been partly begun in us. But Christ, the true Shepherd of our souls, Who has begun this in us, will certainly direct the same and teach [us] to His honor and our salvation, Amen.

Dear brethren and sisters, we who have been assembled in the Lord at Schleitheim on the Border, make known in points and articles to all who love God that as concerns us we are of one mind to abide in the Lord as God's obedient children, [His] sons and daughters, we who have been and shall be separated from the world in everything, [and] completely at peace. To God alone be praise and glory without the contradiction of any brethren. In this we have perceived the oneness of the Spirit of our Father and of our common Christ with us. For the Lord is the Lord of peace and not of quarreling, as Paul points out. That you may understand in what articles this has been formulated you should observe and note [the following].

* The words in brackets are inserted by the translator to clarify the text. The words in parentheses are a part of the original text. [J. C. W.]

A very great offense has been introduced by certain false brethren among us, so that some have turned aside from the faith, in the way they intend to practice and observe the freedom of the Spirit and of Christ. But such have missed the truth and to their condemnation are given over to the lasciviousness and self-indulgence of the flesh. They think faith and love may do and permit everything, and nothing will harm them nor condemn them, since they are believers.

Observe, you who are God's members in Christ Jesus, that faith in the Heavenly Father through Jesus Christ does not take such form. It does not produce and result in such things as these false brethren and sisters do and teach. Guard yourselves and be warned of such people, for they do not serve our Father, but their father, the devil.

But you are not that way. For they that are Christ's have crucified the flesh with its passions and lusts. You understand me well and [know] the brethren whom we mean. Separate yourselves from them for they are preverted. Petition the Lord that they may have the knowledge which leads to repentance, and [pray] for us that we may have constancy to persevere in the way which we have espoused, for the honor of God and of Christ, His Son, Amen.

The articles which we discussed and on which we were of one mind are these: 1. Baptism; 2. The Ban [Excommunication]; 3. Breaking of Bread; 4. Separation from the Abomination; 5. Pastors in the Church; 6. The Sword; and 7. The Oath.

First. Observe concerning baptism: Baptism shall be given to all those who have learned repentance and amendment of life, and who believe truly that their sins are taken away by Christ, and to all those who walk in the resurrection of Jesus Christ, and wish to be buried with Him in death, so that they may be resurrected with Him, and to all those who with this significance request it [baptism] of us and demand it for themselves. This excludes all infant baptism, the highest and chief abomination of the pope. In this you have the foundation and testimony of the apostles. Mt. 28, Mk. 16, Acts 2, 8, 16, 19. This we wish to hold simply, yet firmly and with assurance.

Second. We are agreed as follows on the ban: The ban shall be employed with all those who have given themselves to the Lord, to walk in His commandments, and with all those who are baptized into the one body of Christ and who are called brethren or sisters, and yet who slip sometimes and fall into error and sin, being inadvertently overtaken. The same shall be admonished twice in secret and the third time openly disciplined or banned according to the command of Christ. Mt. 18. But this shall be done according to the regulation of the Spirit (Mt. 5) before the breaking of bread, so that we may break and eat one bread, with one mind and in one love, and may drink of one cup.

Third. In the breaking of bread we are of one mind and are agreed [as follows]: All those who wish to break one bread in remembrance of the broken body of Christ, and all who wish to drink of one drink as a remembrance of the shed blood of Christ, shall be united beforehand by baptism in one body of Christ which is the church of God and whose Head is Christ. For as Paul points out we cannot at the same time be partakers of the Lord's table and the table of devils; we cannot at the same time drink the cup of the Lord and the cup of the devil. That is, all those who have fellowship with the dead works of darkness have no part in the light. Therefore all who follow the devil and the world have no part with those who are called unto God out of the world. All who lie in evil have no part in the good.

Therefore it is and must be [thus]: Whoever has not been called by one God to one faith, to one baptism, to one Spirit, to one body, with all the children of God's church, cannot be made [into] one bread with them, as indeed must be done if one is truly to break bread according to the command of Christ.

Fourth. We are agreed [as follows] on separation: A separation shall be made from the evil and from the wickedness which the devil planted in the world; in this manner, simply that we shall not have fellowship with them [the wicked] and not run with them in the multitude of their abominations. This is the way it is: Since all who do not walk in the obedience of faith, and have not united themselves with God so that they wish to do His will, are a great abomination before God, it is not possible for anything to grow or issue from them except abominable things. For truly all creatures are in but two classes, good and bad, believing and unbelieving, darkness and light, the world and those who [have come] out of the world, God's temple and idols, Christ and Belial; and none can have part with the other.

To us then the command of the Lord is clear when He calls upon us to be separate from the evil and thus He will be our God and we shall be His sons and daughters.

He further admonishes us to withdraw from Babylon and the earthly Egypt that we may not be partakers of the pain and suffering which the Lord will bring upon them.

From this we should learn that everything which is not united with our God and Christ cannot be other than an abomination which we should shun and flee from. By this is meant all popish and antipopish works and church services, meetings and church attendance,* drinking houses, civic affairs, the commitments [made in] unbelief and other things of that kind, which are highly regarded by the world and yet are carried on in flat contradiction to the command of God, in accordance with all the unrighteouness which is in the world. From all these things we shall be separated and have no part with them for they are nothing but an abomination, and they are

* This severe judgment on the state churches must be understood in the light of sixteenth century conditions. The state clergymen were in many cases careless and carnal men. All citizens in a given province were considered members of the state church because they had been made Christians ("chrisened") by infant baptism. Also, in 1527 Zurich had begun to use capital punishment on the Swiss Brethren, with the full approval of the state church leaders. Sattler himself was burned at the stake less than three months after the Schleitheim conference.

the cause of our being hated before our Christ Jesus, Who has set us free from the slavery of the flesh and fitted us for the service of God through the Spirit Whom He has given us.

Therefore there will also unquestionably fall from us the unchristian, devilish weapons of force—such as sword, armor and the like, and all their use [either] for friends or against one's enemies—by virtue of the word of Christ, Resist not [him that is] evil.

Fifth. We are agreed as follows on pastors in the church of God: The pastor in the church of God shall, as Paul has prescribed, be one who out-and-out has a good report of those who are outside the faith. This office shall be to read, to admonish and teach, to warn, to discipline, to ban in the church, to lead out in prayer for the advancement of all the brethren and sisters, to lift up the bread when it is to be broken, and in all things to see to the care of the body of Christ, in order that it may be built up and developed, and the mouth of the slanderer be stopped.

This one moreover shall be supported of the church which has chosen him, wherein he may be in need, so that he who serves the Gospel may live of the Gospel as the Lord has ordained. But if a pastor should do something requiring discipline, he shall not be dealt with except [on the testimony of] two or three witnesses. And when they sin they shall be disciplined before all in order that the others may fear.

But should it happen that through the cross this pastor should be banished or led to the Lord [through martyrdom] another shall be ordained in his place in the same hour so that God's little flock and people may not be destroyed.

Sixth. We are agreed as follows concerning the sword: The sword is ordained of God outside the perfection of Christ. It punishes and puts to death the wicked, and guards and protects the good. In the Law the sword was ordained for the punishment of the wicked and for their death, and the same [sword] is [now] ordained to be used by the worldly magistrates.

In the perfection of Christ, however, only the ban is used for a warning and for the excommunication of the one who has sinned, without putting the flesh to death,—simply the warning and the command to sin no more.

Now it will be asked by many who do not recognize [this as] the will of Christ for us, whether a Christian may or should employ the sword against the wicked for the defence and protection of the good, or for the sake of love.

Our reply is unanimously as follows: Christ teaches and commands us to learn of Him, for He is meek and lowly in heart and so shall we find rest to our souls. Also Christ says to the heathenish woman who was taken in adultery, not that one should stone her according to the law of His Father (and yet He says, As the Father has commanded me, thus I do), but in mercy and forgiveness and warning, to sin no more. Such [an attitude] we also ought to take completely according to the rule of the ban.

Secondly, it will be asked concerning the sword, whether a Christian shall pass sentence in worldly disputes and strife such as unbelievers have with one another. This is our united answer: Christ did not wish to decide or pass judgment between brother and brother in the case of the inheritance, but refused to do so. Therefore we should do likewise.

Thirdly, it will be asked concerning the sword, Shall one be a magistrate if one should be chosen as such? The answer is as follows: They wished to make Christ king, but He fled and did not view it as the arrangement of His Father. Thus shall we do as He did, and follow Him, and so shall we not walk in darkness. For He Himself says, He who wishes to come after me, let him deny himself and take up his cross and follow me. Also, He Himself forbids the [employment of] the force of the sword saying, The worldly princes lord it over them, etc., but not so shall it be with you. Further, Paul says, Whom God did foreknow He also did predestinate to be conformed to the image of His Son, etc. Also Peter says, Christ has suffered (not ruled) and left us an example, that ye should follow His steps.

Finally it will be observed that it is not appropriate for a Christian to serve as a magistrate because of these points: The government magistracy is according to the flesh, but the Christians' is according to the Spirit; their houses and dwelling remain in this world, but the Christians' are in heaven; their citizenship is in this world, but the Christians' citizenship is in heaven; the weapons of their conflict and war are carnal and against the flesh only, but the Christians' weapons are spiritual, against the fortification of the devil. The worldlings are armed with steel and iron, but the Christians are armed with the armor of God, with truth, righteousness, peace, faith, salvation and the Word of God. In brief, as is the mind of Christ toward us, so shall the mind of the members of the body of Christ be through Him in all things, that there may be no schism in the body through which it would be destroyed. For every kingdom divided against itself will be destroyed. Now since Christ is as it is written of Him, His members must also be the same, that His body may remain complete and united to its own advancement and upbuilding.

Seventh. We are agreed as follows concerning the oath: The oath is a confirmation among those who are quarreling or making promises. In the Law it is commanded to be performed in God's Name, but only in truth, not falsely. Christ, who teaches the perfection of the Law, prohibits all swearing to His [followers], whether true or false,—neither by heaven, nor by the earth, nor by Jerusalem, nor by our head,—and that for the reason which He shortly thereafter gives, For you are not able to make one hair white or black. So you see it is for this reason that all swearing is forbidden: we cannot fulfill that which we promise when we swear, for we cannot change [even] the very least thing on us.

Now there are some who do not give credence to the simple command of God, but object with this question: Well now, did not God swear to Abraham by Himself (since He was God) when He promised him that He would be with him and that He would be his God if he would keep His commandments, —why then should I not also swear when I promise to someone? Answer: Hear what the Scripture says: God, since He wished more abundantly to show unto the heirs the immutability of His counsel, inserted an oath, that by two immutable things (in which it is impossible for God to lie) we might have a strong consolation. Observe the meaning of this Scripture: What God forbids you to do, He has power to do, for everything is possible for Him. God swore an oath to Abraham, says the Scripture, so that He might show that His counsel is immutable. That is, no one can withstand nor thwart His will; therefore He can keep His oath. But we can do nothing, as is said above by Christ, to keep or perform [our oaths]: therefore we shall not swear at all [*nichts schweren*]

Then others further say as follows: It is not forbidden of God to swear in the New Testament, when it is actually commanded in the Old, but it is forbidden only to swear by heaven, earth, Jerusalem and our head. Answer: Hear the Scripture, He who swears by heaven swears by God's throne and by Him who sitteth thereon. Observe: it is forbidden to swear by heaven, which is only the throne of God: how much more is it forbidden [to swear] by God Himself! Ye fools and blind, which is greater, the throne or Him that sitteth thereon?

Further some say, Because evil is now [in the world, and] because man needs God for [the establishment of] the truth, so did the apostles Peter and Paul also swear. Answer: Peter and Paul only testify of that which God promised to Abraham with the oath. They themselves promise nothing, as the example indicates clearly. Testifying and swearing are two different things. For when a person swears he is in the first place promising future things, as Christ was promised to Abraham Whom we a long time afterwards received. But when a person bears testimony he is testifying about the present, whether it is good or evil, as Simeon spoke to Mary about Christ and testified, Behold this [child] is set for the fall and rising of many in Israel, and for a sign which shall be spoken against.

Christ also taught us along the same line when He said, Let your communication be Yea, yea; Nay, nay; for whatsoever is more than these cometh of evil. He says, Your speech or word shall be yea and nay. [However] when one does not wish to understand, he remains closed to the meaning. Christ is simply Yea and Nay, and all those who seek Him simply will understand His Word. Amen.

Dear brethren and sisters in the Lord: These are the articles of certain brethren who had heretofore been in error and who had failed to agree in the true understanding, so that many weaker consciences were perplexed, causing the Name of God to be greatly slandered. Therefore there has been a great need for us to become of one mind in the Lord, which has come to pass. To God be praise and glory!

Now since you have so well understood the will of God which has been made known by us, it will be necessary for you to achieve perseveringly, without interruption, the known will of God. For you know well what the servant who sinned knowingly heard as his recompense.

Everything which you have unwittingly done and confessed as evil doing is forgiven you through the believing prayer which is offered by us in our meeting for all our shortcomings and guilt. [This state is yours] through the gracious forgiveness of God and through the blood of Jesus Christ. Amen.

Keep watch on all who do not walk according to the simplicity of the divine truth which is stated in this letter from [the decisions of] our meeting, so that everyone among us will be governed by the rule of the ban and henceforth the entry of false brethren and sisters among us may be prevented.

Eliminate from you that which is evil and the Lord will be your God and you will be His sons and daughters.

Dear brethren, keep in mind what Paul admonishes Timothy when he says, The grace of God that bringeth salvation hath appeared to all men, teaching us that, denying ungodliness and worldly lusts, we should live soberly, righteously, and godly, in this present world; looking for that blessed hope, and the glorious appearing of the great God and our Saviour Jesus Christ; Who gave Himself for us, that He might redeem us from all iniquity, and purify unto Himself a people of His own, zealous of good works. Think on this and exercise yourselves therein and the God of peace will be with you.

May the Name of God be hallowed eternally and highly praised, Amen. May the Lord give you His peace, Amen.

The Acts of Schleitheim on the Border [Canton Schaffhausen, Switzerland], on Matthias' [Day],* Anno MDXXVII.

* February 24

IV

The Dordrecht Confession of Faith

Adopted by a Dutch Mennonite Conference April 21, 1632

Editorial Note: Mennonites are not a creedal church. No human system of doctrine stands between them and the Word of God. It is to the Scriptures that they are bound. Yet it must also be stated that Mennonites actually hold to rather well defined doctrinal views. Many confessions of faith were produced beginning with the Schleitheim articles of 1527. The best of these confessions, although they all resemble each other rather closely, is undoubtedly the one adopted at Dordrecht, Holland, in 1632.

In the days of Menno Simons, 1496-1561, the Mennonites of the Netherlands were one brotherhood. But beginning in 1567 a number of schisms occurred. Bishop Dirck Philips, 1504-68, the great co-worker of Menno, affiliated himself with the Flemish Mennonites, while Bishop Peter Janz Twisck, 1565-1636, who was married to Menno's granddaughter, adhered to the Frisians. Hendrik Roosevelt, a Flemish bishop, and others, labored unsuccessfully for union.

About 1630 another series of efforts were made to unite various Mennonite groups. The "Olive Branch" confession of 1627 (printed on pages 27-33 of the 1938 *Martyrs' Mirror*) was an effort to provide a basis for union between the Friesian and Flemish churches. The Jan Cents' Confession of 1630 (pages 33-38, *Martyrs' Mirror*) was subscribed to by fourteen Friesian and High German ministers.

The Dordrecht Confession of 1632 was written in the first draft by Adrian Cornelis, bishop of the Flemish Mennonite Church in Dordrecht. About the middle of April 1632 a number of Mennonite ministers assembled in Dordrecht in spite of the protest of the Reformed clergy against "this extraordinary gathering of Anabaptists from all provinces." The conference was successful in forming a union, a united brotherhood. At the close of the sessions the ministers extended to each other the right hand of fellowship, greeted each other with the holy kiss, and observed the Lord's Supper together. Of the fifty-one Flemish and Frisian ministers who signed this confession of faith, two were of Crefeld, Germany and two represented "the upper country" (central or south Germany).

The Alsatian Mennonites adopted the Dordrecht Confession in 1660, when thirteen ministers and deacons subscribed to it. The Palatine and German Mennonite Churches also subsequently adopted it. However, the Swiss Mennonite churches never subscribed to it. In 1725 the Pennsylvania Mennonites, mostly Swiss, of what are now the Franconia and Lancaster Conferences, adopted the Dordrecht Confession, undoubtedly through the influence of the Dutch Mennonites of Germantown, near Philadelphia. Sixteen ministers signed a statement of adoption. A number of the more conservative Mennonite bodies of America, including the *Mennonite Church,* now recognize the Dordrecht Confession as the official summary of their doctrinal beliefs. Historically this confession of faith was used as a basis of instruction to classes of young people who were being prepared for baptism and church membership. At the present time in the *Mennonite Church* the chief significance of the Dordrecht Confession is undoubtedly its value as a symbol of the Mennonite heritage of faith and way of life.

The text of the Dordrecht Confession printed below is basically that which is now in circulation in the Mennonite Church in America. It is apparently a translation of a German translation of the Dutch original. In Van Braght's *Bloedigh Tooneel* of 1660 the Dordrecht Confession is printed in the unpaginated introduction. The names of the signers given below were taken from the 1660 edition. For an English translation made directly from the original Dutch, see the 1938 edition of the *Martyrs' Mirror,* pages 38-44. The *Martyrs' Mirror* text of the Dordrecht Confession was used to correct the text which is in common circulation among American Mennonites. The corrections were merely a matter of wording, not a change in sense.

The Alsatian Mennonite statement which follows the Dordrecht Confession was corrected from the *Christliche Glaubens-Bekentnos* . . . , Amsterdam, 1664, pages 35, 36.

Article I.

Of God and the Creation of all Things

Whereas it is declared, that "without faith it is impossible to please God" (Heb. 11:6), and that "he that cometh to God must believe that he is, and that he is a rewarder of them that diligently seek him," therefore we confess with the mouth, and believe with the heart, together with all the pious, according to the Holy Scriptures, that there is one eternal, almighty, and incomprehensible God, Father, Son, and the Holy Ghost, and none more and none other, before whom no God existed, neither will exist after him. For from him, through him, and in him are all things. To him be blessing, praise, and honor, for ever and ever. Gen. 17:1; Deut. 6:4; Isaiah 46:9; I John 5:7.

In this one God, who "worketh all in all," we believe. Him we confess as the creator of all things, visible and invisible; who in six days created and prepared "heaven and earth, and the sea, and all things that are therein." And we further believe, that this God still governs and preserves the same, together with all his works, through his wisdom, his might, and the "word of his power." Gen. 5:1, 2; Acts 14:15; I Cor. 12:6; Heb. 1:3.

When he had finished his works and, according to his good pleasure, had ordained and prepared each of them, so that they were right and good according to their nature, being and quality, he created the first man, Adam, the father of all of us, gave him a body formed "of the dust of the ground, and breathed into his nostrils the breath of life," so that he "became a living soul," created by God "in his own image and likeness," in "righteousness and true holiness" unto eternal life. He also gave him a place above all other creatures and endowed him with many high and excellent gifts, put him into the garden of Eden, and gave him a commandment and an interdiction. Thereupon he took a rib from the said Adam, made a woman out of it, brought her to him, and gave her to him as a helpmate and housewife. Consequently he has caused, that from this first man, Adam, all men who "dwell on the face of the earth," have been begotten and have descended. Gen. 1:27; 2:7, 15-17, 22; 5:1; Acts 17:26.

Article II.

Of the Fall of Man

We believe and confess, that, according to the purport of the Holy Scriptures, our first parents, Adam and Eve, did not long remain in the happy state in which they were created; but did, after being seduced by the deceit and "subtility" of the serpent, and envy of the devil, violate the high command of God, and became disobedient to their Creator; through which disobedience "sin entered into the world, and death by sin;" so that "death passed upon all men, for that all have sinned," and thereby incurred the wrath of God and condemnation. For which reason our first parents were, by God, driven out of Paradise, to cultivate the earth, to maintain themselves thereon in sorrow, and to "eat their bread in the sweat of their face," until they "returned to the ground, from which they were taken." And that they did, therefore, through this one sin, so far apostatize, depart, and estrange themselves from God, that they could neither help themselves, nor be helped by any of their descendants, nor by angels, nor by any other creature in heaven or on earth, nor be redeemed, or reconciled to God; but would have had to be lost forever, had not God, who pitied his creatures, in mercy, interposed in their behalf and made provision for their restoration. Gen. 3:6, 23; Rom. 5:12-19; Psalm 47:8, 9; Rev. 5:3; John 3:16.

Article III.

Of the Restoration of Man through the Promise of the Coming of Christ

Regarding the restoration of our first parents and their descendants, we believe and confess: That God, notwithstanding their fall, transgression and sin, and although they had no power to help themselves, he was nevertheless not willing that they should be cast off entirely, or be eternally lost; but again called them unto him, comforted them, and showed them that there were yet means with him for their reconciliation; namely, the immaculate Lamb, the Son of God; who "was fore-ordained" to this purpose "before the foundation of the world," and who was promised to them and all their descendants, while they (our first parents) were yet in paradise, for their comfort, redemption, and salvation; yea, who was given to them thenceforward, through faith, as their own; after which all the pious patriarchs, to whom this promise was often renewed, longed and searched, beholding it through faith at a distance, and expecting its fulfillment—expecting that he (the Son of God), would, at his coming, again redeem and deliver the fallen race of man from their sins, their guilt, and unrighteousness. John 1:29; 11:27; I Pet. 1:18, 19; Gen. 3:15; I Jno. 2:1, 2; 3:8; Gal. 4:4, 5.

Article IV.

Of the Advent of Christ into This World, and the Reason of His Coming

We believe and confess further: That "when the fullness of the time was come," after which all the pious patriarchs so ardently longed, and which they so anxiously awaited—the previously promised Messiah, Redeemer, and Savior, proceeded from God, being sent by Him, and according to the prediction of the prophets and the testimony of the evangelists, came into the world, yea, into the flesh—, so that the word itself thus became flesh and man; and that he was conceived by the Virgin Mary (who was espoused to a man named Joseph, of the house of David), and that she bare him as her first-born son at Bethlehem, "wrapped him in swaddling clothes, and laid him in a manger." John 4:25; 16:28; I Tim. 3:16; Matt. 1:21; John 1:14; Luke 2:7.

Further we believe and confess, that this is the same One, "whose goings forth have been from of old, from everlasting;" who has "neither beginning of days, nor end of life." Of whom it is testified, that he is "Alpha and Omega, the beginning and the end, the first and the last." That this is also he—and none other—who was chosen, promised, and sent; who came into the world; and who is God's only, first, and proper Son; who was before John the Baptist, before Abraham, before the world; yea, who was David's Lord, and who was God of the "whole earth," "the first-born of every creature"; who was sent into the world, and himself delivered up the body prepared for him, as "an offering and a sacrifice to God for a sweet smelling savor;" yea, for the comfort, redemption, and salvation of all—of the human race. Micah 5:2; Heb. 7:3; Rev. 1:8; John 3:16; Rom. 8:32; Col. 1:15; Heb. 10:5.

But how, or in what manner, this worthy body was prepared, or how the word became flesh, and he himself man, we content ourselves with the declaration which the worthy evangelists have given and left in their description thereof; according to which we confess with all the saints, that he is the Son of the living God, in whom exist all our hope, comfort, redemption, and salvation, and which we are to seek in no one else. Luke 1:31-35; John 20:31.

Further, we believe and confess by authority of scripture, that when he had ended his course, and "finished" the work for which he was sent into the world, he was, by the providence of God, delivered into the hands of the unrighteous; suffered under the judge, Pontius Pilate, was crucified, died, was buried, rose again from the dead on the third day, and ascended into heaven, where he now sits at the right hand of the Majesty of God on high; from whence he will come again to judge the living and dead. Luke 23:1, 52, 53; 24:5, 6, 51.

Thus we believe the Son of God died—"tasted death for every man," shed his precious blood, and thereby bruised the head of the serpent, destroyed the works of the devil, "blotted out the hand-writing," and purchased redemption for the whole human race; and thus he became the source of eternal salvation to all who from the time of Adam to the end of the world, shall have believed in him, and obeyed him. Gen. 3:15; I John 3:8; Col. 2:14; Rom. 5:18.

Article V.

OF THE LAW OF CHRIST, WHICH IS THE HOLY GOSPEL, OR THE NEW TESTAMENT

We also believe and confess, that Christ, before his ascension, established and instituted his New Testament and left it to his followers, to be and remain an everlasting testament, which he confirmed and sealed with his own precious blood; and whch he has so highly commended to them, that neither men or angels may change it, neither take therefrom nor add thereto. Jer. 31:31; Heb. 9:15-17; Matt. 26:28; Gal. 1:8; I Tim. 6:3-5; Rev. 22:18, 19; Matt. 5:18; Luke 21:33.

And that he has caused this Testament (in which the whole counsel and will of his heavenly Father, so far as these are necessary to the salvation of man, are comprehended), to be proclaimed, in his name, through his beloved apostles, messengers, and servants (whom he chose and sent into all the world for this purpose)—to all nations, people and tongues; these apostles preaching repentance and remission of sins; and that he, in said Testament, caused it to be declared, that all men without distinction, if they are obedient, through faith, follow, fulfill and live according to the precepts of the same, are his children and rightful heirs; having thus excluded none from the precious inheritance of eternal salvation, except the unbelieving and disobedient, the headstrong and unconverted; who despise such salvation; and thus by their own actions incur guilt by refusing the same, and "judge themselves unworthy of everlasting life." Mark 16:15; Luke 24:46, 47; Rom. 8:17; Acts 13:46.

Article VI.

OF REPENTANCE AND AMENDMENT OF LIFE

We believe and confess, that, as the "imagination of man's heart is evil from his youth," and consequently inclined to all unrighteousness, sin and wickedness, that, therefore, the first doctrine of the precious New Testament of the Son of God is, Repentance and amendment of life. Gen. 8:21; Mark 1:15.

Therefore those who have ears to hear, and hearts to understand, must "bring forth fruits meet for repentance," amend their lives, believe the gospel, "depart from evil and do good," desist from wrong and cease from sinning, "put off the old man with his deeds and put on the new man," which after God is created in "righteousness and true holiness." For neither *Baptism, Supper, nor church-fellowship,* nor any other external ceremony, can, without faith, the new birth, and a change or renewal of life, help, or qualify us, that we may please God, or receive any consolation or promise of salvation from him. Luke 3:8; Eph. 4:22-24; Col. 3:9, 10.

But on the contrary, we must go to God "with a sincere heart in full assurance of faith," and believe in Jesus Christ, as the scriptures speak and testify of him. Through which faith we obtain the pardon of our sins, become sanctified, justified, and children of God; yea, partakers of his mind, nature and image, as we are born again of God through his incorruptible seed from above. Heb. 10:21, 22; John 7:38; II Pet. 1:4.

Article VII.

Of Holy Baptism

Regarding baptism, we confess that all penitent believers, who through faith, the new birth and renewal of the Holy Ghost, have become united with God, and whose names are recorded in heaven, must, on such scriptural confession of their faith, and renewal of life, according to the command and doctrine of Christ, and the example and custom of the apostles, be baptized with water in the ever adorable name of the Father, and of the Son, and of the Holy Ghost, to the burying of their sins, and thus to become incorporated into the communion of the saints; whereupon they must learn to observe all things whatsoever the Son of God taught, left on record, and commanded his followers to do. Matt. 3:15; 28:19, 20; Mark 16:15, 16; Acts 2:38; 8:12, 38; 9:18; 10:47; 16:33; Rom. 6:3, 4; Col. 2:12.

Article VIII.

Of the Church of Christ

We believe in and confess a visible Church of God, consisting of those, who, as before remarked, have truly repented, and rightly believed; who are rightly baptized, united with God in heaven, and incorporated into the communion of the saints on earth. I Cor. 12:13.

And these, we confess, are a "chosen generation, a royal priesthood, an holy nation," who have the testimony that they are the "bride" of Christ; yea, that they are children and heirs of eternal life—a "habitation of God through the Spirit," built on the foundation of the apostles and prophets, of which "Christ himself is the chief cornerstone"—the foundation on which his church is built. John 3:29; Matt. 16:18; Eph. 2:19-21; Tit. 3:7; I Pet. 1:18, 19; 2:9.

This church of the living God, which he has purchased and redeemed through his own precious blood, and with which he will be—according to his own promise—for her comfort and protection, "always, even unto the end of the world;" yea, will dwell and walk with her, and preserve her, that no "winds" nor "floods," yea, not even the "gates of hell shall prevail against her"—may be known by her evangelical faith, doctrine, love, and godly conversation; also by her pure walk and practice, and her observance of the true ordinances of Christ, which he has strictly enjoined on his followers. Matt. 7:25; 16:18; 28:20; II Cor. 6:16.

Article IX.

Of the Election, and Offices of Teachers, Deacons, and Deaconesses, in the Church

Regarding the offices, and election of persons to the same, in the church, we believe and confess: That, as the church cannot exist and prosper, nor continue in its structure, without offices and regulations, that therefore the Lord Jesus has himself (as a father in his house), appointed and prescribed his offices and ordinances, and has given commandments concerning the same, as to how each one should walk therein, give heed to his own work and calling, and do it as it becomes him to do. Eph. 4:11, 12.

For he himself, as the faithful and great Shepherd, and Bishop of our souls, was sent into the world, not to wound, to break, or destroy the souls of men, but to heal them; to seek that which is lost, and to pull down the hedges and partition wall, so as to make out of many one; thus collecting out of Jews and heathen, yea, out of all nations, a church in his name; for which (so that no one might go astray or be lost) he laid down his own life, and thus procured for them salvation, made them free and redeemed them, to which blessing no one could help them, or be of service in obtaining it. I Pet. 2:25; Matt. 18:11; Eph. 2:13, 14; John 10:9, 11, 15.

And that he, besides this, left his church before his departure, provided with faithful ministers, apostles, evangelists, pastors, and teachers, whom he had chosen by prayer and supplication through the Holy Spirit, so that they might govern the church, feed his flock, watch over, maintain, and care for the same: yea, do all things as he left them an example, taught them, and commanded them to do; and likewise to teach the church to observe all things whatsoever he commanded them. Eph. 4:11, 12; Luke 6:12, 13; 10:1; Matt. 28:20.

Also that the apostles were afterwards, as faithful followers of Christ and leaders of the church, diligent in these matters, namely, in choosing through prayer and supplication to God, brethren who were to provide all the churches in the cities and circuits, with bishops, pastors, and leaders, and to ordain to these offices such men as took "heed unto themselves and unto the doctrine," and also unto the flock; who were sound in the faith, pious in their life and conversation, and who had—as well within the church as "without"—a good reputation and a good report; so that they might be a light and example in all godliness and good works; might worthily administer the Lord's ordinances—baptism and supper—and that they (the brethren sent by the apostles) might also, at all places, where such were to be had, appoint faithful men as elders, who were able to teach others, confirm them in the name of the Lord "with the laying on of hands," and who (the elders) were to take care of all things of which the church stood in need; so that they, as faithful servants, might well "occupy" their Lord's money, gain thereby, and thus "save themselves and those who hear them." I Tim. 3:1; 4:14-16; Acts 1:23, 24; Tit. 1:5; Luke 19:13.

That they should also take good care (particularly each one of the charge over which he had the oversight), that all the circuits should be well provided with deacons, who should have the care and oversight of the poor, and who were to receive gifts and alms, and again faithfully to distribute them among the poor saints who were in need, and this is in all honesty, as is becoming. Acts 6:3-6.

Also that honorable old widows should be chosen as deaconesses, who, besides the deacons, are to visit, comfort, and take care of the poor, the weak, afflicted, and the needy, as also to visit, comfort, and take care of widows and orphans; and further to assist in taking care of any matters in the church that properly come within their sphere, according to their ability. I Tim. 5:9, 10; Rom. 16:1, 2.

And as it further regards the deacons, that they (particularly if they are fit persons, and chosen and ordained thereto by the church), may also in aid and relief of the bishops, exhort the church (being, as already remarked, chosen thereto), and thus assist in word and doctrine; so that each one may serve the other from love, with the gift which he has received from the Lord; so that through the common service and assistance of each member, according to his ability, the body of Christ may be edified, and the Lord's vineyard and church be preserved in its growth and structure. II Tim. 2:2.

Article X.

Of the Lord's Supper

We also believe in and observe the breaking of bread, or the Lord's Supper, as the Lord Jesus instituted the same (with bread and wine) before his sufferings, and also observed and ate it with the apostles, and also commanded it to be observed to his remembrance, as also the apostles subsequently taught and observed the same in the church, and commanded it to be observed by believers in commemoration of the death and sufferings of the Lord—the breaking of his worthy body and the shedding of his precious blood—for the whole human race. So is the observance of this sacrament also to remind us of the benefit of the said death and sufferings of Christ, namely, the redemption and eternal salvation which he purchased thereby, and the great love thus shown to sinful man; whereby we are earnestly exhorted also to love one another—to love our neighbor—to forgive and absolve him—even as Christ has done unto us—and also to endeavor to maintain and keep alive the union and communion which we have with God, and amongst one another; which is thus shown and represented to us by the aforesaid breaking of bread. Matt. 26:26; Mark 14:22; Luke 22:19, 20; Acts 2:42, 46; I Cor. 10:16; 11:23-26.

Article XI.

Of the Washing of the Saints' Feet

We also confess a washing of the feet of the saints, as the Lord Jesus did not only institute and command the same, but did also himself wash the feet of the apostles, although he was their Lord and master; thereby giving an example that they also should wash one another's feet, and thus do to one another as he did to them; which they also afterwards taught believers to observe, and all this is a sign of true humiliation; but yet more particularly as a sign to remind us of the true washing—the washing and purification of the soul in the blood of Christ. John 13:4-17; I Tim. 5:9, 10.

Article XII.

Of Matrimony

We also confess that there is in the church of God an "honorable" state of matrimony between two believers of the different sexes, as God first instituted the same in paradise between Adam and Eve, and as the Lord Jesus reformed it by removing all abuses which had crept into it, and restoring it to its first order. Gen. 1:27; 2:18, 21-24.

In this manner the apostle Paul also taught and permitted matrimony in the church, leaving it to each one's own choice to enter into matrimony with any person who would unite with him in such state, provided that it was done "in the Lord," according to the primitive order; the words "in the Lord," to be understood, according to our opinion, that just as the patriarchs had to marry amongst their own kindred or generation, so there is also no other liberty allowed to believers under the New Testament Dispensation, than to marry among the "chosen generation," or the spiritual kindred of Christ; that is, to such—and none others—as are already, previous to their marriage, united to the church in heart and soul, have received the same baptism, belong to the same church, are of the same faith and doctrine, and lead the same course of life, with themselves. I Cor. 7:39; 9:5; Gen. 24:4; 28:6, 7; Num. 36:6-9.

Such are then, as already remarked, united by God and the church according to the primitive order, and this is then called, "Marrying in the Lord." I Cor. 7:39.

Article XIII.

Of the Office of Civil Government

We also believe and confess, that God has instituted civil government, for the punishment of the wicked and the protection of the pious; and also further, for the purpose of governing the world, countries and cities; and also to preserve its subjects in good order and under good regulations. Wherefore we are not permitted to despise, revile, or resist the same, but are to acknowledge it as a minister of God and be subject and obedient to it, in all things that do not militate against the law, will, and commandments of God; yea, "to be ready to every good work;" also faithfully to pay it custom, tax, and tribute; thus giving it what is its due; as Jesus Christ taught, did himself, and commanded his followers to do. That we are also to pray to the Lord earnestly for the government and its welfare, and in behalf of our country, so that we may live under its protection, maintain ourselves, and "lead a quiet and peaceable life in all godliness and honesty." And further, that the Lord would recompense them (our rulers), here and in eternity, for all the benefits, liberties, and favors which we enjoy under their laudable administration. Rom. 13:1-7; Titus 3:1, 2; I Pet. 2:17; Matt. 17:27; 22:20, 21; I Tim. 2:1, 2.

Article XIV.

Of Defense by Force

Regarding revenge, whereby we resist our enemies with the sword, we believe and confess that the Lord Jesus has forbidden his disciples and followers all revenge and resistance, and has thereby commanded them not to "return evil for evil, nor railing for railing;" but to "put up the sword into the sheath," or, as the prophet foretold, "beat them into ploughshares." Matt. 5:39, 44; Rom. 12:14; I Pet. 3:9; Isaiah 2:4; Micah 4:3.

From this we see, that, according to the example, life, and doctrine of Christ, we are not to do wrong, or cause offense or vexation to anyone; but to seek the welfare and salvation of all men; also, if necessity should require it, to flee, for the Lord's sake, from one city or country to another, and suffer the "spoiling of our goods," rather than give occasion of offense to anyone; and if we are struck on our "right cheek, rather to turn the other also," than revenge ourselves, or return the blow. Matt. 5:39; 10:23; Rom. 12:19.

And that we are, besides this, also to pray for our enemies, comfort and feed them, when they are hungry or thirsty, and thus by well-doing convince them and overcome the evil with good. Rom. 12:20, 21.

Finally, that we are to do good in all respects, "commending ourselves to every man's conscience in the sight of God," and according to the law of Christ, do nothing to others that we would not wish them to do unto us. II Cor. 4:2; Matt. 7:12; Luke 6:31.

Article XV.

Of the Swearing of Oaths

Regarding the swearing of oaths, we believe and confess that the Lord Jesus has dissuaded his followers from and forbidden them the same; that is, that he commanded them to "swear not at all;" but that their "Yea" should be "yea," and their "Nay, nay." From which we understand that all oaths, high and low, are forbidden; and that instead of them we are to confirm all our promises and covenants, declarations and testimonies of all matters, merely with "Yea that is yea," and "Nay that is nay;" and that we are to perform and fulfill at all times, and in all things, to every one, every promise and obligation to which we thus affirm, as faithfully as if we had confirmed it by the most solemn oath. And if we thus do, we have the confidence that no one—not even government itself—will have just cause to require more of us. Matt. 5:34-37; James 5:12; II Cor. 1:17.

Article XVI.

Of the Ecclesiastical Ban or Excommunication from the Church

We also believe in and acknowledge the ban, or excommunication, a separation or spiritual correction by the church, for the amendment, and not for the destruction, of offenders; so that what is pure may be separated from that which is impure. That is, if a person, after having been enlightened, and received the knowledge of the truth, and has been received into the communion of the saints, does willfully, or out of presumption, sin against God, or commit some other "sin unto death," thereby falling into such unfruitful works of darkness, that he becomes separated from God, and is debarred from his kingdom—that such an one—when his works are become manifest, and sufficiently known to the church—cannot remain in the "congregation of the righteous;" but must, as an offensive member and open sinner, be excluded from the church, "rebuked before all," and "purged out as a leaven," and thus remain until his amendment, as an example and warning to others, and also that the church may be kept pure from such "spots" and "blemishes;" so that not for the want of this, the name of the Lord be blasphemed, the church dishonored, and a stumbling-block thrown in the way of those "without," and finally, that the offender may not be condemned with the world, but that he may again be convinced of the error of his ways, and brought to repentance and amendment of life. Isaiah 59:2; I Cor. 5:5, 6, 12; I Tim. 5:20; II Cor. 13:10.

Regarding the brotherly admonition, as also the instruction of the erring, we are to "give all diligence" to watch over them, and exhort them in all meekness to the amendment of their ways (James 5:19, 20); and in case any should remain obstinate and unconverted, to reprove them as the case may require. In short, the church must "put away from among herself him that is wicked," whether it be in doctrine or life.

Article XVII.

Of the Shunning of Those Who Are Expelled

As regards the withdrawing from, or the shunning of, those who are expelled, we believe and confess, that if any one, whether it be through a wicked life or perverse doctrine—is so far fallen as to be separated from God, and consequently rebuked by, and expelled from, the church, he must also, according to the doctrine of Christ and his apostles, be shunned and avoided by all the members of the church (particularly by those to whom his misdeeds are known), whether it be in eating or drinking, or other such like social matters. In short, that we are to have nothing to do with him; so that we may not become defiled by intercourse with him, and partakers of his sins; but that he may be made ashamed, be affected in his mind, convinced in his conscience, and thereby induced to amend his ways. I Cor. 5:9-11; Rom. 16:17; II Thess. 3:14; Tit. 3:10, 11.

That nevertheless, as well in shunning as in reproving such offender, such moderation and Christian discretion be used, that such shunning and reproof may not be conducive to his ruin, but be serviceable to his amendment. For should he be in need, hungry, thirsty, naked, sick or visited by some other affliction, we are in duty bound, according to the doctrine and practice of Christ and his apostles, to render him aid and assistance, as necessity may require; otherwise the shunning of him might be rather conducive to his ruin than to his amendment. I Thess. 5:14.

Therefore we must not treat such offenders as enemies, but exhort them as brethren, in order thereby to bring them to a knowledge of their sins and to repentance; so that they may again become reconciled to God and the church, and be received and admitted into the same—thus exercising love towards them, as is becoming. II Thess. 3:15.

Article XVIII.

Of the Resurrection of the Dead and the Last Judgment

Regarding the resurrection of the dead, we confess with the mouth, and believe with the heart, that according to the scriptures all men who shall have died or "fallen asleep," will, through the incomprehensible power of God, at the day of judgment, be "raised up" and made alive; and that these, together with all those who then remain alive, and who shall be "changed in a moment, in the twinkling of an eye, at the last trump," shall "appear before the judgmentseat of Christ," where the good shall be separated from the evil, and where "every one shall receive the things done in his body, according to that he hath done, whether it be good or bad;" and that the good or pious shall then further, as the blessed of their Father, be received by Christ into eternal life, where they shall receive that joy which "eye hath not seen, nor ear heard, nor hath entered into the heart of man." Yea, where they shall reign and triumph with Christ for ever and ever. Matt. 22:30-32; 25:31; Dan. 12:2; Job. 19:25, 26; John 5:28, 29; I Cor. 15:51, 52; I Thess. 4:13.

And that, on the contrary, the wicked or impious, shall, as the accursed of God, be cast into "outer darkness;" yea, into eternal, hellish torments; "where their worm dieth not, and the fire is not quenched;" and where—according to Holy Scripture—they can expect no comfort nor redemption throughout eternity. Isaiah 66:24; Matt. 25:46; Mark 9:46; Rev. 14:10, 11.

May the Lord through his grace make us all fit and worthy, that no such calamity may befall any of us; but that we may be diligent, and so take heed to ourselves, that we may be found of him in peace, without spot, and blameless. Amen.

Now these are, as before mentioned, the chief articles of our general Christian Faith, which we everywhere teach in our congregations and families, and according to which we profess to live; and which, according to our convictions, contain the only true Christian Faith, which the apostles in their time believed and taught; yea, which they testified to by their lives and confirmed by their deaths; in which we will also, according to our weakness, gladly abide, live, and die, that at last, together with the apostles and all the pious we may obtain the salvation of our souls through the grace of God.

Thus were the foregoing articles of faith adopted and concluded by our united churches in the city of Dordrecht, in Holland, on the 21st day of April, in the year of our Lord 1632, and signed by the following ministers and teachers:

DORDRECHT
Isaac de Koning, and in behalf of our minister, Jan Jacobs
Hans Cobryssz
Iacuis Terwen
Claes Dircksz
Mels Gysbertsz
Adriaen Cornelissz

MIDDELBURGH
Bastiaen Willemsen
Ian Winckelmans

VLISSINGEN
Oillaert Willeborts
Iacob Pennen
Lieven Marynesz

AMSTERDAM
Tobias Govertsz
Pieter Iantz Moyer
Abraham Dircksz
David ter Haer
Pieter Iantz van Singel

HAERLEM
Ian Doom
Pieter Gryspeert
Dirck Woutersz Kolenkamp
Pieter Ioosten

BOMMEL
Willem Iansz van Exselt
Gisbert Spiering

ROTTERDAM
Balten Centen Schoenmaker
M. Michielsz
Israel van Halmael
Hendrick Dircksz Apeldoren
Andries Lucken, de jonge [Jr.]

FROM THE UPPER PART OF THE COUNTRY
Peeter van Borsel
Antony Hansz

KREVELT dito
Harman op den Graff
Weylm Kreynen

ZEELANDT
Cornelis de Moir
Isaac Claessz

SCHIEDAM
Cornelis Bom
Lambrecht Paeldinck

LEYDEN
Mr. C. de Kroninck
Ian Weyns

BLOCKZIEL
Claes Claessen
Pieter Peters

ZIERICZEE
Anthonis Cornelissz
Pieter Iansz Timmerman

UTRECHT
Herman Segers
Ian Hendricksen Hooghvelt
Daniel Horens
Abraham Spronck
Willem van Broeckhuysen

GORCUM
Iacob van der Heyde Sebrechts
Ian Iansz V. K.

AERNHEM
Cornelis Iansz
Dirck Rendersen

Besides this confession being adopted by so many churches, and signed by their ministers, all the churches in Alsace, in the Palatinate, and in Germany afterwards adopted it unanimously. Wherefore it was translated from the

Holland into the languages of these countries—into French and German—for the use of the churches there, and for others, of which this may serve as a notice.

The following attestation was signed by the brethren in Alsace, who examined this confession and adopted it as their own:

We, the undersigned, ministers of the word of God, and elders of the church in Alsace, hereby declare and make known, that being assembled this 4th of February in the year of our Lord 1660, at Ohnenheim in the principality of Rappoltstein, on account of the Confession of Faith, which was adopted at the Peace Convention of the *Tauffs-gesinten* which are called the Flemish, in the city of Dort, on the 21st day of April in the year 1632, and which was printed at Rotterdam by Franciscus von Hochstraten, Anno 1658; and having examined the same, and found it in agreement with our judgment, we have entirely adopted it as our own. Which we, in testimony of the truth, and a firm faith, have signed with our own hands, as follows:

Ministers of the Word	*Deacons*
Hans Müller of Magenheym	Jacob Schmidt of Markirch
Hans Ringer of Heydelsheym	Bertram Habigh of Markirch
Jacob Schnewli of Baldenheym	Ulrich Husser of Ohnenheym
Henrich Schneider of Isenheim	Jacob Gachnauwer of Ohnenheim
Rudolph Egli of Kunenheim	Hans Rudi Bumen of Jepsenheim
Adolph Schmidt of Markirch	Jacob Schneider of Dürsantzenheym
	Henrich Frick of Kunenheym

Postscript to the Foregoing Eighteen Articles

From an authentic circular letter of the year 1557, from the Highland to the Netherland churches, it appears that from the Eyfelt to Moravia there were 50 churches, of which some consisted of from 500 to 600 brethren. And that there were about that time, at a conference at Strasburg, about 50 preachers and elders present, who discoursed about matters concerning the welfare of the churches.

These leaders of the nonresistant Christians endeavored earnestly to propagate the truth; so that like a "grain of mustard seed," of small beginning, it grew against all bloody persecution, to the height in which it is to be seen in so many large churches in Germany, Prussia, the Principality of Cleves, &c., and particularly in the United Netherlands.

But finally, alas! there arose disunion amongst them about matters of faith, which so deeply grieved the peaceably disposed amongst them, that they not only thought about means to heal the schism, and restore union, but did also take the matter in hand, and concluded at Cologne, in the year 1591, a laudable peace between the Highland and Netherland churches. Still the schism was not fully healed. Consequently in the years 1628 and 1630, it was deemed necessary at a certain conference, by some lovers of peace to appoint another conference, in order to see whether they could come to an understanding, and the schism be fully healed. Consequently, in order to attain their object in the most effectual manner, there assembled at Dort, from many of the churches in Holland, on the 21st of April, 1632, fifty-one ministers of the word of God, appointed for said purpose; who deemed it advisable that a scriptural confession of faith should be drawn up, to which all parties should adhere, and on which this peace convention and the intended union should be founded and built. Which was then accordingly drawn up, publicly adopted, confirmed, signed, the so much wished for peace obtained, and the light again put on the candlestick, to the honor of the nonresistant Christianity.

V

On Mennonite Historiography

It may be of some value to make a brief list of the more important Mennonite historians. Let us list these historians by their countries, beginning with Holland. One of the earliest Dutch Mennonite writers was Carl van Gent, 1542-1615. Another was the celebrated T. J. van Braght, 1625-64, author of the *Martyrs' Mirror* of 1660, the greatest book ever written by a Mennonite. Other important historians are Herman Schijn, 1662-1727; S. Blaupot ten Cate, 1807-84; J. G. de Hoop Scheffer, 1819-93; Samuel Cramer, 1842-1913; W. J. Kühler, 1874-1946; and Karel Vos, 1875-1926.

Among the German Mennonite historians should be listed Anna Brons, 1810-1902; Wilhelm Mannhardt, 1831-80; Ernst H. Correll, 1894- , now a professor in Washington, D.C.; and the editors of the *Mennonitisches Lexikon,* Christian Hege, 1869-1943, and Christian Neff, 1863-1946.

Among the Russian Mennonite historians should be mentioned P. M. Friesen, 1849-1914, and Franz Isaac (died 1899), both of whom wrote in the German language.

It is only in recent decades that American Mennonites have been devoting attention to the writing of their denominational history. Well known exceptions were Benjamin Eby, 1785-1863, of Ontario, and D. K. Cassel, 1820-98, of Pennsylvania. The late governor of Pennsylvania, S. W. Pennypacker, 1843-1917, wrote in a sympathetic and understanding way of his Mennonite forbears and neighbors. The three American Mennonite historians who have done the most to give both to Mennonites and the world a true account of the Mennonites are John Horsch, 1867-1941, C. Henry Smith, 1876- , and Harold S. Bender, 1897- . These men know thoroughly the European literature on Mennonite history and along with a number of younger scholars are producing first-class articles and books treating of the history, faith and life of their people.

It is indeed true that Mennonite historians sometimes erred by writing more for edification than for historical accuracy, but non-Mennonite historians, especially in the early years of the movement, wrote accounts of its history which were quite unfair. These non-Mennonite writers combined the writing of history with the prosecution of a vigorous polemic. In general it must be said that the old mud-throwing of Reformation days was uncritically copied from 1525 until 1700 A.D. An outstanding exception to this rule was the work of Sebastian Franck, 1499-c. 1543. Franck's writings are remarkably free of personal bias and bitterness. Another pioneer in impartiality was Gottfried Arnold, 1666-1714. An "Old Catholic."

C. A. Cornelius, 1819-1903, also did the Mennonites a great service by his painstaking research. Another writer of the same caliber was Ludwig Keller, 1849-1915. Three of the most significant of the non-Mennonite historians of recent times were the Lutheran pastor and scholar, Gustav Bossert, 1842-1926, of Germany; the scholarly Catholic Professor, Johann Loserth, 1846-1936, of Austria; and Professor Walter Koehler, 1870-1946, of the University of Heidelberg. Among living historians should be mentioned Professor Fritz Blanke, 1900- , of the University of Zurich.

Since 1927 *The Mennonite Quarterly Review* is the leading journal in the field of Anabaptist-Mennonite history and thought. The *Review* contains scores of first-class articles and discussions, the result of thorough research and good scholarship. The *Review* is published by the Mennonite Historical Society, Goshen College, Goshen, Indiana. This Society also publishes a book-series of learned monographs entitled STUDIES IN ANABAPTIST AND MENNONITE HISTORY.

VI

A Brief English Bibliography of Mennonite History

Chronologically Arranged

Works of Special Merit are Indicated by an Asterisk

I. FICTION

NOTE: Most fiction about Mennonites and Amish indicates both misunderstanding and lack of appreciation.

1904. Helen R. Martin: *Tillie, A Mennonite Maid,* The Century Co. [Unfair].
1905. Helen R. Martin: *Sabina, A Story of the Amish,* The Century Co.
1907. Helen R. Martin: *Betrothal of Elypholate and Other Tales,* The Century Co.
1915. Elsie Singmaster: *Katy Gaumer,* Houghton Mifflin.
1924. B. Mabel Dunham: *The Trail of the Conestoga* Macmillan [Good].
1925. Elsie Singmaster: *Bread in the Bone and Other Stories,* Houghton Mifflin.
1927. B. Mabel Dunham: *Toward Sodom,* Macmillan.
1937. Ruth Lininger Dobson: *Straw in the Wind,* Dodd, Mead & Co. [About Indiana Amish].
*1940. J. W. Yoder: *Rosanna of the Amish,* Huntingdon, Pa., pp. 319 [Reliable].

II. CHILDREN'S BOOKS

1906. Sarah E. Ambler: *Dear Old Home,* Little, Brown & Co.
*1937. Marguerite de Angeli: *Henner's Lydia* [Lancaster Amish girl], Doubleday Doran.
*1939. Marguerite de Angeli: *Skippack School* [of Christopher Dock], Doubleday Doran.
1939. Ella M. Seyfert: *Little Amish Schoolhouse,* Crowell.
1940. Katherine Milhous: *Lovina,* Scribner.
1942. Ella M. Seyfert: *Amish Moving Day,* Crowell.
*1944. Marguerite de Angeli: *Yonie Wondernose,* Doubleday Doran.

III. PUBLISHED SOURCE MATERIALS

1712. *The Christian Confession of the . . . Mennonists* [Dordrecht Articles of 1632]. Amsterdam, Holland, pp. 40.
1849. *The Catechism* [First published in 1778 by the Mennonites of Elbing, Prussia]. Translated by I. Daniel Rupp, Lancaster, Pa., pp. 71.
*1871. *The Complete Works of Menno Simon.* [Translated from the Dutch edition of 1681] Elkhart, Ind., pp. 288 and 455.
1904. Cornelis Ris: *Mennonite Articles of Faith* [1766]. [Translated from Dutch to German by C. J. van der Smissen, and from German to English by A. S. Shelly]. Berne, Ind., pp. 75.
1913. P. J. Twisck: *The Peaceful Kingdom of Christ.* Elkhart, Ind., pp. 32.
1914. *Conference Record Containing the Proceedings of the Kansas-Nebraska Mennonite Conference, 1876-1914,* pp. 207.
1915. Dietrich Philip: *Enchiridion or Handbook of the Christian Doctrine and Religion* [Translated from the German and compared with the original Dutch by A. B. Kolb]. Elkhart, Ind., pp. 539.

1915. Henry Funk: *Restitution* [Treatise on the fulfillment of the O. T. by Christ. Translated from the original German of 1763 by A. B. Kolb]. Elkhart, Ind., pp. 448.
1921. *Mennonite General Conference*, Scottdale, Pa., 1921, pp. 232. [Biennial reports have been published, 1923-].
1929. *Minutes of the Indiana-Michigan Conference*, 1864-1929. Scottdale, Pa., pp. 356 [Congregational histories, pp. 297-338].
*1938. T. J. van Braght: *The Bloody Theatre or Martyrs' Mirror* [Translated from the original Dutch of 1660 by Joseph F. Sohm]. Scottdale, Pa., pp. 1152.
1939. *Minutes of the Virginia Mennonite Conference*, pp. 234.

IV. PERIODICALS

1864-1908. *The Herald of Truth*, Elkhart, Ind.
1882- . *The Mennonite*, Berne, Ind.
1895-1930. *Mennonite Year Book and Almanac*, Berne, Ind.
1905-1908. *The Gospel Witness*, Scottdale, Pa.
1905- . *Mennonite Yearbook and Directory*, Scottdale, Pa.
1908- . *Gospel Herald*, Scottdale, Pa. [The organ of the Mennonite Church].
*1927- . *The Mennonite Quarterly Review*, Goshen, Ind.
1931- . *Year Book of the General Conference of the Mennonite Church of N. A.*, Berne, Ind.
1940- . *Mennonite Historical Bulletin*, Scottdale, Pennsylvania.
*1946- . *Mennonite Life*, North Newton, Kansas.
*1947- . *The Mennonite Community*, Scottdale, Pa.

V. GENERAL MENNONITE HISTORY

1883. E. K. Martin: *The Mennonites.* Philadelphia, Pa., pp. 17.
1888. D. K. Cassel: *History of the Mennonites.* Philadelphia, Pa., pp. 450.
1895. Richard Heath: *Anabaptism . . . , 1521-1536.* London, pp. 194.
*1897. A. H. Newman: *A History of Antipedobaptism to A.D. 1609.* Philadelphia, Pa., pp. 414.
1903. E. B. Bax: *Rise and Fall of the Anabaptists.* London & New York, pp. 407.
1905. J. S. Hartzler and Daniel Kauffman: *Mennonite Church History*, Scottdale, Pa., pp. 422.
*1909. C. H. Smith: *The Mennonites of America.* Goshen, Ind., pp. 484.
1911. W. J. McGlothlin: *Baptist Confessions of Faith.* Philadelphia, pp. 368.
*1920. C. H. Smith: *The Mennonites.* Berne, Ind., pp. 324.
1925. L. J. Heatwole: *Mennonite Handbook of Information.* Scottdale, Pa., pp. 187.
1927. Daniel Kauffman: *Mennonite History.* Scottdale, Pa., pp. 147.
*1937. Daniel Kauffman: *Mennonite Cyclopedic Dictionary*, Scottdale, Pa. pp. 443.
*1941. C. H. Smith: *The Story of the Mennonites*, Berne, Ind., pp. 823.
1944. J. J. Friesen: *An Outline of Mennonite History*, Newton, Kans., pp. 114.

VI. MONOGRAPHS

1882. H. S. Burrage: *A History of the Anabaptists in Switzerland.* Philadelphia, Pa., pp. 231.
1898. H. P. Krehbiel: *History of the General Conference of the Mennonite Church of North America.* Canton, Ohio, pp. 505.
*1903. M. S. Steiner: *John S. Coffman, Mennonite Evangelist.* Spring Grove, Pa., pp. 139.
1905. H. C. Vedder: *Balthasar Hübmaier.* New York, pp. 333.

*1908. M. G. Brumbaugh: *The Life and Works of Christopher Dock.* Philadelphia, Pa. pp. 272.

*1916. John Horsch: *Menno Simons, His Life, Labors, and Teachings.* Scottdale, Pa., pp. 324.

1916. W. H. Grubb: *History of the Mennonites of Butler County, Ohio.* Trenton, Ohio, pp. 49.

1917. Committee: *Mennonite Church History of Howard and Miami Counties, Indiana.* Scottdale, Pa., pp. 189.

1917. J. H. Langenwalter: *Christ's Headship of the Church According to Anabaptist Leaders.* Berne, Ind., pp. 187.

1920. J. A. Huffman: *History of the Mennonite Brethren in Christ Church.* New Carlisle, Ohio, pp. 383.

1921. Henry E. Dosker: *The Dutch Anabaptists.* Philadelphia, Pa., pp. 310.

1921. *Memoirs of Peter Jansen . . . An Autobiography.* Beatrice, Neb., pp. 140.

*1921. J. S. Hartzler: *Mennonites in the World War.* Scottdale, Pa., pp. 145.

1925. J. E. Hartzler: *Education Among the Mennonites of North America.* Danvers, Ill., pp. 195.

1926. W. B. Weaver: *History of the Central Conference Mennonite Church.* Danvers, Ill., pp. 254.

1926. *Building on the Rock* [History of the American Mennonite Mission in India]. Scottdale, Pa., pp. 200.

1917. John Horsch: *Infant Baptism; Its Origin Among Protestants . . . .* Scottdale, Pa., pp. 157.

*1927. John Horsch: *The Principle of Nonresistance as Held by the Mennonite Church.* Scottdale, Pa., pp. 60. Second, Revised Edition, 1939, pp. 74.

1927. C. H. Smith: *The Coming of the Russian Mennonites.* Berne, Ind., pp. 298.

*1928. P. C. Hiebert and O. O. Miller: *Feeding the Hungry.* [Russian Famine, 1919-1925]. Scottdale, Pa., pp. 450.

*1929. C. H. Smith: *The Mennonite Immigration to Pennsylvania in the Eighteenth Century.* Norristown, Pa., pp. 412.

1929. *Twenty-five Years with God in India* [History of the General Conference Mennonite Mission]. Berne, Ind., pp. 250.

1931. E. G. Kaufman: *The Development of the Missionary and Philanthropic Interest Among the Mennonites of North America.* Berne, Ind., pp. 416.

1931. John Horsch: *The Hutterian Brethren, 1528-1931.* Goshen, Ind., pp. 168.

1931. M. G. Weaver: *Mennonites of Lancaster Conference.* Scottdale, Pa., pp. 496.

1931. H. F. Weber: *Centennial History of the Mennonites of Illinois.* Goshen, Ind., pp. 680.

1931. S. G. Shetler: *Church History of the Pacific Coast Mennonite Conference District.* Scottdale, Pa., pp. 102.

*1934. W. J. Bender: *Nonresistance in Colonial Pennsylvania.* Scottdale, Pa., pp. 32.

1935. L. J. Burkholder: *A Brief History of the Mennonites in Ontario.* pp. 358.

1935. R. J. Smithson: *The Anabaptists, Their Contribution to Our Present Heritage,* London, pp. 228.

*1936. G. F. Hershberger: *Nonresistance and the State.* Scottdale, Pa., pp. 48.

*1936. Mary Y. Burkhard: *Life and Letters of Jacob Burkhard, Missionary to India.* Goshen, Ind., pp. 214.

*1936. H. S. Bender and John Horsch: *Menno Simons' Life and Writings.* Scottdale, Pa., pp. 111.

1936. C. H. Smith: *Menno Simons, Apostle of the Nonresistant Life.* Berne, Ind., pp. 76.

1936. R. M. Yoder: *Indiana Literaries,* Mennonite Publishing House, Scottdale, Pennsylvania, pp. 184.

1937. Alta Mae Erb: *Studies in Mennonite City Missions.* Scottdale, Pa., pp. 224.

*1937. A. Warkentin: *Who's Who Among the Mennonites,* pp. 221.
1937. H. A. Brunk: *Life of Peter S. Hartman,* pp. 73.
1937. I. D. Landis: *The Missionary Movement Among Lancaster Conference Mennonites.* pp. 119.
1937. J. C. Wenger: *History of the Mennonites of the Franconia Conference.* Telford, Pa., pp. 523.
1938. F. P. Schultz: *The Settlement of German Mennonites from Russia at Mountain Lake, Minnesota.* Minneapolis, Minn., pp. 123.
1938. H. P. Krehbiel: *The History of the General Conference of the Mennonite Church of North America,* Volume II. Newton, Kans., pp. 682.
1938. Eva F. Sprunger: *The First Hundred Years, A History of the Mennonite Church in Adams County, Indiana.* Berne, Ind., pp. 344.
*1939. Melvin Gingerich: *The Mennonites in Iowa.* Iowa City, Ia., pp. 419.
*1940. John Umble: *Mennonite Pioneers.* Scottdale, Pa., pp. 211.
*1940. H. S. Bender: *Mennonite Sunday School Centennial, 1840-1940.* Scottdale, Pa., pp. 64.
*1940. G. F. Hershberger: *Can Christians Fight?* Scottdale, Pa., pp. 180.
*1940. S. C. Yoder: *For Conscience' Sake.* Goshen, Ind., pp. 320.
1941. Daniel Kauffman: *Fifty Years in the Mennonite Church.* Scottdale, Pa. pp. 92.
*1941. John Umble: *Ohio Mennonite Sunday Schools,* Goshen, Indiana, pp. 522.
*1942. C. G. Bachman: *The Old Order Amish of Lancaster County* [Published in Proceedings of the Pennsylvania German Society. Volume XLIX, 1941, pp. 1-297]. Norristown, Pa., 1942.
*1942. H. S. Bender: *Mennonite Origins in Europe.* MCC, Akron, Pa., pp. 71.
*1942. G. F. Hershberger: *Christian Relationships to State and Community.* MCC, Akron, Pa., pp. 108.
1942. P. C. Hiebert: *Life and Service in the Kingdom of God.* MCC, Akron, Pa., pp. 64.
*1942. John Horsch: *Mennonites in Europe.* Scottdale, Pa., pp. 425.
*1942. W. M. Kollmorgen: *Culture of a Contemporary Rural Community: The Old Order Amish of Lancaster County, Pennsylvania.* Washington, D.C., pp. 105.
1942. C. Z. Mast and R. E. Simpson: *Annals of the Conestoga Valley in Lancaster, Berks, and Chester Counties, Pennsylvania.* pp. 689.
*1942. C. H. Smith: *Mennonites in America.* MCC, Akron, Pa., pp. 72.
1942. Edward Yoder: *Our Mennonite Heritage.* MCC, Akron, Pa., pp. 62.
*1942. Edward Yoder: *The Mennonites of Westmoreland County, Pennsylvania.* Scottdale, Pa., pp. 64.
1943. *The Gospel Under the Southern Cross* [History of Argentina Mennonite Missions]. Scottdale, Pa., pp. 272.
*1943. A. Warkentin and M. Gingerich: *Who's Who Among the Mennonites.* North Newton, Kansas, pp. 428.
1943. J. C. Wenger: *Christianity and Dress.* Scottdale, Pa., pp. 28.
1944. Ed. G. Kauffman: *Our Mission as a Church of Christ.* MCC, Akron, Pa., pp. 59.
1944. J. W. Fretz: *Mennonite Colonization: Lessons From the Past For the Future.* MCC, Akron, Pa., pp. 80.
1944. R. M. Yoder: *Clinton Frame Sketches.* Herald Press, Scottdale, Pennsylvania, pp. 106.
1945. M. C. Lehman: *The History and Principles of Mennonite Relief Work . . . .* Akron, Pa., pp. 67.
1945. W. B. Weaver: *Thirty-Five Years in the Congo.* Chicago, Ill., pp. 241.
1945. J. C. Wenger: *Historical and Biblical Position of the Mennonite Church on Attire.* Scottdale, Pa., pp. 32.
1946. Ira D. Landis: *The Faith of Our Fathers on Eschatology,* Lititz, Pa., pp. 423.
1946. Menno Simons: *The Cross of Christ,* Scottdale, Pa., pp. 49.

Index of Scripture References

General Index

Persons, Places, Subjects and Books